I0214339

INDIA'S DEVELOPMENT DILEMMA

PRODUCTIVITY OR BUREAUCRACY?

Management Strategy for the World's Largest Democracy

JAY NATHAN, PH.D.
TOBIN COLLEGE OF BUSINESS
ST. JOHN'S UNIVERSITY
QUEENS, NEW YORK
2017

Copyright © 2017 Jay Nathan

All rights reserved.

No part of this work may be reproduced, or stored in a retrieval system, or transmitted in any form or by any means, electronic, mechanical, photo-copying, recording, or otherwise without written permission of the author.

ISBN: 978-0-692-98364-5

PRAISE FOR *INDIA'S DEVELOPMENT DILEMMA*

"*A thoughtful appreciation of ancient India—and productivity-induced recommendations for sustained future development.*"
—Michael Mensah, Dean, Kania School of Management
The University of Scranton, Pennsylvania, USA

"*Dr. Jay Nathan brings a Fulbrighter's orientation to this intensive analysis of India's economic potential. He demonstrates a real respect for the historical achievements of India and the progress it's making across industrial sectors. He also sees a bright future ahead if the country can also shed its bureaucratic culture and focus on applying science and technology to the challenges ahead.*"
—Nancy Neill, Fulbright Scholar to New Zealand
President, Fulbright Association, USA

"*Dr. Jay Nathan is recognized as one of the top scholars on India, having travelled and studied that nation and the South Asia region for over three decades. His comparisons of the US and Indian business enterprises, sector by sector, is a must-read for every manager and government official in India—as well as for any firm considering business relations with India.*"
—Barry Render, Harwood Professor of Operations Management Emeritus
Rollins College Graduate School of Business, Florida, USA

"Dr. Jay Nathan provides an up-to-date, timely analysis of the Indian economy at the beginning of the 21st century. Each sector of the economy is analyzed from historical, cultural, and governmental viewpoints. As the largest democracy on earth with abundant natural and human resources, one might wonder why India has not done better in terms of economic development and improvement in standard of living. Often the entrenched governmental bureaucracy and over regulation seem to be holding back foreign investment, which could lead to many positive gains. Basic infrastructure needs such and roads and electricity cry for allocation of funds. Nathan points out that over 40 percent of the population own not so much as a bicycle for transportation and only a small percentage use the Internet, due mainly to lack of electricity. Dr. Nathan's work is carefully and extensively researched and documented. The book ends on a positive and hopeful note with suggestions as to how India can progress. This is a must-read for anyone interested in modern India."

—James Pomfret, Professor Emeritus, Bloomsburg University, Pennsylvania Executive Director, Global Awareness Society International

"Dr. Jay Nathan provides a challenging and comprehensive picture of the modern Indian economy and an insightful argument that to bring India's economy to its full potential, a focus on intergenerational development is necessary; the argument is presented in well-organized chapters, with clear and numerous charts."

—Harold W. Baillie, Ph.D.
Former Provost, Professor of Philosophy,
The University of Scranton, Pennsylvania

This book is dedicated to ancient India—for her contributions to Mathematics, Astronomy, Medicine, and Languages, including Sanskrit— and to modern India—for embracing a diversity of cultures and faiths, democracy, and tolerance.

Where the mind is without fear and the head is held high

Where knowledge is free

Where the world has not been broken up into fragments

By narrow domestic walls

Where words come out from the depth of truth

Where tireless striving stretches its arms towards perfection

Where the clear stream of reason has not lost its way

Into the dreary desert sand of dead habit

Where the mind is led forward by thee

Into ever-widening thought and action

Into that heaven of freedom, my Father, let my country awake

Rabindranath Tagore
Nobel Prize for Literature, 1913

CONTENTS

FOREWORD

INDIA, ONE OF THE MOST ANCIENT of civilizations, is today still a relatively young but the most populous democracy in the world. The past, present, and future of this critical nation and its strategic place on the global stage is the subject matter of yet another well-researched text by Jay Nathan, Ph.D., Management Professor of Management at the Tobin College of Business at St. John's University (NY).

Jay Nathan deftly contrasts ancient India with modern India in a study that examines the major industries, institutions, and issues that keep India from achieving sustained development or fall back on a stunted growth pattern. Exploring the growing pains that this ancient country still experiences as it struggles to choose between productivity or bureaucracy, Jay Nathan offers a balance of data, statistics, and substantive research to support the roadmap to sustainability for India that he outlines in this timely text.

A Fulbright Scholar to Thailand, Poland, Kazakhstan, and Mongolia, Jay Nathan combines practical business experience with his management research and almost four decades of full-time teaching. A passionate advocate for the importance of a global business education, Jay Nathan contextualizes his international travels in his teaching, service, research, and writing. From his vantage point at St. John's University, a Catholic and Vincentian university located in the most ethnically diverse urban area in the United States, Jay Nathan takes his readers on a journey through the expansive hills and history of India and its major regional and industrial sectors.

Jay Nathan is a world traveler yet he regularly arrives at the St. John's campus via a local public bus. From his seat on the bus, he peers out a window with a global perspective that is the hallmark of this dynamic scholar. Jay Nathan brings that local and global lens to the classroom, to multi-national corporations and to readers who seek first-hand, real world anecdotes and experiences from an outstanding business professor and practitioner.

This book discusses development strategies and pragmatic suggestions for reform in India as offered by Jay Nathan. The comparative analysis of other developing nations astutely recognizes the unique sense of time and place that is modern India. A "one size fits all" management strategy is not the panacea for the seventh largest country by area with a population of over 1.2 billion people. India is changing fast and while some change has led to greater economic development and opportunity, a more sustained climate of change is needed. Jay Nathan presents a potential pathway for India on a road to promise and possibility.

Since achieving independence, India has made slow but steady progress towards greater economic development, political stability, and advances in science, technology, engineering and mathematics (STEM). Yet all of these advances in social mobility are still harnessed by continuing challenges with poverty, unemployment, illiteracy, and housing. India in the 21st century is on the cusp of breaking through as one of the fastest growing, major global economies. But potential does not equal performance and as Jay Nathan so accurately analyzes; India has real decisions to make and the outcomes of those decisions made today will influence the future of India not only for tomorrow but for centuries to follow.

Conrado "Bobby" Gempesaw, Ph.D.
President, St. John's University

PREFACE

INDIA IS ONE OF the most important nations in the world due to its population, strategic location, history, and civilization. A member of G20, India is in a group of first-world and economically emerging countries with an overall gross domestic product that is higher than approximately 180 countries of the world. However, unlike first-world countries, India is not exporting manufactured goods in large numbers to United States or Europe, whereas South Korea, Singapore, China, and Japan are exporting and manufacturing high-end, sophisticated electronic and technological products to global markets.

This book identifies differences between India and the United States in the use of public spaces, work culture, professionalism, personal growth, economic mobility, and achievement orientation; it explores India's major industries and their strengths and weaknesses and brings into focus the disparities that exist in regional and industrial sectors in India that prevent the country from competing on a global scale. The chapters cover eight major industries: agriculture, banking, retail, textiles, real estate, transportation, information technology, engineering, and biotechnology. Figures and charts are included to show the development challenges, including productivity and performance issues, in these industries.

My hope is that this book will further the debate, promoting effective management strategies to be implemented at the local, state, regional, and national levels in Indian society.

1

THEORIES ABOUT
UNEVEN DEVELOPMENT

INDIA IS ONE OF THE OLDEST CIVILIZATIONS IN THE WORLD.
In many ways, India is perceived as a spiritual nation with rich traditions and a way of life quite different from Western countries. In the twenty-first century, countries are measured in economic development and, in this sphere, the republic's progress is uneven. India's lagging economic growth is in part a result of inefficient systems and excessive bureaucracy, but this has not always been the case in Indian culture.

History shows that ancient Indian civilization had effective systems for planning and management, allowing them to create highly advanced architecture. Susan Gole, author of *Size as a Measure of Importance in Indian Cartography* (1990), explains that, although no early maps have been found, it should not be assumed that the Indians did not know how to conceptualize in a cartographic manner. In the second millennium BCE, towns like Mohenjo-Daro near the Indus and on the Saurashtra coast, which are 420 miles apart, were built with baked bricks of identical size on similar plans. This denotes a widespread recognition of the need for accuracy in planning and management. In the eight century CE the Kailas temple at Ellora in Maharashtra was carved down into mountain for 100 feet, with intricate sculptures lining pillared halls, no easy task with an exact map to follow, impossible without.

Joseph E. Schwartzberg, author of *Maps and Mapmaking in India* (2008), proposes that the Bronze Age Indus Valley civilization (c. 2500–1900 BCE) may have known "cartographic activity" based on a number of excavated surveying instruments and measuring rods. The use of large-scale construction plans, cosmological drawings, and cartographic material was known to India with some regularity since the Vedic period (first millennium BCE). This is evidence that India has had an advanced civilization since ancient times. To produce such intricate architecture would require efficient management—there would have to be a leader who organized the project, a financer, and laborers working in teams.

Indus Valley Civilization with Great Bath
Source: *Science*, 12 June 2016, posted by Scientific India

During and after the Vedic period and Bronze Age Indus Valley Civilization, the Indian subcontinent was constantly invaded by foreigners (Alexander the Great from Macedonia, Moguls, and the British). Despite invasions and immigration, India preserved her culture and has remained one of the oldest civilizations.

MODERN INDIA

India became independent from the British colonial rule in 1947. Since then, the country adopted parliamentary democracy as a form of governance. India continues to be the largest democracy in the world today and pursues a liberal socialist democracy, unlike the United States, which has a capitalist democracy with a president as the chief executive and a congress with legislative powers. Where the United States has inherited Anglo-Saxon cultural values that govern individuals and family, India is, in many ways, rooted in spiritual and traditional values. Many critics who are rooted in Western tradition point to spirituality in thought and action as one of the major obstacles to sustained economic development in India. They argue that Indian culture is less focused on worldly success and more focused on spiritual attainment.

MEASURING UNEVEN DEVELOPMENT

Geographers, management scholars, and economists debate the dramatic difference in the levels of economic development on a world scale, a continental scale (such as the north–south divide in Europe), and on a subnational scale (for example the difference between the southeast and the rest of the UK). Experts even debate how best to characterize unevenness, but the most profound disagreements are about the reasons for uneven development.

According to neoclassical economics, uneven development should be self-correcting because less developed areas have low-cost land and labor, which should attract investment from high-cost areas—there are some examples of this, especially the appearance of newly industrialized countries in the 1970s. But unevenness seems to be extremely persistent over time. Marxists emphasize this point, stressing that development tends toward a concentration of economic and political power. This power can be used to ensure that future investment largely favors the more developed area, so that advantage becomes cumulative. This theory would explain the UK government's adoption of policies that favor the southeast as well as the US domination of the World Bank and IMF.

There are some exceptions to the perpetuation of advantage. British capital, for example, has been keen to invest abroad and the West Midlands region of England has plummeted from privilege to deindustrialization. Conversely, economies in the Far East have advanced rapidly in relation to Europe and the US.

A third set of arguments, known as "spatial divisions of labor," suggests that the pursuit of profit and growth uses the differences between places in different ways at different times to produce changes that are neither self-correcting nor self-perpetuating. This argument is more difficult to refute than the two earlier positions and has the merit of directing attention to the detailed reasons for persistence and change in unevenness. Its critics object that it is more of a detailed description than a general explanation.

UNEVEN DEVELOPMENT, GDP, AND THE BOTTOM OF THE PYRAMID

Uneven development occurs in any country, whether it is poor, developing, or developed, but the severity of unevenness is more pronounced in poor and developing countries. Why? There are a number of contributing factors: (1) unequal distribution of natural resources; (2) unfavorable climate and geography, lack of rivers and fertile soil, and colonial heritage; (3) water scarcity and shortage of electricity and other energy resources; and (4) national and local government's lack of leadership and management skills needed to develop cohesive policies for modernization. In the case of India, leadership is rooted in tradition and culture and is not adaptive to present-day requirements for education, technology, entrepreneurship, and political stability.

The GINI coefficient, a measure frequently used by economists, shows that as countries increase their gross domestic product (GDP) (i.e., growth), they also create income inequality and therefore their GINI coefficients are higher. It is hard to imagine that countries, especially poor and economically disadvantaged ones, do not even acknowledge the disparities in living conditions and quality of life in their various regions. It is not uncommon for leaders and well-meaning elites to point to the economic growth of 5 percent or 6 percent, and that their GDPs fair well, in comparison to some ten or twenty years before. In doing so, some of the leaders in economically and politically disadvantaged countries convey a sense of "feel good economics." Can the leadership and citizens take comfort in national GDP—its growth rate and the fact that the economy has added more cars, televisions, computers, and cell phones; several hundred citizens are enjoying Internet access, foreign travel, and education abroad? Yes, this could be, in some ways, a comforting thought. However, in reality, many citizens are lucky to have electricity and running water during a few hours each day and others have none at all. Can leadership ignore these plights or simply take a devil-may-care attitude? We must call for new growth indicators that promote sustainable development and improve the quality of human life, without impeding economic progress (Costanza, 2009).

Countries with high levels of exports can incur impressive GDP figures, but it is not an indication of their true growth. GDP ignores a number of different factors, such as the quality of social relations, economic security and personal safety, health, and longevity (Fleurbaey, 2009). For instance, let us consider a country that earns a high number of exports from its abundant supply of oil. GDP does not take into consideration the negative effects of oil spills, which could destroy surrounding wildlife and devastate families who depend on the area for fishing. The living conditions of poor families, in particular, are not taken into consideration with this calculation of GDP, and so other measures must be taken to better determine social welfare.

What is the point of raising these facts as a framework for discussion? For one, the present-day media, especially television, newspapers, and magazines with wide circulation, distributed from advanced industrialized nations, focus on GDP, stock markets, technology, and innovation. This may be okay for some parts of the world, but not for struggling poor countries! Those living at the bottom of the pyramid lack economic mobility and most remain at the level of extreme poverty.

The study of a country's economic development has proven to be a crucial step in determining that country's standard of living and its overall economic health. Specifically, it is both a quantitative and qualitative measure of progress in an economy. With the rapid expansion of globalization, the overall economic standing of countries is changing so swiftly that it is becoming increasingly difficult for any country to maintain a stable position in terms of development. The line between what was once firmly considered a "developed" and a "developing" country is being stretched thinner as factors of production steadily change hands and economic mobility has begun to rise. India and China, in particular, were once perceived as merely overpopulated developing countries with too much unskilled labor. Now they have risen to the top of the economic charts due to this very pool of unskilled labor. Thousands of manufacturing firms have relocated their factories to these less-developed countries, where labor is much cheaper and readily available, allowing these economies to thrive and expand their overall well-being.

While the significant development of these countries over the last few decades deserves applause, we tend to overlook the fact that this development may have only occurred in select areas of the country. In today's digital age, where technology has become an important part of everyday life, there are still millions who have no access to a computer and for whom electricity itself remains a luxury. For instance, the city of Hyderabad in India is a metropolitan hub that hosts various financial, manufacturing, and research institutions. Zones of the city are dedicated to the operation of information technology companies, yet within the same state of Andhra Pradesh, 95 percent of the population falls below the poverty line (Srinivasa Rao, 2011) and has no Internet access at all. The problem seems to be the tendency to focus developmental efforts on the easy areas, the areas with some preexisting degree of urbanization. It is a much simpler task to expand on already developed areas, instead of investing in rural ones where lack of electricity, telecommunications, and education may make it difficult to sustain any attempt at development. Regions that attract investment are usually those that have a better geographical location, resource potential, labor force potential, and available capital (Kyrylych, 2013). With the continued spread of globalization throughout the world and the increasingly free movement of goods, services, and capital, the problem of uneven development is steadily worsening.

In particular, the gap between the GDP per capita of different states has been widening, especially in countries like India. Although these figures do not provide an exact measure of the standard of living, they do give some indication of the overall well-being of the state and tend to tie in closely to its development. India's map of GDP per capita, displayed below, shows that the south and the far north are experiencing higher levels of GDP.

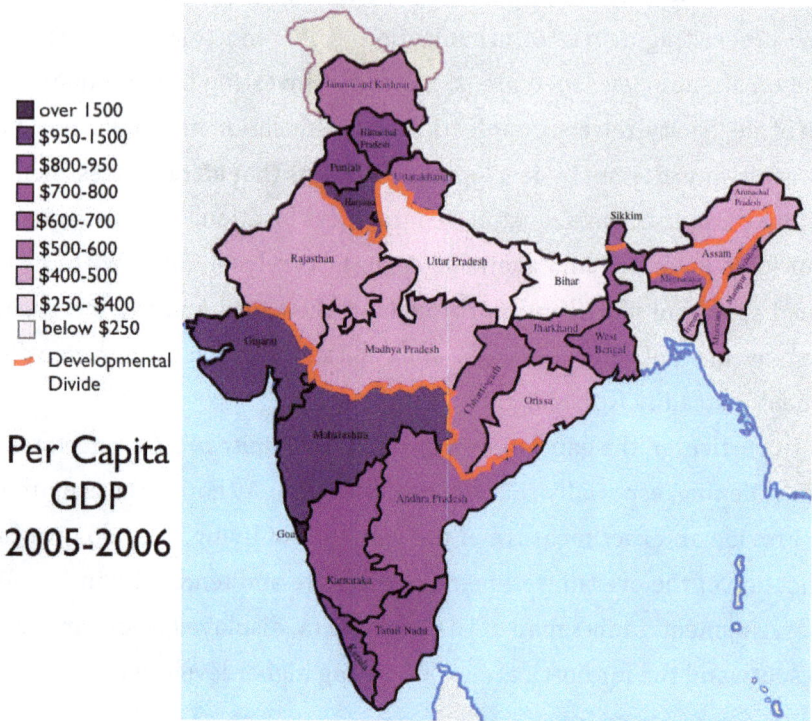

Source: Lewis (2010)

In Andhra Pradesh, there are lower than average levels of per capita GDP, despite the progress made in cities such as Hyderabad. Solely relying on GDP to determine the economic condition of the states is impractical. As we discuss the levels of growth and development within a country, we must consider whether improvements would indeed enable the poorest of the poor to move out of their unfortunate circumstances, or whether their economic mobility is too limited.

In developing countries especially, economic mobility may be limited by both historical and global factors (Kamau, 2005). Those at the bottom of the pyramid have new opportunities for employment as global firms continue their search for cheap, abundant labor, but it may not be enough to propel them out of their current economic status. Even if they manage to achieve great success and a rise in their current income levels, there may be other factors preventing them from truly obtaining socioeconomic mobility, such as geographical location or caste, as in India. There are those who may not be able to cope with the shock associated with these changes, and they may find themselves vulnerable to downward mobility instead of upward mobility.

There are a number of factors to be considered: (1) general education; (2) technology-oriented skill sets (e.g., information technology, engineering, digital media, and others); (3) management and leadership skills; and (4) business-friendly culture and local legal and regulatory environments.

SERVICES ACCESS AND SATISFACTION GAP

As we can see from Figure 1.1, satisfaction gained from public services has been quite poor (Paul et al., 2004).

Figure 1.1: The gap between physical access to services and the quality of services produced leads to an access/satisfaction gap.

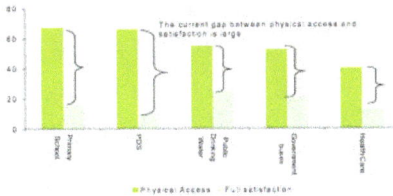

Source: Paul et al. (2004)

To understand the reasons behind this, let us first break this down into individual services. The first is primary school education. The government of India places emphasis on primary school education for children up to the age of fourteen and bans child labor to increase the number of children attending schools. The availability of primary school education has increased greatly, yet the level of satisfaction is still poor. Why is the Indian population so dissatisfied? The government has been unable to increase the number of teachers at a rate proportionate to students. A comparison of the number of primary school teachers to students in 2011 shows there are approximately two to three teachers for 100 students (World Bank, 2014). This can have a big impact on the quality of education that the children receive, mainly because teachers would have little time to give students individual attention and may have to standardize tests for a greater range of ages.

SYSTEMIC REFORM, NOT MORE OF THE SAME

"The existing primary school system is crying out for radical reform."
–Amartya Sen, Nobel Prize Laureate in Economics, 2002

The second service shown in the chart is public distribution service, a government service to distribute rations of grain. The service has wide coverage across the country and the majority of the population own ration cards. The ration card system has become increasingly sophisticated, particularly in Andhra Pradesh, where computer systems are used to prevent retail corruption. The availability of grain in shops is still very low due to issues with the transport of food, so even though the rationing system is widespread, it is inefficient.

Reliance on public and private healthcare systems varies heavily between states; however, most of the population relies on the private sector, because private facilities are closer than public ones. The dissatisfaction with public-sector facilities is due to long wait times, an inadequate number of hospital rooms, and inconvenient hours of operation.

Public transportation services have slowly been improving within the states, but government buses are rated poorly in terms of punctuality and frequency. The buses are often so crowded that people must pack themselves tightly to fit, resulting in unsafe travel conditions.

As of 2012, 93 percent of the population had access to water, with 91 percent in the rural area and 97 percent in urban areas. The government has increased investment and supply of improved water sources for a high percentage of the population, but people living in rural areas often have to travel great distances to obtain water from a safe drinking source. Instead, many of them risk contamination by using unsafe water sources that are more conveniently located.

Figure 1.2: Average hours per day and quantity of water service in selected Indian and comparative cities

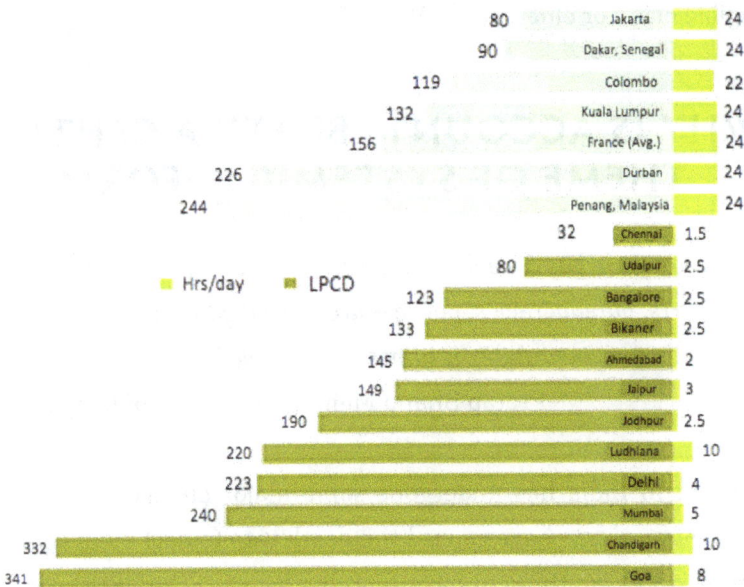

Source: Ministry of Urban Development and Water and Sanitation Program benchmarking study, ADB utilities book, verified with relevant utilities (2006)

The Ministry of Urban Development has provided statistics showing the water supply to various Indian cities is unreliable. We can see from Figure 1.2 that there are very few cities that have access to a continuous water supply. The Indian government is currently working on obtaining a 24/7 water supply system for the city of Coimbatore (Valsan, 2014). The city municipal corporation has also made plans to expand water supply to other cities as well. With continued research and development, India may soon be able to achieve continuous water supplies in the majority of its cities. This is a task that will take an enormous effort and commitment, both by the Indian government and its citizens.

The World Bank is also undertaking a water and sanitation project for low-income states in India. The goal is to improve piped water supply and sanitation services in selected rural communities in the target states through decentralized delivery systems. The World Bank will also increase the capacity of participating states to respond promptly and effectively to an eligible crisis or emergency (World Bank, 2014).

WHY IS ACCOUNTABILITY A CENTRAL THEME OF SYSTEMIC REFORM?

"If the Indian state has a weakness, it is this: most of the institutions and rules—courts, bureaucracies, police—are so riddled with perverse incentives structures that accountability is almost impossible."

–Pratap Bhanu Mehta, *The Burden of Democracy*, 2003

Healthcare in India has undergone some major changes over the years. These improvements have caused the death rate to decline in recent years and most states continue to have high birth rates. The healthcare system has a long way to go, though. According to World Bank statistics, the average life expectancy was lower than the global average in 2012, and the infant and adult mortality rates were both well over the global averages. The cost of an efficient healthcare system poses an immense problem for the Indian government, particularly due to the sheer size of the population. A major stumbling block in the healthcare system is the prevalence of unqualified healthcare workers.

Healthcare is provided through the public health system of hospitals and first responder primary healthcare centers (PHCs) as well as a large number of private providers (Das and Hammer, 2004). In the private sector, training periods vary greatly and some practitioners are severely under-qualified. Given the distance and expense of professional doctors and hospitals within the public health system, the majority of the Indian population seeks healthcare within the private sector, particularly in rural areas. This means they receive unprofessional healthcare in unsanitary conditions. In addition, providers at PHCs often underperform, providing lesser healthcare even when they know better. This problem is particularly rampant in Delhi. There are two parts to the city of Delhi—New Delhi and Old Delhi. New Delhi is the seat of government, many professionals live there, and it has a major medical university. Old Delhi is located in the heart of the city. It is a congested area with narrow roads and dilapidated buildings. It has a poorer population and many of those citizens seek healthcare from PHCs where the healthcare is of a lower quality.

Figure 1.3: The "effort deficit"—the gaps between what medical practitioners knew to do and what they actually did—is present in all public facilities, and enormous in PHCs in Delhi

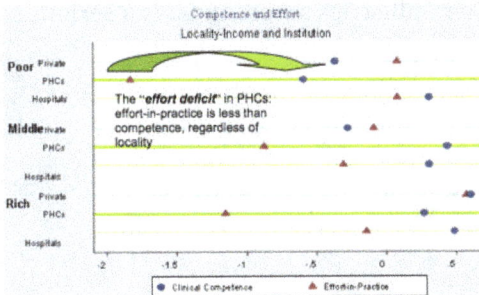

Source: Das and Hammer (2004)

Education is another area where lack of accountability and professionalism is an issue. Teachers have a high rate of absenteeism in many of India's states. According to a study in 2004 (figure 1.4), during unannounced visits to a nationally representative sample of government primary schools in India, 25 percent of teachers were absent from school, and only about half were teaching. Absentee rates varied from 15 percent in Maharashtra to 42 percent in Jharkhand, with higher rates concentrated in the poorer states.

Out of twenty-one states, more than half the teachers were absent in fourteen states (Kremer et al., 2004). When we consider such alarming percentages, we can assume that the problem is not with the individuals but with the system. Older teachers, more educated teachers, and head teachers were all paid more but were also more frequently absent; contract teachers were paid much less than regular teachers but had similar absentee rates. Although relative teacher salaries were higher in poorer states, absentee rates were also higher. The issue appears to stem from a lack of work culture—teachers and other workers don't feel motivated to succeed at their jobs the way workers do in other cultures.

Teacher absenteeism seemed to correlate with daily incentives to attend work: teachers were less likely to be absent at schools that had been inspected recently, had better infrastructure, and were closer to a paved road (Kremer et al., 2004). The lack of work culture and professionalism in education and other industries across India is a serious societal issue.

Figure 1.4: In a nationwide survey using unannounced visits the nationwide average was that less than half of teachers were both present and engaged in classroom activity

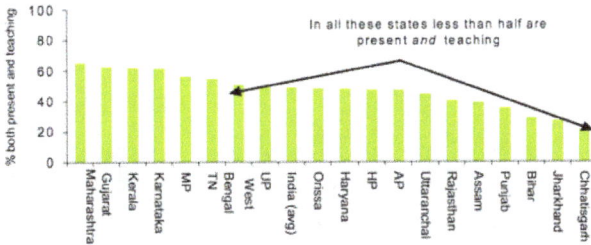

Source: Kremer et al. (2004)

COMMON PRINCIPLES OF ACCOUNTABILITY-ENHANCING REFORMS

"I must caution that outlays do not necessarily mean outcomes. The people of the country are concerned with outcomes. The prime minister has repeatedly emphasized the need to improve the quality of implementation and enhance the efficiency and accountability of the delivery mechanism."
                                        –Minister of Finance, "Budget Speech," February 28, 2005

Studies show that improved accountability comes from citizens' increased involvement. This can be achieved either by giving citizens more direct involvement in the government that oversees the programs or through a system where providers are directly accountable to the citizens who are their clients. Citizens will demand greater professionalism and accountability because they are the ones set to gain or lose from the service.

Figure 1.5: Relationships of accountability between citizens and the state and between citizens and service providers are central to improving services

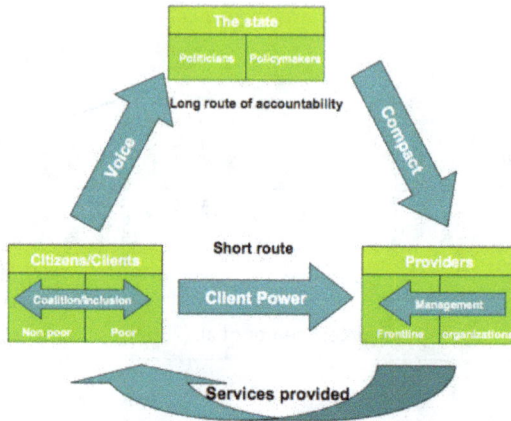

Source: World Bank (2003)

Such a system has been successful in Bangalore, where citizens monitor government services and give feedback in the form of a report card. Citizen's' ratings of the services put pressure on the agencies to improve. As shown in Figure 1.6, the satisfaction rate rose from 9 percent to 49 percent in only nine years.

Figure 1.6: Improvement in services in Bangalore following the introduction of the citizen report cards

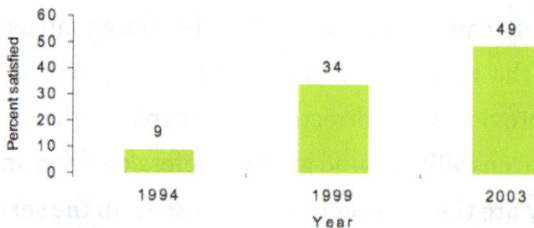

Source: Paul (2006)

As the government reforms and growth increases, the next hurdle will be to avoid a pattern of deceleration. Studies show that government investment can actually lead to a decrease in growth over time, because of bureaucracy and lack of work culture.

Figure 1.7: India needs to avoid the common pattern of growth deceleration following superior performance

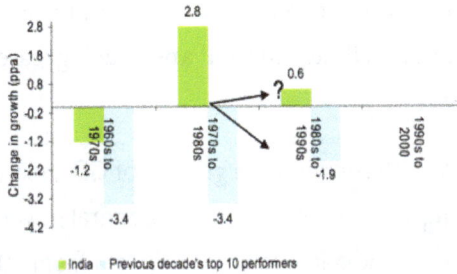

Source: Murgai, Pritchett and Wes (2006)

Using World Bank 2014 data, the study calculated a linear regression relationship between GDP and imports of goods and services, exports of goods and services, final consumption expenditure, and general government final consumption expenditure. The R square value for this sample is extremely high, indicating that the data are an excellent fit, almost 100 percent. This would make sense, given that imports, exports, consumption, and government expenditure are four of the five basic components of GDP using the expenditure approach.

From the regression, it was noted that each of these variables has a p value below 0.05, indicating that they are all statistically significant. There were no significant changes to GDP for an increase in each of these variables (i.e., more than a 100 percent difference); however, it is interesting to note that the government expenditure value is negative. This would mean that with each additional dollar contributed by government expenditure, GDP would decrease by $1.90.

The reason for this negative correlation is unusual, but not impossible. By contributing more money, the government actually decreases economic growth. This is most likely because government spending is inefficient, particularly in a developing country such as India. High ratios of government spending to GDP could mean excessive use of resources, impeding growth.

When comparing the data trends throughout the 2004 to 2012 period, we can calculate that government was spending at a faster rate than the population was consuming, even though consumption was expected to be the most significant contributor to GDP and much greater overall, as shown in the figure below.

Figure 1.8: Graph showing the growth of GDP, exports, imports, final consumption expenditure, and general government final expenditure of India in current US dollars from 2004 to 2012

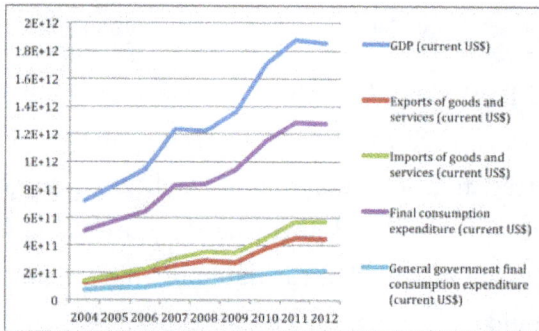

Source: World Bank (2014)

Figure 1.9: China has an enormous—
and growing—advantage in infrastructure

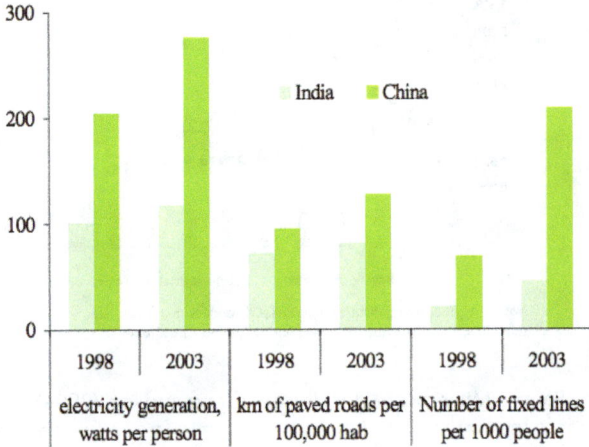

hab = 100,000 people

Source: Murgai, Pritchett, and Wes (2006)

Figure 1.10: Organized private-sector
unemployment—daily status (2001–2003)

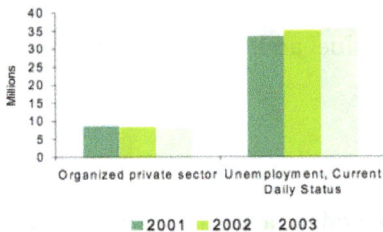

Source: GOI Planning Commission (2005), tables 8.1 and 8.2

Figure 1.11: Subsidies have gone up, productive investments down

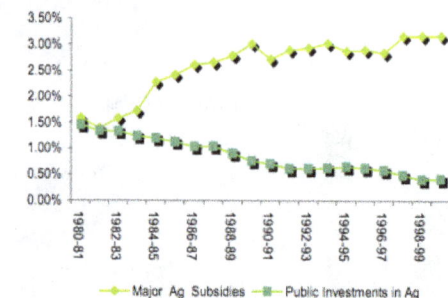

Notes: Agricultural subsidies include GOI foodgrain and fertilizer subsidies, state government power and irrigation subsidies.

Source: Ministry of Agriculture, Acharya and Jogi (2004)

Using World Bank data as of 2014, a regression analysis was conducted to investigate the relationship of agriculture, industry, and services to GDP in India for the period from 2004 to 2012. The independent variables used in the analysis can be defined as follows:

(1) AGRICULTURE

Agriculture includes forestry, hunting, and fishing, as well as cultivation of crops and livestock production.

(2) INDUSTRY

Industry comprises value added in mining, manufacturing, electricity, water, and gas.

(3) SERVICE

Services include value added in wholesale and retail trade (including hotels and restaurants); transport; and government, financial, professional, and personal services such as education, healthcare, and real estate services. Also included are imputed bank service charges, import duties, and any statistical discrepancies noted by national compilers as well as discrepancies arising from rescaling.

The coefficients of each of the variables of agriculture, industry, and services all had insignificant values when tested against GDP. This shows that changes in each factor produced minor changes in GDP. Agriculture had the most significant impact out of all the independent variables in the sample, resulting in a $3.56 increase in GDP for each additional dollar spent on agriculture. Agriculture in India has been growing at a steady rate and has now led the country to one of the leading positions in agricultural production around the world.

It was also noted that the p values for both industry and service were above 0.05, indicating that they are not statistically significant. Agriculture, however, has a low p value and overall the data seem to be a good fit, as indicated by the high R square value (99.96 percent).

Figure 1.12: Graph showing the growth of GDP, agriculture, industry, and services in India for the period 2004–2012

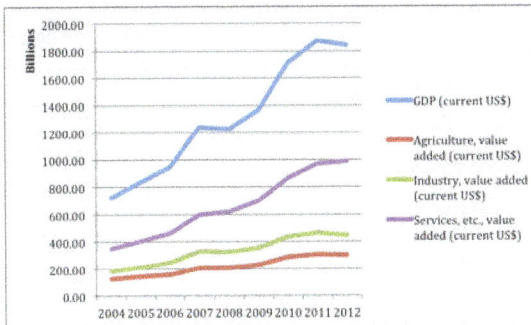

Source: World Bank (2014)

Figure 1.13: Growth accelerated in nearly all states in the 1980s, but gaps widened dramatically in the 1990s

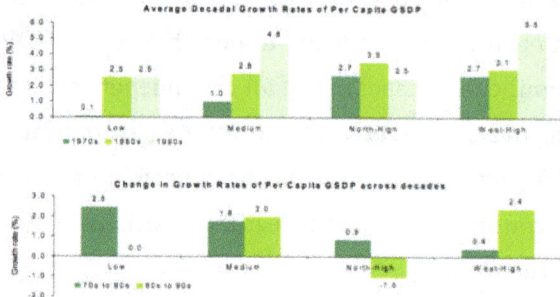

Decadal growth of per capita gross domestic product in Indian states, by income group or region, 1970s to 1990s

Note: Low-income states include Bihar, Madhya Pradesh, Orissa, Uttar Pradesh, and Rajasthan. Medium-income states include Andhra Pradesh, Karnataka, Kerala, Tamil Nadu, and West Bengal. North-High includes Punjab and Haryana, and West-High refers to Gujarat and Maharashtra.

Source: Murgai, Pritchett, and Wes (2006)

Figure 1.14: In most of the lagging states, over half of the residencies are not connected by roads

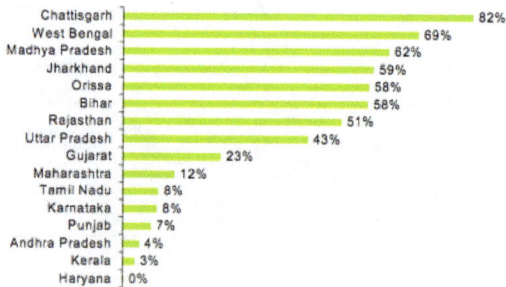

State	Percent
Chattisgarh	82%
West Bengal	69%
Madhya Pradesh	62%
Jharkhand	59%
Orissa	58%
Bihar	58%
Rajasthan	51%
Uttar Pradesh	43%
Gujarat	23%
Maharashtra	12%
Tamil Nadu	8%
Karnataka	8%
Punjab	7%
Andhra Pradesh	4%
Kerala	3%
Haryana	0%

Source: Ministry of Rural Development, government of India

Figure 1.15: The poorer sections of the wealthier Indian
states have nearly the same income as those in the poorer states

Distribution of per capita expenditures, by state, 1999–2000

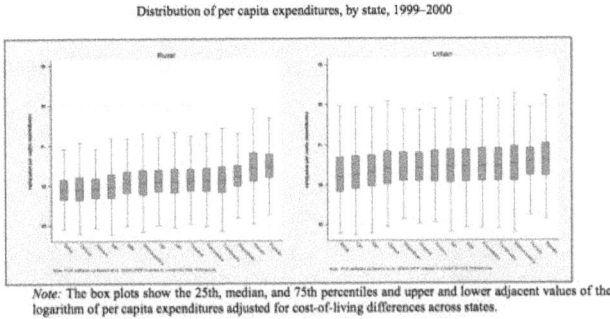

Note: The box plots show the 25th, median, and 75th percentiles and upper and lower adjacent values of the
logarithm of per capita expenditures adjusted for cost-of-living differences across states.

Source: Murgai, Pritchett, and Wes (2006)

In 1991, the Indian government shifted its policies toward economic liberalization. Regulations around foreign direct investment (FDI) were loosened, allowing Indian companies to issue shares to foreign investors. In some cases FDI could be made under an automatic route, meaning no government approval was required. Liberalization resulted in high growth but may also have contributed to increased inequality.

Urbanization in India has been experiencing speedy growth due to increased vehicle ownership, telephone usage, and electricity usage in rural areas. Rural GDP on its own has experienced an increase, due to rapid strides in rural road and electricity development. The urban population, however, has been expanding in size and has managed to achieve a population growth rate triple that of its rural counterpart.

According to a Barclays Equity Research, studies have shown that the urban contribution to India's GDP will reach 75 percent by 2020. Following current trends and using Excel data to compute future values, the urban population was found to be about half of the predicted rural population. If these predictions are correct, the urban population will contribute significantly more labor than rural populations. India's large pool of low-skilled labor may become drastically more urbanized and contribute to exports to increase GDP.

2

AGRICULTURE

OVERVIEW

According to the 2010 FAO (Food and Agriculture Organization) world agriculture statistics, India is the world's largest producer of many fresh fruits and vegetables, dairy, spices, select fibrous crops such as jute, and several staples such as millet and castor seed oil. India is the second-largest producer of wheat and rice, the world's major food staples. India is also the world's second- or third-largest producer of several dried fruits, material for agriculture-based textiles, roots and tuber crops, legumes, farmed fish, eggs, coconut, sugarcane, and numerous vegetables.

In 2010, India is one of the world's five largest producers of agricultural products, including many cash crops such as coffee and cotton. As of 2011, India is among the world's five largest producers of livestock and poultry, with one of the fastest growth rates. From canned, processed, and frozen food to dairy, seafood, meat, poultry, and grains, the Indian agricultural industry has plenty of choices for business.

The Department of Agriculture and Cooperation, under the Ministry of Agriculture, is the nodal organization responsible for the development of the agriculture sector in India. Under it, several other bodies, such as the National Dairy Development Board, develop other allied agricultural sectors.

One report from 2008 claimed India's population is growing faster than its ability to produce rice and wheat. Other recent studies claim that if India can reduce food staple spoilage, improve its infrastructure, and raise its farm productivity to levels achieved by other developing countries such as Brazil and China, then it can easily feed its growing population and still produce wheat and rice for global exports.

During the fiscal year ending in June 2011, when there was a normal monsoon season, Indian agriculture accomplished an all-time record production of 85.9 million tons of wheat, a 6.4 percent increase from the previous year. Rice output in India also hit a record high at 95.3 million tons, a 7 percent increase from the year earlier. The production of lentils and many other food staples also increased year over year. Indian farmers thus produced about 71 kilograms of wheat and 80 kilograms of rice for every member of the Indian population in 2011. The per capita supply of rice every year in India is now higher than the yearly per capita consumption of rice in Japan.

Aquaculture and catch fishery—the farming of fish and shellfish—is among the fastest-growing industries in India. Between 1990 and 2010, Indian fish capture harvest doubled, while aquaculture harvest tripled. In 2008, India was the world's sixth-largest producer of marine and freshwater capture fisheries and the second-largest aquaculture farmed fish producer. India exported 600,000 metric tons of fish products to nearly half of all the world's countries.

India has annually shown a steady nationwide average increase in the kilograms produced per hectare for various agricultural items over the last sixty years. These gains have come mainly from India's green revolution, improving road and power generation infrastructure, knowledge of gains, and reforms. Despite these recent accomplishments, agriculture in India has not reached its full potential in productivity and total output gains. Crop yields in India are still just 30 to 60 percent of the best sustainable crop yields of the farms in developed and developing countries. Additionally, poor infrastructure and disorganized retail have caused India to experience some of the highest food losses in the world.

INDIAN AGRICULTURE
AFTER INDEPENDENCE

Since 1947, India's economy, particularly agriculture, became increasingly self-reliant, and domestic production of various crops, poultry, and other commodities grew rapidly. Still, India was reliant on imports and foreign aid until the mid-1960s. In 1965 and 1966, India experienced severe drought. Indian leadership learned that they could not rely on food aid and was forced to reform the country's agricultural policy with a focus on self-sufficiency. India embraced the Green Revolution, a movement to adopt superior farming techniques and use varieties of high-yielding, disease-resistant wheat.

The major beneficiaries were the states of Punjab, Haryana, and western Uttar Pradesh. Agricultural production mainly increased in areas with a close proximity to rivers and other water sources. In these states, both farmers and governments set priorities on knowledge transfer and farm productivity—and this produced a substantial increase in food-grain production.

A hectare of land that produced 0.8 tons in 1948 began to produce 4.7 tons by 1975. India became self-sufficient by the late 1970s. This gave small landowners opportunities for further growth, and many became entrepreneurs in both production and distribution of agricultural products. New methods and techniques were employed—and so, by the end of 2000, many

Indian farms became high-yielding ones, producing about eight tons of wheat per hectare.

After achieving success in wheat farming, India turned its attention to improving rice production. By applying new Green Revolution methods, technology, and seeds, rice production reached new highs in 1970s and 1980s. This was especially evident in the heavily irrigated regions of Bihar, Odisha, and West Bengal. Later, in the 1980s, Indian agricultural policy made a shift to a pattern of production aligning with the demand, which also necessitated diversification of crops and other agricultural products. For example, farmers adopted new methods and applied science to dairy, fish, and livestock farming. This diversification in agriculture, along with population growth and increased movement to urban areas, has created the need for better agricultural infrastructure, reliable electricity and cold storage to preserve food, and improved retail systems.

Agriculture has been a major contributor to India's GDP over the years. As shown in Figure 2.1 below, agriculture accounted for 32 percent of GDP between 1990 and 1991. However, this number has been decreasing over the years as the industry and service sectors have expanded. Between 1970 and 2011, the GDP share of agriculture has fallen from 43 to 16 percent. This isn't a consequence of agricultural policy or because agriculture has become less important. The change is largely because of the rapid economic growth in services, industrial output, and nonagricultural sectors in India from 2000 to 2010. Today, agriculture is still an important part of the Indian economy, even though it is not as significant as it was in the past.

Figure 2.1: India's Sector wise Contribution to GDP

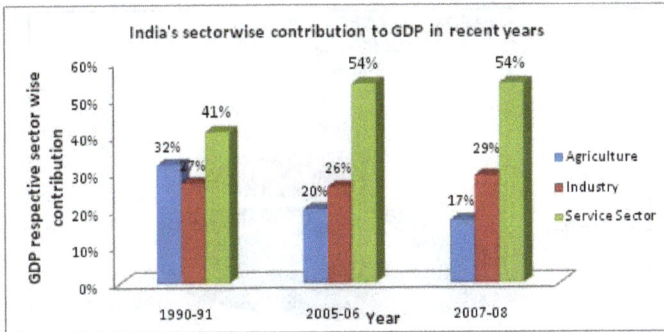

Source: Trade Chakra (2008)

OUTPUT

As of 2011, India had a large and diverse agricultural sector, accounting, on average, for about 16 percent of GDP and 10 percent of export earnings. India's arable land area of 159.7 million hectares (394.6 million acres) is the second-largest in the world, after the United States. Its gross irrigated crop area of 82.6 million hectares (215.6 million acres) is the largest in the world. As of 2011, India had the world's largest herds of buffalo and cattle, is the largest producer of milk, and has one of the largest and fastest growing poultry industries. India exported around 2 million metric tons of wheat and 2.1 million metric tons of rice in 2011 to Africa, Nepal, Bangladesh, and other regions around the world.

As we can see from Figure 2.2 below, Indian exports of agricultural products for the year 2004 to 2005 consisted of a variety of different products, primarily APEDA products (Agricultural and Processed Food Products Export Development Authority). APEDA is powered by the Ministry of Commerce and Industry in India and is mandated with the responsibility of export promotion and development for many different agricultural products.

Figure 2.2: Indian Exports of Agro Products

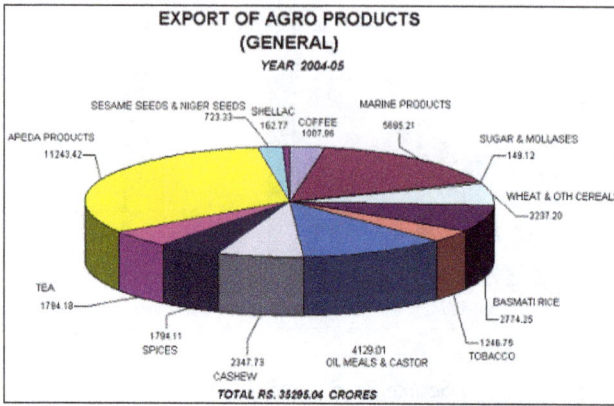

EXPORT OF AGRO PRODUCTS
(GENERAL)
YEAR 2004-05

SESAME SEEDS & NIGER SEEDS
723.33

SHELLAC
162.77

COFFEE
1007.96

MARINE PRODUCTS
5695.21

APEDA PRODUCTS
11243.42

SUGAR & MOLLASES
149.12

WHEAT & OTH CEREALS
2237.20

TEA
1794.18

BASMATI RICE
2774.25

1794.11
SPICES

2347.73
CASHEW

4129.01
OIL MEALS & CASTOR

1246.75
TOBACCO

TOTAL RS. 35295.04 CRORES

Source: India Exports

Figure 2.3 below shows the change in value added (in 2013 US dollars) from 2008 to 2012. As we can see from the chart, agriculture has been experiencing an almost steady incline, despite a slight dip between 2011 and 2012.

Figure 2.3: World Bank Agricultural Data

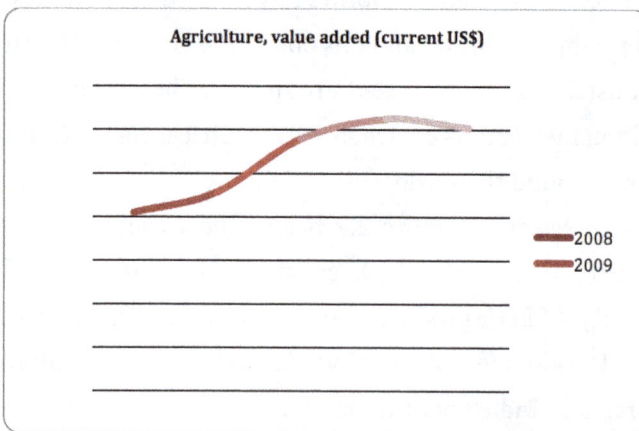

Agriculture, value added (current US$)

2008
2009

Source: World Bank (2014)

WORLD BANK OVERVIEWS

The World Bank is an international financial institution with the goal of ending extreme poverty. One of the functions of the World Bank is to provide status reports on the economy of various countries every few years. In the World Bank's overview of India in 2008, it mentioned the speedy growth of India's economy between 1998 and 2008. The overview also acknowledged that income inequality was rising. The overview asserted that developing the agriculture sector and making farming a viable living would be crucial to curbing poverty.

The World Bank's overview from 2011 argues that the growth rate of the agriculture sector is falling due to systemic issues. The overview cites a 2003 analysis: "For food staples, the annual growth rate in production during the six-year segments 1970–76, 1976–82, 1982–88, 1988–1994, and 1994–2000 were found to be respectively 2.5, 2.5, 3.0, 2.6, and 1.8 percent per annum. Corresponding analyses for the index of total agricultural production show a similar pattern, with the growth rate for 1994—2000 attaining only 1.5 percent per annum."

The poverty found in the area of agriculture affects women disproportionately to men. Figure 2.4 below shows the share of workers in Indian agriculture. Women workers remain stuck doing low-value and arduous agriculture work. Around two-thirds of women workers are still employed in agriculture as their principal economic activity, while the share for male workers has fallen to less than half (Chandrasekhar and Ghosh, 2011).

Figure 2.4: Share of Workers in Agriculture

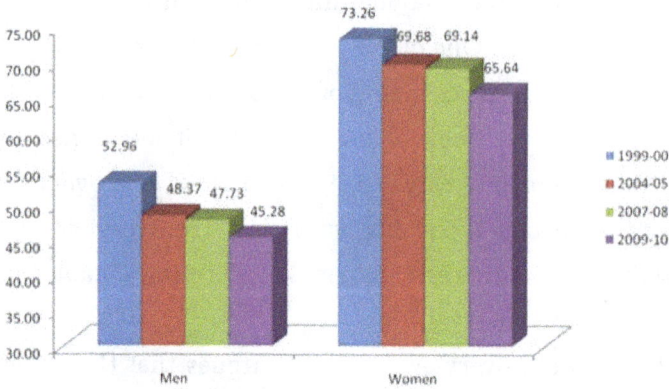

Source: Chandrasekhar and Ghosh (2011)

The sections below outline the many factors contributing to the lack of growth and low wages in the agriculture sector.

IRRIGATION

Irrigation in India refers to the supply of water from Indian rivers, tanks, wells, canals, and other artificial projects for the purpose of cultivation and agricultural activities. In a country such as India, 64 percent of cultivated land is dependent on monsoon rain. The economic significance of irrigation in India is to reduce over-dependence on monsoons, advance agricultural productivity, bring more land under cultivation, reduce instability in output levels, create job opportunities, provide electricity and transport facilities, control of floods, and prevent droughts.

INFRASTRUCTURE

India has very poor rural roads, which affects the timely supply of inputs and the timely transfer of outputs from Indian farms. Irrigation systems are inadequate and lack of water leads to crop failures in some parts of the country. In other areas, regional floods, poor seed quality, inefficient farming practices, lack of cold storage, and harvest spoilage causes over 30 percent of farmers' produce to go to waste. The lack of organized retail and competing buyers limit the ability of Indian farmers to sell surplus and commercial crops.

Figure 2.5 below shows the land use map of India. As we can see, India is primarily covered with stretches of farmable land and forestry. Out of the 304 million hectares of land in India for which records are available, roughly 40 million hectares are considered unfit for vegetation, as they are either in urban areas, occupied by roads and rivers, or under permanent snow, rock, or desert. Of the remaining 264 million hectares of land that have some potential for vegetation, 142 million hectares are cultivated, 67 million hectares are classified as forestland, and 55 million hectares are classified as fallow, wasteland, or land with pastures or groves (PACS, n.d.).

In percentage terms, according to World Bank estimates:

♦ Cultivable land amounts to around 58 percent of land that has potential for vegetation.

♦ 22 percent is forestland.

♦ 7 percent is uncultivated (revenue) or wasteland.

♦ 7 percent is rocky, barren land.

♦ 7 percent is urban/non-agricultural land.

Roughly 20 percent of the total land area is considered commons, which includes both cultivable and uncultivable wasteland and some forestland.

Figure 2.5: Land Use Map of India

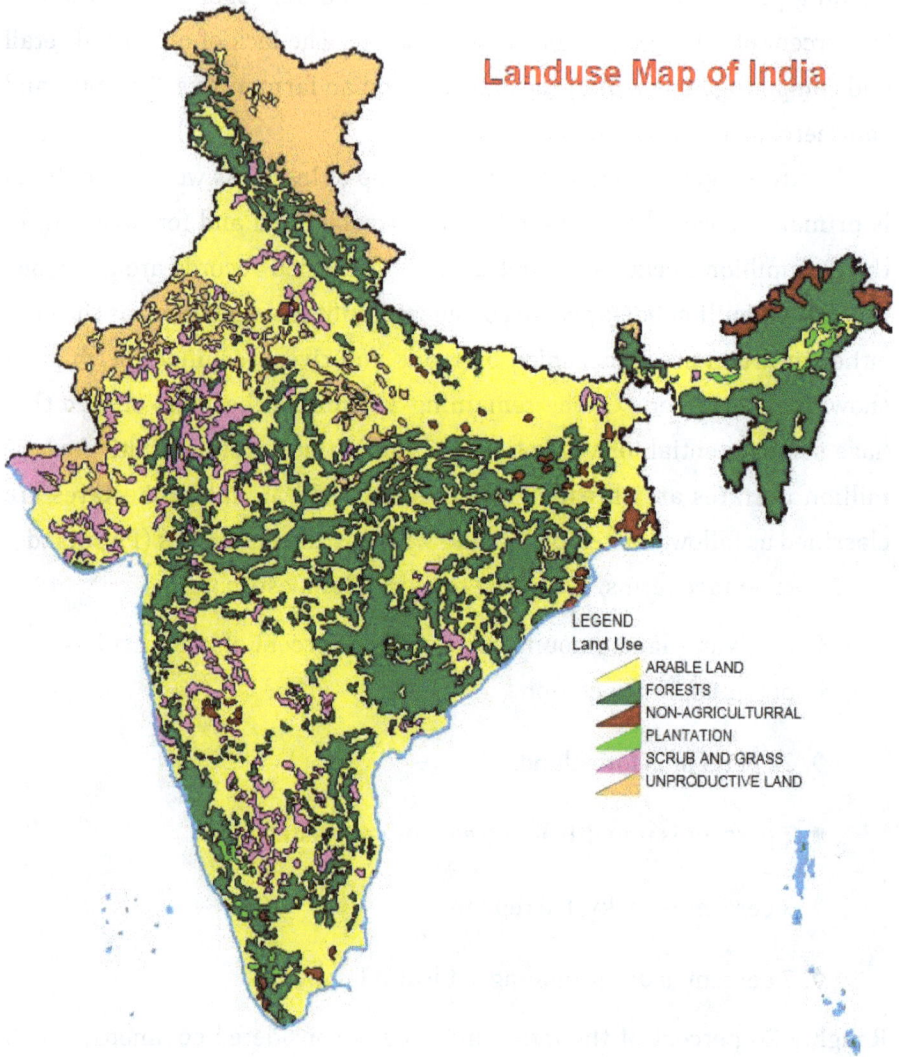

Source: National Institute of Hydrology (2009)

Figure 2.6: Indian Crop Production and Population

India – Crop Production and Population
Indian financial years

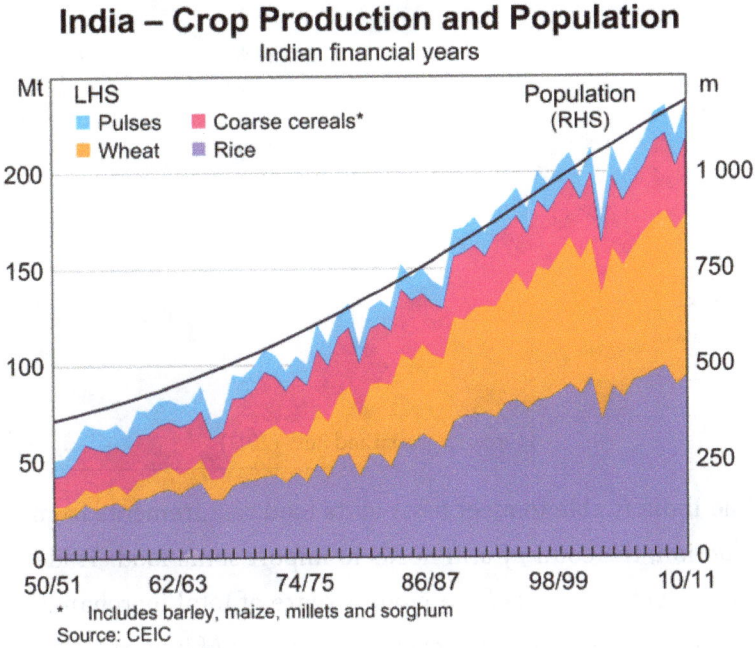

| Mt | LHS | | | Population | m |

* Includes barley, maize, millets and sorghum
Source: CEIC

Source: Cagliarini and Rush (2011)

The increase in agricultural production from the Green Revolution boosted rural incomes and caused food prices to fall. This had the effect of reducing rural poverty.

Figure 2.7 below shows the major agricultural products produced in India in 2008. Around the turn of the century, India overtook the United States as the world's largest producer of milk and is also a major producer of pulses, such as chickpeas and lentils, which are major sources of protein in vegetarian diets (Cagliarini and Rush, 2011).

Figure 2.7: Major Agricultural Products in 2008

Commodity	World Rank	Production Mt
Buffalo milk	1	60.9
Bananas	1	26.2
Paddy rice	2	148.7
Cow milk	2	44.1
Wheat	2	78.6
Sugar cane	2	348.2
Fresh vegetables	2	31.4
Cotton lint	2	3.8

Source: Cagliarini and Rush (2011)

While India is able to meet most of its food requirements from domestic production, the country still needs to import some food. Trade in agricultural products accounts for a modest share of total merchandise trade, currently about 8 percent of exports and 2 percent of imports. Agricultural trade has, however, grown rapidly over the past decade with the value of exports and imports both recording average annual growth rates of about 15 percent. Rice, animal feed, and seafood are India's principal food exports, while fruit and vegetables are its largest food imports (Figure 2.8). The diversification of agricultural production over the past couple of decades is also reflected in the changing composition of India's food exports, with the share of traditional exports like tea and coffee declining and the share of meat exports increasing. Food grain imports are relatively low, because India is broadly self-sufficient in grain production. Much of India's trade is with economies within a relatively short shipping distance, except for imports of wheat and sugar, which come from more distant sources, such as Russia and Brazil.

Figure 2.8: India's Agricultural Trade
Annual average, 2005–2009

	Average trade value US$ million	Average volume kt	Largest export/ import partner	Share of trade with largest partner Per cent
Exports				
Rice	2,137	4,287	Saudi Arabia	24.6
Animal feed	1,636	6,188	Vietnam	23.4
Crustaceans, molluscs	1,093	237	United States	21.6
Fruit and nuts	943	686	United States	22.9
Bovine meat	826	464	Vietnam	15.3
Imports				
Vegetables	1,257	2,650	Myanmar	39.3
Fruit and nuts	935	1,066	United States	19.0
Wheat	374	1,440	Russia	40.3
Sugar, mollasses and honey	258	713	Brazil	74.0

Source: Cagliarini and Rush (2011)

Private investment in the agricultural sector has also been limited by restricted access to credit and insurance, although access has generally improved over the past decade, with credit to the agricultural sector growing, on average, by more than 20 percent annually over the period. Nevertheless, credit extension remains predominately focused on assisting farmers through the annual cycle rather than helping them to finance the building and purchase of assets, such as tractors and pump sets. Government programs have been used to improve access to credit for farmers through a number of channels, including interest rate subsidies, debt relief, collateral-free loans, improving administration, and mandating banks to increase the flow of credit to rural customers. Much of this expansion has been through so-called microfinance facilities. While such lending has increased significantly over the past decade, borrowers have often faced interest rates as high as 40 percent. Furthermore, many have had difficulties repaying debts after crops have failed. In 2009—2010, the Indian government spent roughly 0.2 percent of GDP on debt waivers and debt relief for farmers.

The government is also gradually improving access to insurance through the National Insurance Scheme, although in 2009 only 18 million farmers were insured under the scheme. The scheme covers farmers who produce cereals, millets, legumes, oilseeds, sugarcane, cotton, and potatoes. In certain areas, farmers growing these crops and accessing Seasonal Agricultural Operations loans from financial institutions are required to purchase this insurance, while others can opt in voluntarily. Importantly, the scheme covers and other weather events as well as loss of production due to pests and disease. Premium rates are typically between 1.5 percent and 3.5 percent of the value insured, with those farming less than 2 hectares receiving a 50 percent subsidy. In 2009, the government tried a modified insurance scheme, expanding coverage to more areas and providing premium subsidies of between 40 and 75 percent. By reducing credit risk faced by lending institutions, increased coverage of insurance should give farmers better access to credit and encourage further investment in the agricultural sector.

The increase in the flow of credit to the agricultural sector has doubled investment from the private sector over the past decade, although public sector investment still dominates (Figure 2.9). Since the early 1990s, investment growth in the agriculture sector has averaged over 4 percent, although prior to the onset of the global financial crisis, investment growth exceeded 10 percent, suggesting that the improved flow of credit to the sector, and higher food prices, had encouraged capital, deepening on the sector (Figure 2.10).

Figure 2.9: India—Investment in Agriculture

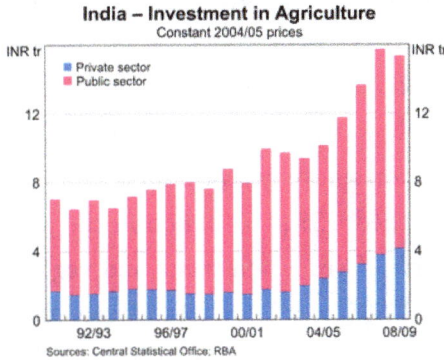

India – Investment in Agriculture
Constant 2004/05 prices

Source: Cagliarini and Rush (2011), Central Statistical Office, RBA

Figure 2.10: Indian Agricultural Investment—
Real Annual Growth in Gross Capital Formation

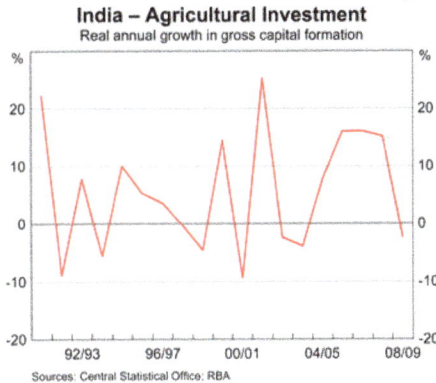

India – Agricultural Investment
Real annual growth in gross capital formation

Source: Cagliarini and Rush (2011), Central Statistical Office, RBA

In recent years, India has emerged as a major agricultural export-er, with exports climbing from just over $5 billion in 2003 to a record of more than $39 billion in 2013. India became the world's seventh-largest ex-porter of agricultural products in 2013, surpassing Australia. In terms of net exports, India is now the world's sixth-largest net exporter, with net exports double those of the EU- 28. The Indian government's support for both production and exports has contributed to the rapid growth in shipments, which are increasingly destined for developing nations, including the least developed nations (as classified by the United Nations).

Figure 2.11 below shows the breakdown of agricultural exports in 2003. Since then, Indian exports have grown immensely. The export of agriculture products has reached US$44.59 billion in the period of April 2013 to February 2014. Exports of processed fruits and vegetables and other processed foods reached US$5.24 billion, fresh fruits and vegetables reached US$1.45 billion, cereals were at US$10.54 billion, and animal products registered US$5.36 billion worth of exports in the same period of 2013 to 2014.

Figure 2.11: Indian Agricultural Exports

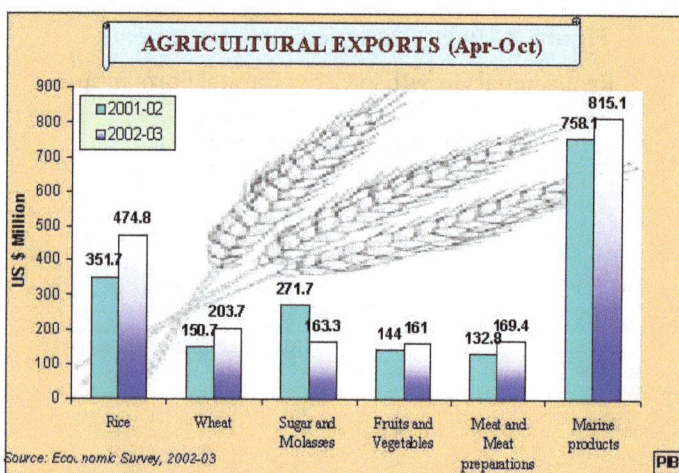

Source: Press Information Bureau, India (2003)

CHALLENGES FOR INDIAN AGRICULTURE

India lacks cold storage, food packaging, as well as a safe and efficient rural transport system. The result is one of the world's highest food spoilage rates, particularly during Indian monsoons and other adverse weather conditions.

Food travels to the Indian consumer through a slow and inefficient chain of traders. Indian consumers buy agricultural produce in suburban markets known as *sabzi mandi*. India has only 5,386 stand-alone cold storage facilities, which have a total capacity of 23.6 million metric tons. However, 80 percent of this storage is used only for potatoes. The remaining infrastructure capacity is less than 1 percent of the annual farm output of India, and grossly inadequate during peak harvest seasons. This leads to an average of 30 percent losses in certain perishable agricultural output every year.

Indian agriculture includes a mix of traditional and modern . In some parts of India, farmers still use cattle to plough fields. Traditional farms have some of the lowest per capita productivity and income for farmers. Since 2002, India has become the world's largest manufacturer of tractors, with 29 percent of world's output in 2013; it is also the world's largest tractor market.

The following is an excerpt from an article by the Navjivan Foundation, a nonprofit organization dedicated to the growth of India's economy:

> *Slow agricultural growth is a concern for policymakers as some two-thirds of India's people depend on rural employment for a living. Current agricultural practices are neither economically nor environmentally sustainable and India's yields for many agricultural commodities are low. Poorly maintained irrigation systems and almost universal lack of good extension services are among the factors responsible. Farmers' access to markets is hampered by poor roads, rudimentary market infrastructure, and excessive regulation.*

PRODUCTIVITY

Although India has attained self-sufficiency in food staples, the productivity of Indian farms is below that of Brazil, the United States, France, and other nations. Indian wheat farms, for example, produce about a third of the wheat per hectare per year compared to farms in France. Rice productivity in India was less than half that of China. Production of other staples is similarly low. The total factor productivity growth in India remains below 2 percent per annum. In contrast, China's total factor productivity growth is about 6 percent per annum, even though China also has smallholding farmers, and they constitute over 97 percent of China's farming population. The difference is that Chinese smallholder farmers are able to rent their land to larger farmers, and China's organized retail and extensive Chinese highways are able to provide the incentive and infrastructure necessary for sharp increases in farm productivity.

Several studies suggest India could eradicate hunger and malnutrition within its borders and be a major source of food for the world by achieving productivity comparable with other countries.

By contrast, Indian farms in some regions post the best yields for sugarcane, cassava, and tea crops. Crop yields for some farms in India are within 90 percent of the best yields achieved by farms in developed parts of the world, such as the United States and the European Union.

No single state in India is the best in every crop. Tamil Nadu achieved the highest yields in rice and sugarcane, Haryana in wheat and coarse grains, Karnataka in cotton, Bihar in legumes, while other states do well in horticulture, aquaculture, and flower and fruit plantations. These differences in agricultural productivity within India are a function of local infrastructure, soil quality, microclimates, local resources, farmer knowledge, and innovations.

The Indian food distribution system is highly inefficient. Movement of agricultural produce within India is heavily regulated, with interstate and even interdistrict restrictions on marketing and moving agricultural goods. One study suggests Indian agricultural policy would best focus on improving rural infrastructure primarily in the form of irrigation and flood control infrastructure as well as the transfer of knowledge about better yielding and more disease-resistant seeds. Additionally, cold storage, hygienic food packaging, and efficient modern retail to reduce waste can improve output and rural incomes.

The low productivity in India is a result of the following factors:

♦ The average size of land holdings is very small (less than 2 hectares) and is subject to fragmentation due to land ceiling acts and, in some cases, family disputes. Such small land holdings are often over manned, resulting in disguised unemployment and low productivity of labor.

♦ Adoption of modern agricultural practices and use of technology is inadequate, hampered by ignorance of such practices, high costs, and impracticality in the case of small land holdings.

♦ According to the World Bank, Indian Branch: Priorities for Agriculture and Rural Development, India's large agricultural subsidies are hampering productivity-enhancing investment. Overregulation of agriculture has increased costs, price risks, and uncertainty. The government intervenes in labor, land, and credit markets. India has inadequate infrastructure and services. The World Bank also says that the allocation of water is inefficient, unsustainable, and inequitable. The irrigation infrastructure is deteriorating. The overuse of water is currently being covered by over pumping aquifers, but these are falling by one foot of groundwater each year, so this is a limited resource. The Intergovernmental Panel on Climate Change released a report that food security may be a big problem in the region after 2030.

♦ Illiteracy, general socioeconomic backwardness, slow progress in implementing land reforms, and inadequate or inefficient finance and marketing services for farm produce contribute to inefficiency.

♦ Government policy is inconsistent. Agricultural subsidies and taxes often changed without notice for short-term political ends.

♦ Irrigation facilities are inadequate, as revealed by the fact that only 52.6 percent of the land was irrigated in 2003–2004. The result is that farmers are still dependent on rainfall, particularly during the monsoon season. A good monsoon results in a robust growth for the economy as a whole, while a poor monsoon leads to sluggish growth. Farm credit is regulated by NABARD, which is the statutory apex agent for rural development in the subcontinent. At the same time, over pumping made possible by subsidized electric power is leading to an alarming drop in aquifer levels.

♦ A third of all food that is produced rots due to inefficient supply chains. Investors are blocked from using the Walmart business model (low prices on a large scale at minimal cost), which would improve efficiency, because of laws against foreign investment in the retail sector.

FARMER SUICIDES

Following the liberalizing economic reforms of 1991, the government withdrew support from the agricultural sector. These reforms, along with other factors, led to a rise in farmer suicides. The rise in farmer suicides showed that conditions for farmers had become dire. Various studies identify the important factors in farmer suicides as the withdrawal of government support, insufficient or risky credit systems, the difficulty of farming semiarid regions, poor agricultural income, absence of alternative income opportunities, a downturn in the urban economy that forced nonfarmers into farming, and the absence of suitable counseling services.

DIVERSION OF AGRICULTURAL LAND FOR NON AGRICULTURAL PURPOSE

Rezoning is another threat to the agriculture sector. The National Policy for Farmers (2007) calls for the protection of productive farmland, allowing rezoning only in "exceptional circumstances." The 2013 draft National Land Utilization Policy notes that as food demands rise and less land is available for farming, it becomes even more important to protect the remaining farms from development. The Foreign Exchange Management Act regulations prohibit foreign ownership of farmland. Real estate companies have been trying to circumvent this rule, since foreign ownership is permitted in urban areas. The Ministry of Urban Development has formed a committee to investigate.

INITIATIVES

The estimated level of investment required for the development of marketing, storage, and cold storage infrastructure would be huge. The government has not been able to implement various schemes to raise investment in marketing infrastructure. Among these schemes are construction of rural godowns—building storage for grains—and market research and information networks as a means for farmers to gather information about the market and set their prices accordingly.

DEVELOPING AND STRENGTHENING AGRICULTURAL MARKETING INFRASTRUCTURE

Agriculture marketing is the service of moving the product to the consumer. These services could be developed and strengthened to ensure farmers receive better prices. Grading and standardization are means of regulating the quality of agricultural products, for example food items can be graded based on factors like size, ripeness, location of origin, and so on. Food products can be standardized so that they must meet certain specifications to be sold.

The government of India has adopted and implemented several initiatives in the past few months. Some of the recent major initiatives are as follows:

◆ The Ministry of Food Processing Industries has taken some new initiatives to develop the food-processing sector, which will help to enhance the incomes of farmers and export of agricultural and processed foods, among others. These include the reduction in excise duties for food processing machinery and opening Mega Food Parks, a network of farm collection and processing centers aimed at increasing the processing of perishable foods to expand India's share in global food trade.

◆ The government of Telangana has allocated Rs 4,250 crore (US$ 687.38 million) for the first phase of a farm loan waiver scheme. The scheme is expected to benefit 3.6 million farmers who had taken loans of Rs 100,000 (US$1,617.37) or below before March 31, 2014.

◆ The government of India plans to launch a new insurance scheme to protect farmers and their incomes against production and price risks. The new insurance scheme is expected to encourage farmers toward crop diversification.

◆ The Ministry of Agriculture has signed a memorandum of understanding with fifty-two countries to provide better agricultural facilities for cooperation in the field of agriculture and allied sectors.

◆ India and Bhutan plan to strengthen strategic cooperation in the field of agriculture and allied sectors.

♦ The government of India plans to invest Rs 50,000 crore (US$8.08 billion) to revive four fertilizer plants and set up two new plants to produce farm nutrients. In addition, the government is also in talks with the government of Iran to set up a 1.2 million tons per annum (MTPA) urea plant in Iran on the lines of India's joint venture (JV) with Oman.

THE ROAD AHEAD

The government's liberal FDI policies have opened the doors for several foreign companies to set up operations in India. Also, there is scope for the use of genetically modified crops to increase the yield in farms. The Twelfth Five-Year Plan's estimates of expanding the storage capacity to 35 million ton (MT) and the target of achieving an overall growth of 4 percent will help in improving the growth of the agriculture sector. Furthermore, Dairy Vision 2025 has been planned to take stock of the current situation across the dairy value chain and evolve strategies for increasing productivity and profitability of farmers. Agriculture is a major aspect of India's economy. For the country to achieve more uniform development, it is vital for farming to be a fair and profitable business.

3

TEXTILES

OVERVIEW

Second to agriculture, the textile industry has traditionally generated huge employment for both skilled and unskilled labor. Textiles provide direct employment to over 35 million people in India and accounted for 11.04 percent of all exports from April to July 2010 according to the Ministry of Textiles. From 2009 to 2010, the Indian textile industry was pegged at US$55 billion—64 percent of the domestic demand for services. In 2010, there were 2,500 textile weaving factories and 4,135 textile finishing factories in all of India.

Figure 3.1 below shows the value of the apparel retail industry. The Indian apparel industry grew from US$19.2 billion in 2005 and was estimated to grow to US$28.1 billion in 2009. The compound annual growth rate (CAGR) of the Indian apparel industry during that period was 10 percent. Capacity has built over the years, leading to low costs per unit, making India's players more competitive. Outsourcing has increased over the years as 25 Indian players went from being traders of global retail giants to vendor partners.

Figure 3.1: India Apparel Retail Industry Value (USD billion)

India apparel retail industry value (USD billion)

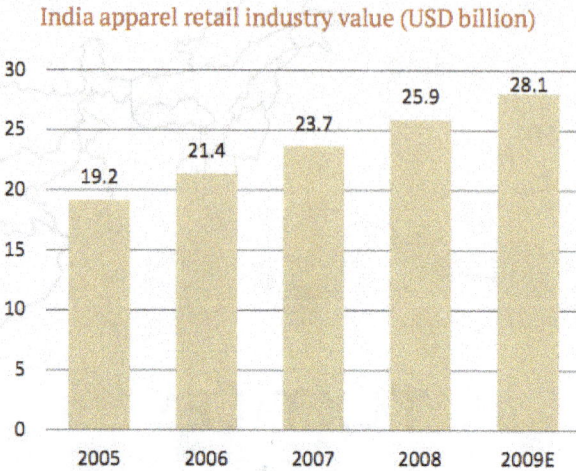

Source: Datamonitor, Aranca Research, IBEF (2011)

HISTORY

Archaeological surveys and studies have found that four thousand years ago, the people of Harrapan civilization knew how to weave and spin cotton. Vedic literature, dating back to 1500 BCE, also contains references to weaving and spinning materials.

There was also textile trade in early centuries. Block-printed and resist-dyed fabrics that originated in Gujarat were found in tombs of Fostat, Egypt, showing that cotton textiles were largely exported to the Egypt or the Nile civilization in medieval times. Large quantities of north Indian silk were traded to western countries on the Silk Route in China. During the late seventeenth and eighteenth centuries, the early Industrial Revolution in Europe, Indian cotton was a major export to meet the need of the European industries. Indian silk and Muslin cloth of Bengal, Bihar, and Orissa were also exported to other countries by the East Indian Company. Consequently, nationalist movements developed, such as the famous Swadeshi movement headed by Aurobindo Ghosh, aimed at improving conditions in India by removing the British from power, for example by boycotting British products.

Figure 3.2 below shows the primary locations of different textile-related industries throughout India, such as the cotton and silk industries. As we can see from the map, these industries mostly seem to be located in the northeastern area and along the southwest border. The cotton industry is particularly prominent in Mumbai and Ahmedabad, due to their locations and nearby markets in neighboring states, as well as their abundant supply of labor and skills for the cotton industry.

Figure 3.2: Textile Map of India

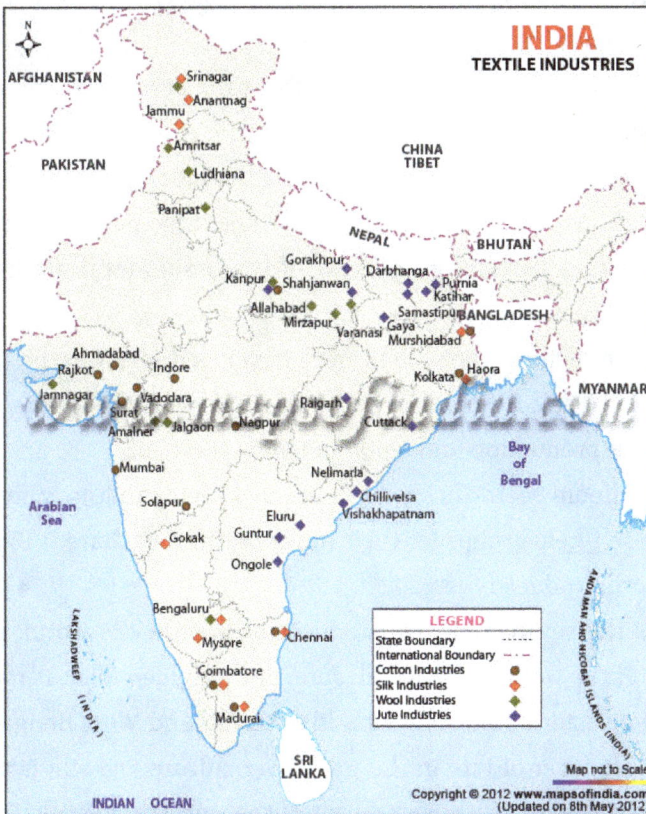

Source: Maps of India (2012)

PRODUCTION IN
THE DECENTRALIZED SECTOR

India is the second-largest producer of fiber in the world, with industries in cotton, silk, jute, wool, and man-made fibers. Cotton is the most produced fiber, making up 60 percent of the Indian textile industry.

The strong domestic demand and the revival of the economic markets in 2009 has led to huge growth of the Indian textile industry. In December 2010, the domestic cotton price was up by 50 percent compared to the December 2009 prices. High cotton prices are a result of floods in Pakistan and China. India projected a high production of textiles (325 lakh bales for 2010–2011). India's share of global textile trading has increased by 7 percent in five years. The rising prices are the major concern of the domestic producers in the country.

The following sectors make up India's textile production. Man-made fibers account for the largest sector of the textile production in India. These include clothes manufactured using synthetic fiber or filament or synthetic yarns. Man-made fibers are produced in the large power loom factories. This sector has a share of 62 percent of the India's total production and provides employment to about 4.8 million people.

The cotton sector is the second-most developed sector in the Indian textile industries. The cotton sector provides employment to several thousand people, but its production and employment is seasonal.

The handloom sector is a well-developed sector that is mainly dependent on the self-help groups for their funds. Its market share is 13 percent of the total cloth produced in India.

India is the seventh-largest producer of wool in the world, producing 1.8 percent of the world's total wool. Jute, or the golden fiber, is mainly produced in the eastern states of India like Assam and West Bengal. India is the largest producer of jute in the world. Sericulture and silk is a labor-intensive sector that produces 18 percent of the world's total silk. India is the second-largest producer in the world after China. The main types of silk produced are mulberry, eri, tasar, and muga.

INDIAN TEXTILE POLICY

NATIONAL TEXTILE POLICY 2000

In 2000, the government of India announced the National Textile Policy of 2000, which replaced the previous Textile Policy of 1985. One of the main objectives of the new policy was to enable the textile industry to attain and sustain a preeminent global standing in the manufacture and export of clothing.

Other key objectives of the policy:

♦ Equipping the industry to withstand pressures of import penetration and maintaining dominant presence in the domestic market

♦ Liberalizing controls and regulations so that different segments of the textile industry are able to perform in a greater competitive environment

♦ Developing a strong multifiber base with emphasis on product upgrade and diversification

♦ Sustaining and strengthening the traditional knowledge, skills, and capabilities of the weavers and craftsmen.

DERESERVATION OF THE GARMENT SECTOR

Prior to the National Textile Policy of 2000, the Indian garment sector was reserved for the small-scale industries (SSI) sector; large enterprises could manufacture apparel, provided they met the export obligation of mini-mum 50 percent of output. This policy acted as an impediment to growth by preventing the capacity for expansion and the technological upgrade of garment manufacturing units. To improve competitiveness of garment manufacturers, the Textile Policy of 2000 removed this restriction and dereserved garments, hosiery, and knitwear from the SSI sector.

SUB SEGMENTS
OF THE TEXTILE INDUSTRY

Most companies in the textile industry operate in the cotton segment (Fig-ure 3.3). Forty-two percent of the companies dealing in cotton earn more than 50 percent of their revenue from the international market. The aver-age revenue growth of the companies dealing in silk was 44 percent. For cotton, it was 35 percent over the past two years.

Figure 3.3: Textile Industry Sub segments

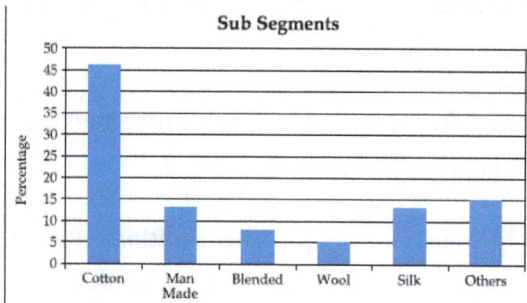

Source: D&B India (2008)

INVESTMENTS

Figures 3.4 and 3.5 below give an overview of the investments in the Indian textile sector. The textiles sector has witnessed a spurt in investment during the last five years. The industry (including dyed and printed fabric) attracted FDI worth US$1,495.07 million from April 2000 to September 2014. These figures show the volume of exports and their composition, respectively. Cotton plays an important role in the Indian economy, as the country's textile industry is predominantly cotton based. The Indian textile industry contributes about 11 percent to industrial production, 14 percent to the manufacturing sector, 4 percent to the GDP, and 12 percent to the country's total export earnings. The cotton cultivation in India in 2013-2014 was estimated at 37 million bales (170 kg each) of cotton, making it the second-largest producer of cotton worldwide after China.

Figure 3.4: Investment in Textile Industry in India

Investment in Textile industry in India

Sl.No	Segment	Investment (Rs.in crore)
1.	Ginning & Processing	1,800
2.	Spinning	10,600
3.	Weaving	22,950
4.	Knitting	3,150
5.	Woven Processing	25,800
6.	Knit Processing	8,550
7.	Clothing	24,000
8.	Jute	500
9.	Silk, Wool	1,200
	Total	98,550

Source: http://texmin.nic.in

Source: Chellasamy and Karuppaiah (n.d.), Ministry of Textiles

Figure 3.5: Investment in Textile Industry in India

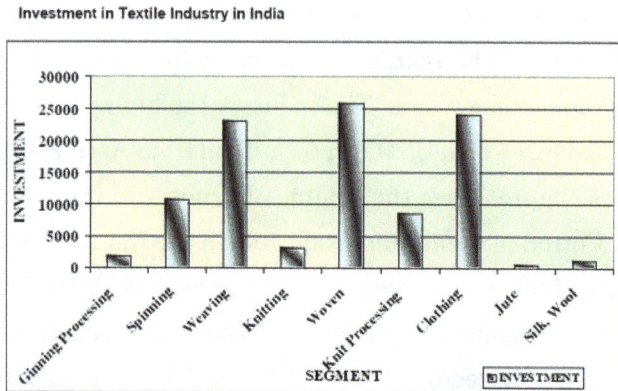

Source: Chellasamy and Karuppaiah (n.d.) Ministry of Textiles

Some of the major investments in the Indian textiles industry are as follows:

♦ Arvind Lifestyle, a manufacturer that produces clothing for international brands such as The Gap and Aeropostale, invested Rs 126 crore (US$20.37 million) as capital expenditure in the 2013 fiscal year to expand its footprint. "We are looking at Rs 126 crore (US$20.37 million) capex this fiscal, up from Rs 90 crore (US$14.54 million) spent last fiscal, as we plan to open around 200 stores," said Mr. J. Suresh, managing director and chief executive of Arvind Lifestyle.

♦ Arvind Lifestyle brands also made a foray into the children's wear retail segment in India. The company signed a franchise agreement worth US$1.8 billion with the US-based company The Children's Place.

♦ Sangam India ventured into the seamless garment segment with an investment of Rs 120 crore (US$19.39 million). The company set up 10,000 spindles for slub yarn and a mercerize unit, in addition to modernizing the processing division.

◆ Nonresident Indian businessman Apurv Bagri acquired controlling stake in leading Indian denim maker Spykar Lifestyle. Mr. Bagri's Metmin Investment Holdings bought a 30 percent stake from private equity firm Avigo Capital, which owns a majority stake in Spykar.

◆ Private equity firm Everstone invested Rs 100 crore (US$ 16.16 million) for an undisclosed minority stake in the fashion label of designer Ritu Kumar.

FOREIGN DIRECT INVESTMENT

One hundred percent FDI is allowed in the textiles sector under the automatic route; this encourages international textile companies to set up base in India. Figure 3.6 depicts inflow of FDI into the Indian textiles industry. The drop in 2008–2009 was due to the worldwide recession.

Figure 3.6: Inflow of FDI into the Textiles Sector (in billions of rupees)

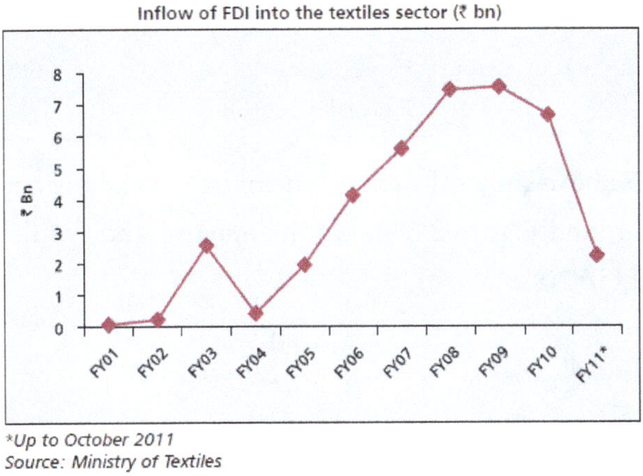

Inflow of FDI into the textiles sector (₹ bn)

*Up to October 2011
Source: Ministry of Textiles

Source: D&B India, Ministry of Textiles (2011)

MARKET SIZE

The Indian textile industry is set for strong growth, buoyed by strong domestic consumption as well as export demand. The most significant change in the Indian textile industry has been the advent of man-made fibers (MMF). India has successfully placed its innovative range of MMF textiles in almost every country across the globe. MMF production recorded an increase of 3 percent during the period April to July 2014.

In addition, the production of cotton yarns also increased by 4 percent from April to July 2014. Blended and 100 percent synthetic yarn production increased by 5 percent from April to July 2014. Cloth production by mill sector registered a growth of 6 percent from April 2013 to July 2014. The hosiery sector of cloth production increased by 8 percent from April to July 2014. Total cloth production grew by 2 percent from April to July 2014.

Figure 3.7: India's Textile Market Size

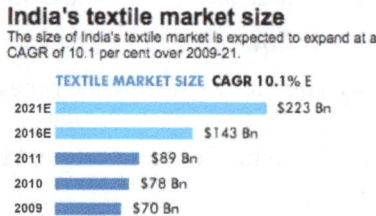

India's textile market size
The size of India's textile market is expected to expand at a
CAGR of 10.1 per cent over 2009-21.

TEXTILE MARKET SIZE **CAGR 10.1% E**

2021E	$223 Bn
2016E	$143 Bn
2011	$89 Bn
2010	$78 Bn
2009	$70 Bn

Source: IBEF (2014)

Figure 3.7 above shows the expected volume of expansion of the Indian textile market, and Figure 3.8 shows the apparel and textile share of the overall market in 2012.

Figure 3.8: India's Textile and Apparel Sector

India's textile and apparel sector
In 2012, apparel had a share of 69 per cent of the overall market; textiles contributed the remaining 31 per cent.

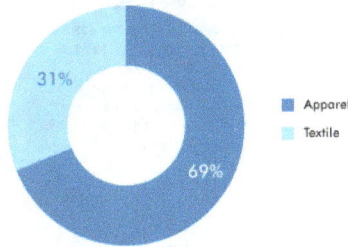

31%

69%

■ Apparel
  Textile

Source: IBEF (2014)

ORGANIZED SECTOR

The Indian textile industries are mainly dominated by government, semi government, and large private institutions rather than small businesses and individuals. According to Kearney's Retail Apparel Index, India ranked as the fourth most promising market for apparel retailers in 2009. There is a large scope of improvement in the textile industry of India due to the huge increase in personal disposable income among Indians after the 1991 liberalization. There is also a large growth of the organized sector in the Indian textile industries. Foreign brands in collaboration with Indian companies established business in India, including Puma, Armani, Benetton, Esprit, Levi Strauss, Hugo Boss, Liz Claiborne, Crocs, and so on.

The major Indian Industries include Bombay Dyeing, Fabindia, Grasim Industries, JCT Limited, Lakshmi Machine Works, Lakshmi Mills, and Mysore Silk.

Figure 3.9: India's Textile Exports

India's textile exports
Exports grew to US$ 33.3 billion in FY12 from US$ 17.6 billion in FY06, implying a CAGR of 11.2 per cent.

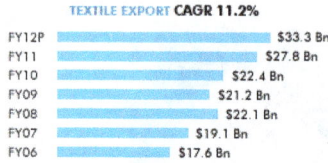

TEXTILE EXPORT **CAGR 11.2%**

FY12P	$33.3 Bn
FY11	$27.8 Bn
FY10	$22.4 Bn
FY09	$21.2 Bn
FY08	$22.1 Bn
FY07	$19.1 Bn
FY06	$17.6 Bn

Source: IBEF (2014)

During 2013 and 2014 in India, cotton yarn production increased by 2 percent, and cloth production by the mill and power loom sector increased by 5 percent and 6 percent, respectively. The states of Gujarat, Maharashtra, Andhra Pradesh, Haryana, Punjab, Madhya Pradesh, Rajasthan, Karnataka, and Tamil Nadu are the major cotton producers in India.

Figure 3.10: India's Textile Exports Share

India's textile exports share
Readymade garments was the largest contributor to total textile and apparel exports from India in FY12P; the segment had a share of 39 per cent.

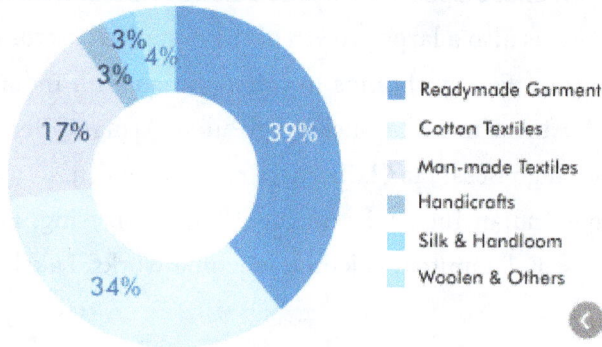

- Readymade Garment
- Cotton Textiles
- Man-made Textiles
- Handicrafts
- Silk & Handloom
- Woolen & Others

Source: IBEF (2014)

KEY MARKETS
AND EXPORT DESTINATIONS

India accounted for about 4.72 percent of the global textile and clothing trade in 2011. The total value of textile products exported from India was estimated at US$40 billion in FY 2013. India has overtaken Italy and Germany and is now the second-largest textile exporter in the world. India was the third-largest supplier of textiles and clothing to the US in 2013, contributing about 6.01 percent of its total imports. China is the biggest importer of raw cotton from India. The other major cotton importing countries from India are Bangladesh, Egypt, Taiwan, and Hong Kong, among others.

Figure 3.11: Indian Cotton Exports to Other Countries, 2002–2003

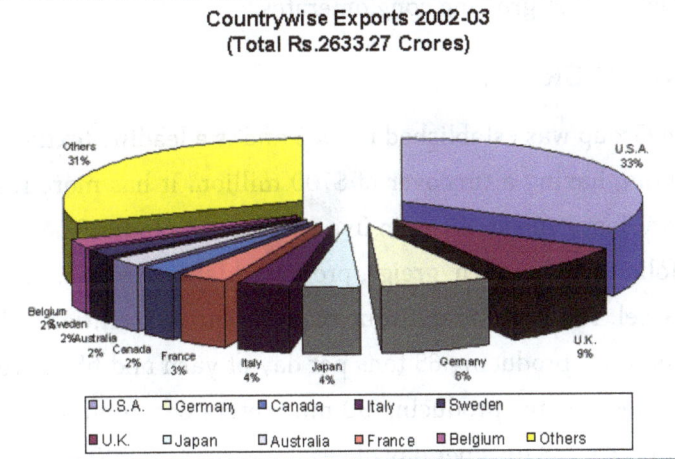

Countrywise Exports 2002-03
(Total Rs.2633.27 Crores)

Source: Texprocil

Figure 3.11 above shows the countries where India exported cotton during 2002–2003. The United States accounted for the majority of exporters within that year.

PROFILES OF MAJOR PLAYERS IN THE INDIAN TEXTILE INDUSTRY

WELSPUN INDIA LIMITED

Welspun India, Ltd. (WIL), is the flagship company of Welspun Group, with an enterprise value of US $3 billion. WIL is an ISO 9001:2000, 14001 and SA 8000-certified company. WIL is a composite textile mill producing cotton yarn, terrycloth towels, and rugs for the international market. It is one of the largest home textile producers in Asia and among the top four producers of terrycloth towels in the world. WIL is located in the village Morai in the Valsad district of Gujarat State. Its annual sales for 2009–2010 was Rs 681.881 crores. WIL has a presence in more than fifty countries, employs over 24,000 people, and has more than100, 000 shareholders. Welspun is one of India's fastest-growing conglomerates.

VARDHMAN GROUP

Vardhman Group was established in 1965 and is a leading textile conglomerate in India, having a turnover of $700 million. It has more than twenty-four manufacturing facilities in five states across India. The group business portfolio includes yarn, greige, processed fabric, thread, acrylic fiber, and alloy steel. The Vardhman Group manufacturing facilities include over 800,000 spindles, producing 65 tons per day of yarn and fiber dyeing, and 900 shuttle less looms, producing 90 mn meters per annum of processed fabric; it produces 33 tons per day of sewing thread, 18,000 metric tons per annum of acrylic fiber, and 100,000 tons per annum of special and alloy steel.

ALOK INDUSTRIES LIMITED

Alok Industries, Ltd., is a private India-based textile manufacturing company and was established in 1986. Alok Industries has manufacturing bases spread over six locations in Navi Mumbai, Vapi, Silvassa, and Maharashtra.

Its business domain involves weaving, knitting, processing, home textiles, and ready-made garments. It's a diversified manufacturer of world-class home textiles, apparel fabrics, garments, and polyester yarns. Its buyers include manufacturers, exporters, importers, retailers, and branded apparel manufacturers of the world. Further, it operates its embroidery business through its sister company, Grabal Alok Impex, Ltd. Today, Alok Industries is one of the largest private exporters of textiles in India. Its business operations are spread across all the continents. Moreover, the manufacturing lab has been certified for ISO 9001:2000 quality standards.

Alok Industries became a public limited company in 1993 and its shares are listed in Bombay. The group business portfolio includes yarn, greige, and processed fabric, sewing thread, acrylic fiber, and alloy steel.

RAYMOND LIMITED

Raymond was incorporated in 1925 and has over 60 percent of the market share in worsted suiting in India. The company has a diverse product range of nearly 20,000 designs and colors of suiting fabric. It exports its products to over fifty-five countries, including the USA, Canada, Europe, Japan, and the Middle East. The company has registered a turnover of US$636.7 million for the FY 2011, as compared to US$364 million turnover in 2006. Its suiting is available in India in over 400 towns, through 3,000 retailers, as well as over 500 exclusive retail shops. Raymond is among the largest integrated manufacturers of worsted fabrics in the world. Raymond Limited owns some of the most highly respected apparel brands, like Raymond, Manzoni, Park Avenue, ColorPlus, Parx, Park Avenue, Be, Zapp!, Notting Hill, and GAS. Raymond manufactures and markets brands like Kamasutra condoms and even surgical gloves. The Raymond Group also has an expansive retail presence.

BOMBAY DYEING

Bombay Dyeing is one of the leading companies in the textile business worldwide. In fact, India has carved out a position in the world textile sector by holding hands with Bombay Dyeing. The company's products are exported to different nations all across the world like the United States, countries in the European Union, Australia, and New Zealand. Bombay Dyeing is, at present, the largest exporter of sophisticated ready-made items as well as cotton and poly-cotton products. Bombay Dyeing has created a sizable market in the production of a wide range of fabrics and ready-mades. This includes both formal and casual wear. Its ready-made collection is changing its production pattern with evolving fashion trends. The consumer section of Bombay Dyeing includes bed linen, towels, furnishings, suiting and shirting fabrics, and cotton and polyester-blended dresses and saris.

CLUSTER INSIGHTS

Cluster insights are aimed at highlighting the performance and expectations of the small and medium enterprises operating in the textile sector in the Kolkata cluster. The sample considered for this analysis are the textile companies profiled in this book. The variables considered for analysis include operational structure, business practices, and future plans.

KEY CHARACTERISTICS
OF THE KOLKATA TEXTILE CLUSTER

- ◆ The average revenue growth of the textile companies in the last two years was around 27 percent.

- ◆ The companies operated at an average capacity utilization of 90 percent.

- ◆ Around 38 percent of the companies were relatively older and started operations prior to the 1990s, while 18 percent were established after the year 2000.

♦ Garmenting is the preferred service for the textile companies in the Kolkata region.

♦ 23 percent of the companies operated with two or more manufacturing facilities.

♦ Around 33 percent of the companies manufacture and market branded products.

♦ 65 percent of the companies were involved in exports.

♦ Around 40 percent of the companies generated more than 50 percent of their revenue from exports.

♦ Europe is the preferred destination for export of textile goods, followed by America and the Middle East.

OWNERSHIP PATTERN

The ownership pattern of textile companies was inclined toward proprietary firms (Figure 3.12).

Figure 3.12: Textile Industry Company Ownership Pattern

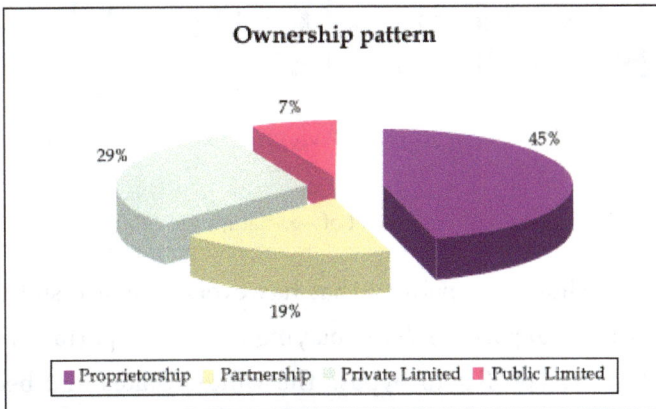

Source: D&B India (2008)

♦ Of the total proprietary concerns covered, 95 percent fall into the turnover bracket of Rs 10–100 mn.

♦ 29 percent of the private limited companies have been involved in manufacturing as well as trading activities.

Proprietary and private limited companies showed an average revenue growth of 26 percent in 2007 and 2008, while public limited companies and partnership firms showed 27 percent and 31 percent revenue growth during the same two years.

PRODUCTION AND EXPORTS

Figure 3.13: India's Cotton Production and Exports

India's Production and Exports Continue to Grow

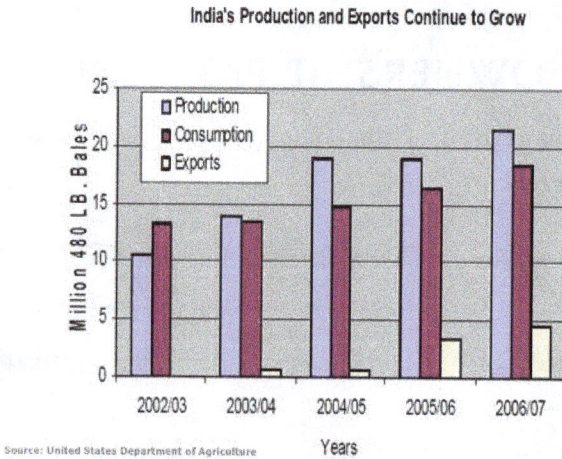

Source: United States Department of Agriculture

Source: US Department of Agriculture, PBS (2007)

Figure 3.13 shows the pattern that has evolved as a result of the increased growth of exports. India is playing an ever-important role in the world's cotton market. Set to bypass the United States and become the world's second-largest producer of cotton in 2007, India has seen its cotton sector undergo critical changes in recent years.

Ever since the government of India authorized the commercialization of Bt cotton in 2002, cotton production has soared. From 2002 to 2006, production doubled from 11 million bales to 23 million bales. India is expected to overtake the US as the world's second-largest cotton producer in 2007. The recent increase in Indian cotton production has outpaced the domestic needs for cotton, making India the third-largest exporter of cotton—most of which goes to China. Less than a decade ago, India's cotton exports were insignificant.

GROWTH IN CLOTH PRODUCTION ACCELERATED IN FY 2010

Between FY 2003 and FY 2011, India's cloth production recorded year-on-year growth in each of the years except FY 2003 and FY 2009. After the 2 percent decline in production in FY 2009, cloth production grew 9.8 percent to 60,333 mn square meters during FY 2010.

Figure 3.14: Trends in Cloth Production

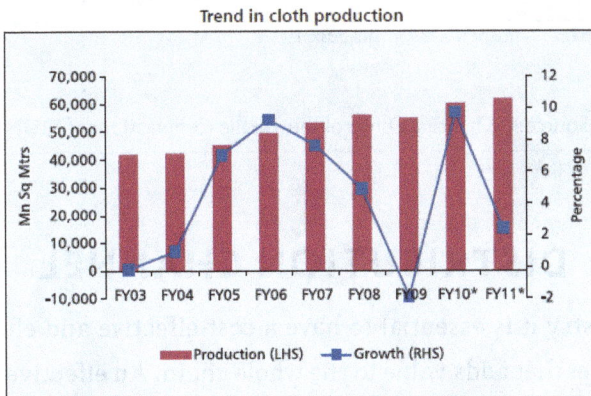

*Provisional
Source: Office of the textile commissioner

Source: D&B India, Office of the Textile Commissioner (2011)

COMPOSITION OF CLOTH PRODUCTION

The composition of cloth production remains the same even today. Production of cotton made up 47.4 percent of total cloth production during FY 2002–FY 2011. Production of other cloth was a share of 37.8 percent during this period. During FY 2011, production of cotton cloth grew 7.9 percent to 31,201 million square meters. Production of noncotton cloth declined to 5.2 percent, or 21,663 million square meters.

Figure 3.15: Composition of Cloth Production

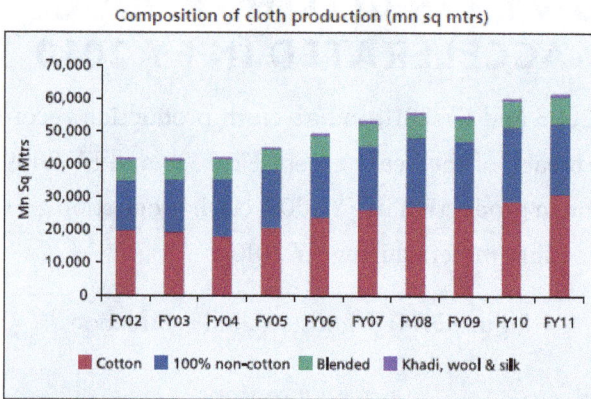

Composition of cloth production (mn sq mtrs)

Source: Office of the textile commissioner

Source: D&B India, Office of the Textile Commissioner (2011)

DISTRIBUTION CHANNEL

For any industry it is essential to have a cost-effective and efficient distribution channel that adds value to the whole chain. An effective distribution channel and integrated supply chain management help the growth of the industry and make it more competitive. India has a large and diversified textile industry with different segments and sectors; therefore it has a fragmented sales and distribution network.

Figure 3.16: Textile Industry Distribution Channel

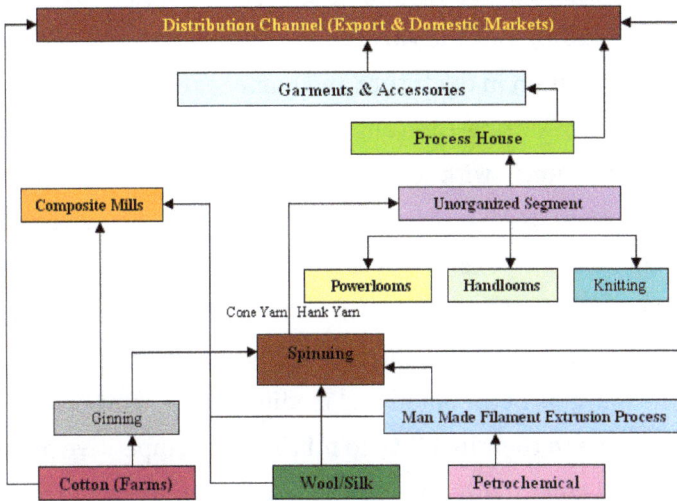

Source: India Crafts

In the Indian textile industry products are distributed mainly through following intermediaries as a part of the distribution network: importers, indenting agents, distributors, wholesalers, retailers, dealers, commission agents. Products are sold mainly through following marketplaces: small and large retail outlets, supermarkets, retail outlets situated in malls, shopping websites, and company owned showrooms, and retail chains.

Figure 3.17: Export of Indian Textiles

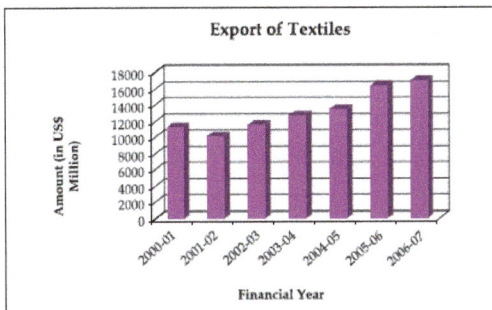

Source: D&B India (2008)

According to Dun and Bradstreet (D&B) Industry Research Service estimates, India's domestic textile market is expected to grow at 10.4–10.6 percent CAGR until 2010, with the garments segment expected to grow at 10.5–12.6 percent per annum in the future and home textiles segment at 15.0–17.3 percent per annum during the same period. The retail boom has provided the Indian consumer with a variety of clothing brands to choose from. In the future, many textile manufacturers may find domestic sales more attractive compared to exports, due to the growing textile demand from domestic apparel manufacturers. Also, the appreciating rupee has taken its toll on the export of textile and apparel products from India, adversely affecting the margins of the small and medium-sized firms, which have lost sizable orders due to their inability to fill them at competitive prices.

Figure 3.18 below shows the top ten textile exporters to the US in the first quarter of 2014. India has been continually rising up in the rankings as it expands its textile industry.

Figure 3.18: Top Ten Textile Exporters to the US

TOP TEN TEXTILE EXPORTERS TO THE US IN JAN-APRIL 2014			
COUNTRY	APRIL 2013*	APRIL 2014*	%CHANGE
CHINA	11,412	11,490	0.68
VIETNAM	2,667	3,081	15.51
INDIA	2,215	2,347	5.96
INDONESIA	1,917	1,838	-4.11
BANGLADESH	1,781	1,778	-0.21
MEXICO	1,473	1,487	0.97
PAKISTAN	982	1,006	2.44
CAMBODIA	873	891	2.12
HONDURAS	725	745	2.87
SALVADOR	544	568	4.31
WORLD	31,864	32,894	3.23

* In million dollars   Source: US Department of Commerce's Office of Textiles and Apparel

Source: Sasi (2014)

TRADE COMPOSITION

Figure 3.19 below shows the textile trade composition from 2012 to 2013.

♦ *Import basket:*
   Dependency on fabric imports is falling, but technical textiles imports are increasing.

♦ *Export basket:*
   Share of apparel in exports is high but that of raw cotton & cotton yarn is also significant.

Figure 3.19: Textile Trade Composition, 2012–2013

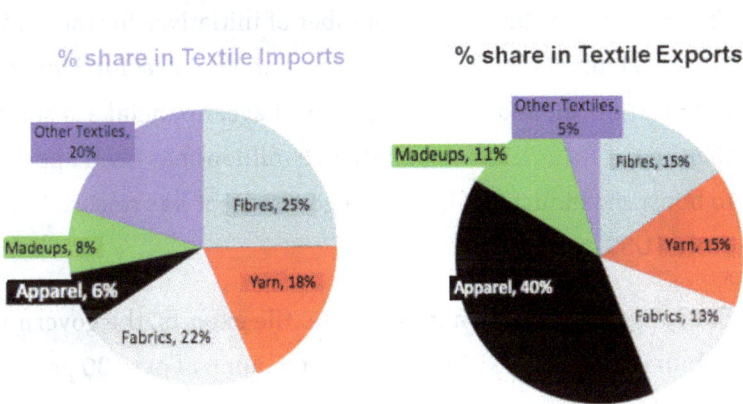

% share in Textile Imports

Other Textiles, 20%
Fibres, 25%
Madeups, 8%
Apparel, 6%
Yarn, 18%
Fabrics, 22%

% share in Textile Exports

Other Textiles, 5%
Madeups, 11%
Fibres, 15%
Yarn, 15%
Apparel, 40%
Fabrics, 13%

Source CITI India (2013)

GOVERNMENT INITIATIVES

The Indian government has come up with a number of export promotion policies for the textile sector. It has also allowed 100 percent FDI in the textiles sector under the automatic route.

The following are some of initiatives taken by the government to further promote the industry:

♦ The Ministry of Textiles inked a deal with Flipkart to provide an online platform to handloom weavers to sell their products.

♦ The Ministry of Textiles implemented the scheme to upgrade plain power looms for the SSI sector in Surat and the Ahmedabad power loom clusters in Gujarat.

♦ The government has taken a number of initiatives for the welfare and development of the weaving and handloom sector. Under a revival, reform, and restructuring package, financial assistance to the tune of Rs 1,019 crore (US$164.72 million) has been approved to boost the industry. The Indian government has released Rs 741 crore (US$119.78 million).

♦ Encouraged by the turnaround in textile exports, the government of India set up a US$60 billion target, a jump of over 30 percent from the previous financial year.

♦ The Cabinet Committee on Economic Affairs has approved an Integrated Processing Development Scheme with a corpus of Rs 500 crore (US$80.82 million) to make textiles processing units more environmentally friendly and globally competitive.

THE ROAD AHEAD

The Indian textile industry is set for strong growth, buoyed by both strong domestic consumption and export demand. The industry is expected to reach US$220 billion by 2020, according to estimates by Alok Industries, Ltd.

With consumerism and disposable income on the rise, the retail sector has experienced a rapid growth in the past decade, with several international players like Marks & Spencer, Guess, and Next having entered the Indian market. The organized apparel segment is expected to grow at a CAGR of more than 13 percent over a ten-year period.

4

RETAIL

OVERVIEW

Retail is one of the pillars of the Indian economy and accounts for 14 to 15 percent of its GDP. The Indian retail market is estimated to be worth US$500 billion. It is one of the top five retail markets in the world by economic value and one of the fastest-growing retail markets in the world, with 1.2 billion consumers. Figure 4.1 shows the Indian retail market as of 2007.

Figure 4.1: Indian Retail Markets

Indian Retail Markets (at 2007 Market Prices)

Segments	Total retail market (Rs billion)			Organised retail market (Rs billion)		
	2006	2007	Share in 2007	2006	2007	Share in 2007
Clothing & accessories	1,135	1,313	9.5%	214	298	38.1%
Food and grocery	7439	7,920	62.0%	58	90	11.5%
Footwear	137.5	160	1.1%	52	77.5	9.9%
Electronics	481	575	4.0%	50	71	9.1%
Catering services (F&B)	570	713	4.8%	39.4	57	7.3%
Home & office improvement	406.5	455	3.4%	37	50	6.4%
Telecom	216.5	272	1.8%	17.4	27	3.4%
Entertainment	380	456	3.2%	15.6	24	3.1%
Jewellery	602	694	5.0%	16.8	23	2.9%
Books, music & gifts	133	164	1.1%	16.8	22	2.8%
Watches	39.5	44	0.3%	18	21.5	2.7%
Pharmaceuticals	422	488	3.5%	11	15.4	2.0%
Beauty & wellness	38	46	0.3%	4	6.6	0.8%
Total	12,000	13,300		550	783	

Source: Images India Retail Report

As of 2013, India's retailing industry was essentially made up of small-owner shops. In 2010, larger-format convenience stores and supermarkets accounted for about 4 percent of the industry, and these were present only in large urban centers. India's retail and logistics industry employs about 40 million Indians (3.3 percent of the population).

LOCAL TERMS

Organized retail in India refers to trading activities undertaken by licensed retailers, that is, those who are registered for sales tax, income tax, etc. These include the publicly traded supermarkets, corporate-backed hypermarkets and retail chains, and also the privately owned large retail businesses.

Unorganized retailing refers to the traditional formats of low-cost retailing, for example, the local corner shops, owner-manned general stores, paan/beedi shops, convenience stores, hand cart and pavement vendors, etc.

Organized retailing was absent in most rural and small towns of India in 2010. Supermarkets and similarly organized retail accounted for just 4 percent of the market.

Figure 4.2 shows the most sought after target segments by India's retail companies.

Figure 4.2: Retail Company Target Segments

Apparel and textile segment is the most sought after by the retail companies

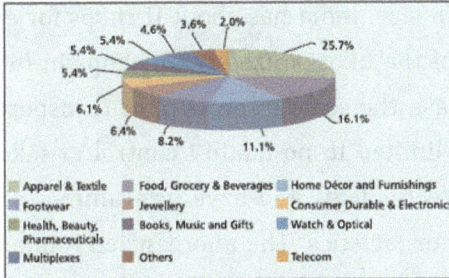

25.7%

5.4% 5.4% 4.6% 3.6% 2.0%
5.4%
6.1%
6.4% 8.2% 11.1%
16.1%

- Apparel & Textile
- Footwear
- Health, Beauty, Pharmaceuticals
- Multiplexes
- Food, Grocery & Beverages
- Jewellery
- Books, Music and Gifts
- Others
- Home Décor and Furnishings
- Consumer Durable & Electronics
- Watch & Optical
- Telecom

Each segment's share is calculated on the cumulative shares of all segments served by the respondent companies.

Source: D&B India (2014)

Most Indian shopping happens in open markets or small grocery and retail shops. If you were to go shopping at a nearby grocery, you would typically wait outside the shop and ask for whatever item you needed to buy. This is because shops usually have limited space. For example, if you wanted a toothbrush, you wouldn't be able to look at a shelf with a selection of toothbrushes, comparing each brand and model, and choosing the one you like the best. Instead, the shopkeeper would go to the back of the store and bring out a toothbrush to sell you. If you requested a specific brand of toothbrush, the shopkeeper might bring a substitute, claiming it is similar or equivalent to the one you requested. In most cases, there would be no price tag on the item; however by law, all packaged products must display the maximum retail price, and it is a criminal offense to sell the product for a higher price. The shopkeeper is allowed to price food staples and household products arbitrarily, and two consumers may pay different prices for the same product on the same day, but those prices can never be above the maximum retail price. Price is rarely negotiated between the shopper and shopkeeper. The shoppers usually do not have time to examine the product label and are not given the choice between competitive products.

India's retail and logistics industry, the organized and unorganized sectors combined, employs about 40 million people (3.3 percent of Indian population). The typical Indian retail shops are very small. Over 14 million outlets operate in the country and only 4 percent of them are larger than 500 sq. ft. (46 m²) in size. India has about 11 shops for every 1,000 people. The vast majority of the unorganized retail shops in India employ family members, do not have the scale to procure or transport products at high volume level, have limited to no quality control or fake-versus-authentic product screening technology, and have no training in safe and hygienic storage, packaging, or logistics. The unorganized retail shops source their products from a chain of middlemen who mark up the products as they move from farmer or producer to consumer. The unorganized retail shops typically offer no after-sales support or service. Finally, most transactions at unorganized retail shops are done in cash, with all sales being final.

Figure 4.3: Indian Wholesale Price Inflation, 2007–2008

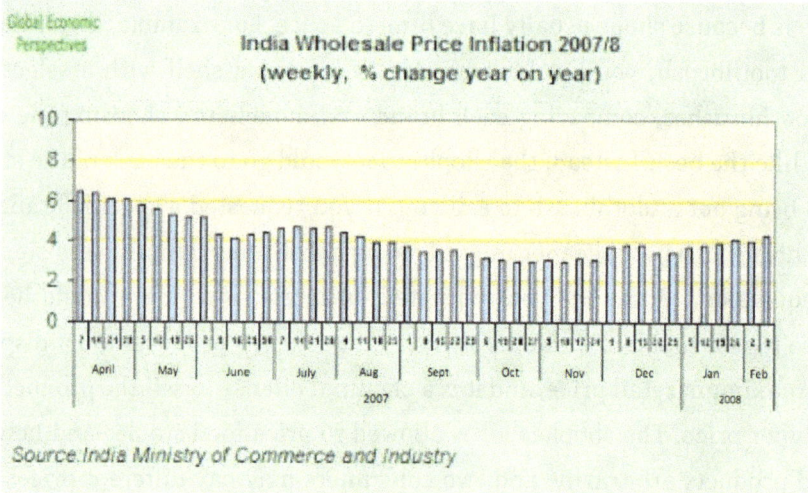

Source: India Ministry of Commerce and Industry

Until the 1990s, regulations prevented innovation and entrepreneurship in retail. Some retailers were faced with over thirty regulations, such as "signboard licenses" and "anti-hoarding measures" before they could open their doors. Taxes are incurred by moving goods to other states, from other states, and even within states in some cases. Farmers and producers had to go through middlemen monopolies to get their products in retail stores. The logistics and infrastructure were very poor, with losses exceeding 30 percent.

Through the 1990s, India introduced widespread free market reforms, including some related to retail. Between 2000 and 2010, consumers in select Indian cities gradually began to experience the quality, choice, convenience, and benefits of an organized retail industry.

GROWTH

Figure 4.4: Growth Drivers for the Indian Retail Industry

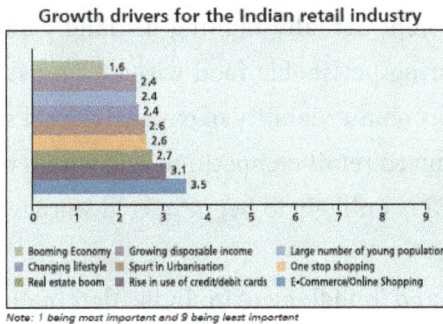

Growth drivers for the Indian retail industry

Note: 1 being most important and 9 being least important

Source: Technopak Advisers Pvt., Ltd.

GROWTH FROM 1997 TO 2010

In 1997, India allowed FDI in cash-and-carry wholesale. At that time, government approval was required. In 2006, the approval requirement was relaxed, and automatic permission was granted for FDI. Between 2000 and 2010, Indian retail attracted about $1.8 billion in FDI, representing a mere 1.5 percent of the total investment flow into India.

Single-brand retail is when a store that sells one brand of products, for example the Apple store or Banana Republic. In India, single-brand retail attracted ninety-four proposals between 2006 and 2010, of which fifty-seven were approved and implemented. For a country of 1.2 billion people, this is a very small number. Some claim that one of the primary restraints inhibiting better participation was India's requirement that single-brand retailers limit their ownership in Indian outlets to 51 percent. China, in contrast, allows 100 percent ownership by foreign companies in both their single-brand and multibrand retail presence.

Indian retail has experienced limited growth and, as mentioned earlier, its rate of food spoilage is among the highest in the world, because of limited integrated cold chain and other infrastructure issues. Indian law already allows 100 percent FDI in cold-chain infrastructure and there has been no interest in FDI in cold storage infrastructure build-out. Experts claim that cold storage infrastructure will become economically viable only when there is strong and contractually binding demand from organized retail. The risk of cold-storing perishable food without an assured way to move and sell it puts the economic viability of expensive cold storage in doubt. In the absence of organized retail competition and with a ban on FDI in multibrand retailers, FDI is unlikely to begin in cold storage and farm logistics infrastructure.

Intermediaries and middlemen in India dominate the value chain. This means that norms are flouted and pricing lacks transparency. Small-time farmers earn only one-third the total price paid by the end consumer. Farmers in nations with a higher share of organized retail earn two-thirds of the final price. The margins of 60 percent and more for middlemen and traditional retail shops have limited growth and prevented innovation in the retail industry.

India has had years of debate and discussions about the risk and prudence of allowing innovation and competition within its retail industry. Numerous economists repeatedly recommended to the government of India that legal restrictions on organized retail be removed and the retail industry in India be opened to competition. For example, in an invited address to the Indian Parliament in December 2010, Jagdish Bhagwati, professor of economics and law at Columbia University, analyzed the relationship between growth and poverty reduction, then urged the Indian Parliament to extend economic reforms by freeing up of the retail sector, further liberating trade in all sectors, and introducing labor market reforms. Such reforms, Professor Bhagwati argued, will accelerate economic growth and make a sustainable difference in the lives of India's poorest citizens.

A 2007 report noted that an increasing number of people in India are turning to the services sector for employment due to the relatively low compensation offered by agriculture and manufacturing sectors. The organized retail market is growing at 35 percent annually while the growth of the unorganized retail sector is pegged at 6 percent.

The retail business in India is currently at the point of inflection. In 2008, rapid change in investments to the tune of US$25 billion was planned by several Indian and multinational companies and realized by 2015. Retail is a huge industry, and according to the India Brand Equity Foundation (IBEF), it is valued at about US$395.96 billion. Organized retail garnered about 16 to 18 percent of the total retail market (US$65–75 billion) between 2008 and 2013.

India has topped the A.T. Kearney annual Global Retail Development Index for the third consecutive year, maintaining its position as the most attractive market for retail investment. In 2007, the Indian economy registered a growth of 8 percent and in 2008 it was 7.9 percent. The enormous growth of the retail industry has created a huge demand for real estate. Property developers are creating retail real estate at an aggressive pace; in 2010 alone, three hundred malls became operational in the country.

Figure 4.5: Indian Retail Market Growth (2006–2007 to 2011–2012 (E))

INDIAN RETAIL MARKET GROWTH (2006-07 to 2011-12 (E))

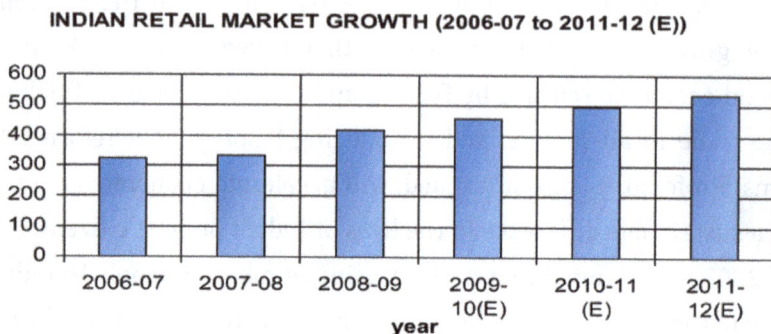

2009 - 2011 are estimates.
F&S sources: CSO, NSSO and Technopak Advisers Pvt. Ltd.

Source: CSO, NSSO and Technopak Advisers Pvt., Ltd.

GROWTH AFTER 2011

Until 2011, the Indian central government denied FDI in multibrand retail, forbidding foreign groups from any ownership in supermarkets, convenience stores, or any retail outlets. Even single-brand retail was limited to 51 percent ownership and a bureaucratic process. The government regulation of retail was meant to protect small businesses, but has instead eliminated competition and allowed large domestic companies to dominate the market.

Several studies claim that the lack of infrastructure and an uncompetitive retail industry are the key causes of India's persistently high inflation. Furthermore, because of unorganized retail, in a nation where malnutrition remains a serious problem, India is rife with food waste. Well over 30 percent of food staples and perishable goods that are produced in India spoil.

In November 2011, India's central government announced retail reforms for both multibrand stores and single-brand stores. These market reforms paved the way for retail innovation and competition with multibrand retailers such as Walmart, Carrefour, and Tesco, as well single-brand majors such as IKEA, Nike, and Apple. The announcement sparked intense activism, both in opposition and in support of the reforms. Those opposed feared that international companies would take over the retail sector in India, pushing out Indian companies and destroying small businesses. Those in favor of the reforms saw the potential for growth in the retail sector and the improvements in quality, pricing, and customer experience that competition would bring. In December 2011, under pressure from the opposition, the Indian government placed the retail reforms on hold until it reached a consensus.

In 2011 the Indian retail market generated sales of about $470 billion a year, of which a minuscule $27 billion came from organized retail such as supermarkets, chain stores with centralized operations, and shops in malls. Some claimed that opening the retail industry to free market competition would enable rapid growth in the retail sector of the Indian economy. Others believed the growth of the Indian retail industry would take time, and that organized retail might take a decade to grow to a 25 percent share.

In 2011, food accounted for 70 percent of Indian retail, but was underrepresented by organized retail. A.T. Kearney estimates India's organized retail had a 31 percent share in clothing and apparel, while home supplies retail was growing between 20 percent and 30 percent per year. These data correspond to retail prospects prior to the November announcement of the retail reform.

It might be true that India has the largest number of shops per inhabitant. In Belgium, the number of outlets is approximately 8 outlets per 1,000 people and in the Netherlands it is 6 outlets per 1,000 people. So the Indian number must be far higher.

Figure 4.6: Indian Retail Market Growth Expectation

India Retail Market	2007 Retail Sales ($US bn)	CAGR 2007-2012
Total Market	$339.7	10.2%
Organized Sector	$13.9	43.7%

(CAGR = compound annual growth rate)
Source: CSO, NSSO, and Technopak Advisers Pvt., Ltd.

In January 2012, India approved reforms for single-brand stores. The new laws allowed anyone in the world to innovate in the Indian retail market with 100 percent ownership but imposed the requirement that the single-brand retailer source 30 percent of its goods from India. The Indian government continues the hold on retail reforms for multibrand stores.

In June 2012, IKEA announced that it applied for permission to invest $1.9 billion in India and set up twenty-five retail stores. An analyst from Fitch Group stated that the 30 percent requirement was likely to significantly delay, if not prevent, most single-brand majors from Europe, the USA, and Japan from opening stores and creating associated jobs in India.

On September 14, 2012, the government of India announced the opening of FDI in multibrand retail, subject to approval by individual states. This decision was welcomed by economists and the markets, but caused protests and upheaval in the Indian central government's political coalition structure. Protestors from opposition parties and trade unions stopped trains, shouting slogans and waving signs saying things like, "FDI in retail: curse to Indian retailers and farmers." They argued that opening FDI to multibrand retail would put small shops out of business. Those in favor of the reform argued that there was room in the market for both small businesses and multibrand retailers. They claimed that the reform would create new jobs. On September 20, 2012, the government of India formally notified the FDI reforms for single- and multibrand retail, thereby making it effective under Indian law.

On December 7, 2012, the federal government of India allowed 51 percent FDI in multibrand retail in India. The government managed to get approval for multibrand retail from Parliament despite heavy uproar from the opposition (the NDA and leftist parties). Some states will allow foreign supermarkets like Walmart, Tesco, and Carrefour to open, while other states will not.

Given the expected growth of the retail industry through 2021, a 25 percent market share is estimated to be over $250 billion a year. That is equal to the 2009 revenue share from Japan for the world's 250 largest retailers. The *Economist* forecasts that Indian retail will nearly double in economic value, expanding by about $400 billion by 2020. The projected increase alone is equivalent to the current retail market size of France.

Figure 4.7 shows the division of India's retail sector.

Figure 4.7: India's Retail Market Division

India's retail market

HOW THE SECTOR IS DIVIDED

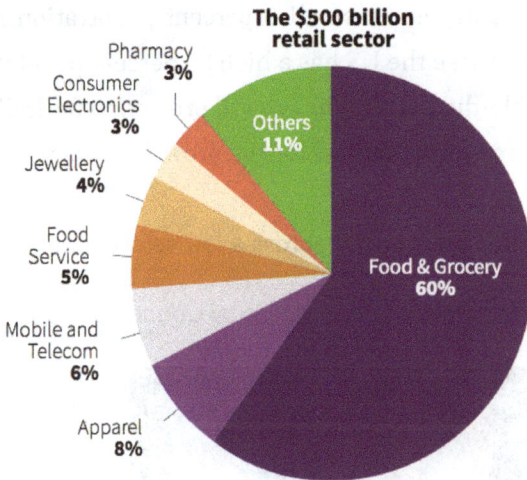

The $500 billion retail sector

Pharmacy **3%**
Consumer Electronics **3%**
Jewellery **4%**
Food Service **5%**
Mobile and Telecom **6%**
Apparel **8%**

Others **11%**

Food & Grocery **60%**

92% of the sector is *unorganised*, those that fall under "mom and pop" stores, and only 8% is *organised*, those dominated by retailers who have multiple stores

Source: Deloitte, Jan 2013

HOW IT COMPARES TO OTHER MARKETS

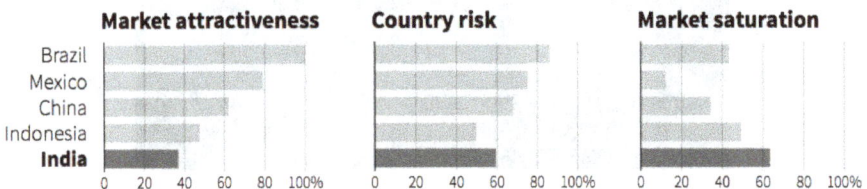

Market attractiveness

Brazil
Mexico
China
Indonesia
India
0 20 40 60 80 100%

Country risk

0 20 40 60 80 100%

Market saturation

0 20 40 60 80 100%

Source: Fastest growing retail markets according to AT Kearney Global Retail Development Index 2013

Staff 19/03/2014   REUTERS

Source: Kearney Global Retail Development Index (2013)

THE INDIAN RETAIL MARKET

The Indian market is highly complex in terms of the wide geographic spread and the variation in consumer preferences by region. This necessitates localization, even within the geographic zones. India has the highest number of outlets per person (7 per one thousand), but Indian retail space per capita, at 2 square feet per person (0.19 m²), is the lowest in the world. Indian retail density, at 6 percent, is highest in the world. Approximately 1.8 million households in India have an annual income of over ₹4.5 million (US$72,900.00).

Organized retail in India is still in its nascent stage and therefore offers immense potential. India currently has a small 6 percent penetration in organized retail, while a country like the US has a high 85 percent penetration. Given that there is a double-digit economic growth projection for India in the next decade, there is immense potential for the growth of organized retail in the future.

Figure 4.8 below shows retail penetration across a few select countries.

Figure 4.8: Comparative Retail Penetration by Country

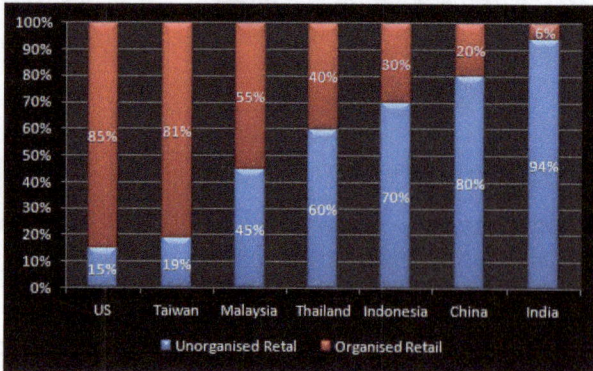

Source: Ernst & Young Report, Aranca Research

INDIAN RETAILERS

A 2012 PricewaterhouseCoopers (PWC) report states that modern retailing has a 5 percent market share in India with about $27 billion in sales, and is growing at 15 to 20 percent per year. Retail may be shifting away from small shops to modern retail formats and mall companies.

CHALLENGES

While India presents a large market opportunity, given the number of consumers and their increased purchasing power, there are still significant challenges. Over 90 percent of trade is conducted through independent local stores, the population is geographically dispersed, ticket sizes are small, the distribution network is complex, there is little use of information technology (IT) systems, mass media is limited, and counterfeit goods are prevalent. Regardless of these challenges, a number of merger and acquisitions have begun in Indian retail market. PWC expects the multibrand retail market to grow to $220 billion by 2020.

A D&B survey revealed that apart from the slowdown in the economy, understanding consumer behavior and customer retention are the other major challenges that the Indian retailers face. Retailers are concerned about decreasing consumer spending, as consumers are deferring their purchases, and the sector is witnessing a paradigm shift from what is being called "conspicuous consumption to conscious consumption." Moreover, any dip in customer footfall and weak conversion ratio has an impact on retailer's inventory turnover, which increases their working capital requirements.

Figure 4.9: Challenges in the Indian Retail Industry

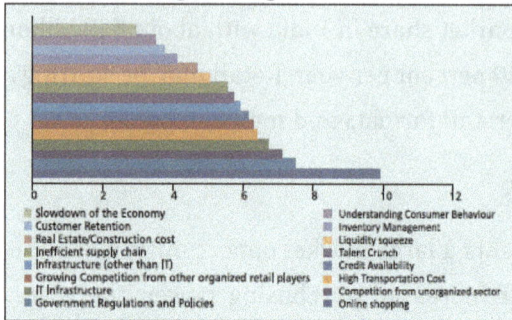

Issues and challenges facing the Indian retail industry

Slowdown of the Economy
Customer Retention
Real Estate/Construction cost
Inefficient supply chain
Infrastructure (other than IT)
Growing Competition from other organized retail players
IT Infrastructure
Government Regulations and Policies

Understanding Consumer Behaviour
Inventory Management
Liquidity squeeze
Talent Crunch
Credit Availability
High Transportation Cost
Competition from unorganized sector
Online shopping

Note: 1 being most important and 12 being least important

Source: Technopak Advisers Pvt., Ltd.

A McKinsey study claims retail productivity in India is very low compared to international peer measures. For example, the labor productivity in Indian retail was just 6 percent of the labor productivity in United States in 2010. India's labor productivity in food retail is about 5 percent, compared to Brazil's 14 percent, while India's labor productivity in nonfood retailing is about 8 percent, compared to Poland's 25 percent.

Total retail employment in India, both organized and unorganized, accounts for about 6 percent of the current work force, most of which is unorganized. This about a third of the levels in the United States and Europe and about half the levels in other emerging economies. A complete expansion of the retail sector to reach levels and productivity similar to other emerging economies and developed economies such as the United States would create over 50 million jobs in India. Training and developing labor and management for higher retail productivity is expected to be a challenge.

INDIA RETAIL REFORMS

Until 2011, Indian central government denied FDI in multibrand Indian retail, forbidding foreign groups from any ownership in supermarkets, convenience stores, or any retail outlets, and the sales of multiple products from different brands directly to Indian consumers.

On November 24, 2011, the government of Manmohan Singh, prime minister, announced the following:

♦ India will allow foreign groups to own up to 51 percent in "multibrand retailers," as supermarkets are known in India. This was the most radical pro-liberalization reform passed by an Indian cabinet in years.

♦ Single-brand retailers, such as Apple and Ikea, can own 100 percent of their Indian stores, up from the previous cap of 51 percent.

♦ Both multibrand and single-brand stores in India will have to source nearly a third of their goods from small and medium-sized Indian suppliers.

♦ All multibrand and single brand stores in India must confine their operations to approximately fifty-three cities with a population over one million, out of some 7,935 towns and cities in India. It is expected that these stores will now have full access to over 200 million urban consumers in India.

♦ Multibrand retailers must have a minimum investment of US$100 million with at least half of the amount invested in back-end infrastructure, including cold chains, refrigeration, transportation, packing, sorting, and processing to considerably reduce the postharvest losses and bring remunerative prices to farmers.

♦ The opening of retail competition will be within India's federal structure of government. In other words, the policy is an enabling legal framework for India. The states of India have the prerogative to accept and implement it or not. Actual implementation of policy is within the parameters of state laws and regulations.

The opening of retail industry to global competition is expected to spur a retail rush to India. It has the potential to transform not only the retailing landscape but also the nation's ailing infrastructure.

A *Wall Street Journal* article claims that fresh investments in Indian organized retail will generate ten million new jobs between 2012 and 2014, with about five to six million jobs in logistics alone, even though the retail market is being opened in just fifty-three cities out of about 8,000 towns and cities in India.

INDIAN RETAIL REFORMS ON HOLD

According to *Bloomberg*, on December 3, 2011, the chief minister of the Indian state of West Bengal, Mamata Banerjee, who is against the policy and whose Trinamool Congress brings nineteen votes to the ruling Congress Party–led coalition, claimed that India's government may put the FDI retail reforms on hold until it reaches consensus within the ruling coalition. Reuters reports that this risked a possible dilution of the policy rather than a change of heart.

Several newspapers claimed on December 6, 2011, that Indian Parliament is expected to shelve retail reforms while the ruling Congress Party seeks consensus from the opposition and the Congress Party's own coalition partners. Suspension of retail reforms on December 7, 2011, would be, the reports claimed, an embarrassing defeat for the Indian government, suggesting it is weak and ineffective in implementing its ideas.

Anand Sharma, India's commerce and industry minister, after a meeting of all political parties on December 7, 2011, said, "The decision to allow foreign direct investment in retail is suspended until consensus is reached with all stakeholders."

On February 19, 2013, Tamil Nadu became the first state in the country to stoutly resist multinational company (MNC) "invasion" into the domestic retail sector. In Chennai, Tamil Nadu Chennai Metropolitan Development Authority authorities placed a seal on the massive warehouse spreading across 7 acres that had reportedly been built for one of the world's leading multinational retail giants, Walmart.

In February 2014, Vasundhara Raje, who led the newly elected Rajasthan government, reversed the earlier government's decision to allow FDI in retail in the state. He reasoned that the sources of domestic retail are primarily local, whereas international retail affects domestic manufacturing activity and therefore reduces employment opportunities.

SINGLE-BRAND RETAIL REFORMS APPROVED

On January 11, 2012, India approved increased competition and innovation in single-brand retail. The reform seeks to attract investments in operations and marketing; improve the availability of goods for the consumer; encourage increased sourcing of goods from India; and enhance competition in Indian enterprises through access to global designs, technologies, and management practices. India requires single-brand retailers with greater than 51 percent foreign ownership to source at least 30 percent of the value of products from Indian small industries, village and cottage industries, artisans, and craftsmen.

Mikael Olsson, chief executive of IKEA, announced that IKEA is postponing its plan to open stores in India. He claimed that IKEA's decision reflects India's requirements that single-brand retailers such as IKEA source 30 percent of their goods from local small and medium-sized companies. This was an obstacle to IKEA's investment in India and it will take IKEA some time to source goods and develop reliable supply chains inside India. IKEA announced that it plans to double the amount of goods it sources from India for its global product range to over $1 billion a year within three years. In the short term, IKEA plans to focus on expansion in China and Russia instead, where such restrictions do not exist.

SOCIAL IMPACT AND CONTROVERSY
WITH RETAIL REFORMS

The November 2011 retail reforms in India sparked intense activism, both in opposition and in support of the reforms. Critics of deregulating retail in India are making one or more of the following claims:

♦ Independent stores will close, leading to massive job loss. Walmart employs very few people in the United States. If allowed to expand in India to the same extent it has expanded in the United States, a few thousand jobs could be created but millions would be lost.

♦ Walmart's efficiency at supply chain management leads to direct procurement of goods from the supplier. In addition to eliminating the middleman, due to its status as the leading retailer, suppliers of goods are pressured to drop prices in order to ensure consistent cash flow.

♦ The small retailer and the middleman present in the retail industry play a large part in supporting the local economy, since they typically procure goods and services from the area where their retail shops are located. This leads to increased economic activity and wealth redistribution. With large, efficient retailers, goods are acquired in other regions, hence reducing the local economy.

♦ Walmart will lower prices to dump goods, get competition out of the way, become a monopoly, and then raise prices. It is argued that this was the case of the soft drink industry—Pepsi and Coca-Cola came in and wiped out all the domestic brands.

♦ India doesn't need foreign retailers, since homegrown companies and traditional markets have been able to do the job.

♦ Work will be done by Indians, and profits will go to foreigners.

♦ Like the East India Company, Walmart could enter India as a trader and then take over politically.

♦ There will be sterile homogeneity and Indian cities will look like cities anywhere else.

♦ The government hasn't built consensus.

♦ The government claims modern retail will create 4 million new jobs. This cannot be true because Walmart, with over 9,000 stores worldwide, has only 2.1 million employees.

♦ The Democratic staff of the US House Committee on Education and the Workforce report Walmart's low wages and their effect on taxpayers and economic growth.

Supporters of the reforms claim none of these objections have merit. They claim the following:

♦ Organized retail will need workers. Walmart employs 1.4 million people in United States alone. The population of the United States is about 300 million and India's population is about 1.2 billion. If Walmart-like retail companies were to expand in India as much as they have in the United States, and the staffing level in Indian stores was at same level as it is in the United States, Walmart alone would employ 5.6 million Indian citizens. Walmart has a 6.5 percent market share of total retail in the United States. Adjusted for this market share, the expected jobs created by future organized retail in India would total over 85 million. In addition, millions of additional jobs would be created in the building and maintenance of retail stores, roads, cold storage centers, software, electronic cash registers, and other supporting organizations. Instead of job losses, retail reforms are likely to be massive boost to Indian job availability.

♦ Klynveld Peat Marwick Goerdeler (KPMG), one of the world's largest audit companies, finds that after China opened retail to foreign and domestic innovation and competition, the employment in both retail and wholesale trade increased from 4 percent in 1992 to about 7 percent in 2001. In absolute terms, China experienced the creation of 26 million new jobs within nine years after announcing FDI retail reforms. Contrary to some concerns, after retail reforms in China, the number of traditional small retailers also grew by 30 percent over five years.

♦ India needs trillions of dollars to build its infrastructure, hospitals, housing, and schools for its growing population. The Indian economy is small, with limited surplus capital. The government is already operating on budget deficits. It is simply not possible for Indian investors or the government to fund this expansion, job creation, and growth at the rate India needs. Global investment capital through FDI is necessary. Beyond capital, the Indian retail industry needs knowledge and global integration. Global retail leaders, some of which are partly owned by people of Indian origin, can bring this knowledge. Global integration can potentially open export markets for Indian farmers and producers. For example, since Walmart came into the Indian wholesale retail market, it expects to source and export some $1 billion worth of goods from India every year.

♦ Walmart, Carrefour, Tesco, Target, Metro, and Coop are among over 350 global retail companies with annual sales over $1 billion. These retail companies have operated for over 30 years in numerous countries. They have not become monopolies. Competition between Walmart-like retailers has kept food prices in check. Canada credits its very low inflation rates to the Walmart effect. Antitrust laws and state regulations, such as those in the

Indian legal code, have prevented food monopolies from forming anywhere in the world. Price inflation in these countries has been five to ten times lower than price inflation in India. The current consumer price inflation in Europe and the United States is less than 2 percent, compared to India's double-digit inflation.

♦ The Pepsi and Coca-Cola example is meaningless in the context of the Indian beverage market. Competition is lacking because of limited demand. The Indian consumer has limited interest in soft drinks; they represent less than 5 percent of Indian beverage market. Indian consumers prefer milk-based tea and coffee and these account for 90 percent of the Indian beverage market with plenty of competing domestic brands and even European brands like Nestlé. The next most important market in India is bottled water, which outsells the combined soft drink sales of Pepsi and Coca-Cola. Organized retail too will have numerous brands and strong competition.

♦ Comparing the twenty-first century to the eighteenth century is inappropriate. Conditions today are different. India wasn't a democracy then. Global awareness and news media have also changed. For example, China has over 57 million square feet of retail space owned by foreigners, employing millions of Chinese citizens. Yet, China hasn't become a vassal of imperialists, enjoying respect from all global powers. Other Asian countries like Malaysia, Taiwan, Thailand, and Indonesia see foreign retailers as catalysts of new technology and price reduction and they have benefited by welcoming FDI in retail. India too will benefit by integrating into the world, rather than isolating itself.

♦ With a 51 percent FDI limit in multibrand retailers, nearly half of any profits will remain in India. All profits will be subject to taxes, and such taxes will reduce the Indian government's budget deficit.

Many years ago, China adopted the retail reform policy India has announced, allowing FDI in its retail sector. FDI-financed retailers in China took five to ten years to post profits, in large part because of the huge investments that were made initially. Like China, it is unlikely foreign retailers will earn any profits in India for the first five to ten years. Ultimately, retail companies must earn profits by creating value.

♦ States have a right to say no to retail FDI within their jurisdiction, and states have the right to add restrictions to the retail policy before they implement it. Thus, they can place limits on number, market share, style, diversity, homogeneity, and other factors to suit their cultural preferences. Finally, in the future, states can always introduce regulations and India can change the law to ensure the benefits of retail reforms reach the poorest and weakest segments of Indian society. Free and fair retail competition does indeed lead to sharply lower inflation than current levels, small farmers get better prices, the jobs created by organized retail pay well, and healthier food becomes available to more households.

♦ As much as 40 percent of food production doesn't reach consumers due to inbuilt inefficiencies and wastage in distribution and storage. Fifty million children in India are malnourished. Food often rots in farms, in transit, or in antiquated state-run warehouses. Cost-conscious organized retail companies will avoid waste and loss, making food available to the weakest and poorest segment of Indian society, while increasing the income of small farmers. For example, since Walmart's arrival in Indian wholesale retail market, it has successfully introduced the "Direct Farm Project" at Haider Nagar near Malerkotla in Punjab. There, 110 farmers have been connected with Bharti Walmart for sourcing fresh vegetables directly, thereby reducing waste and bringing fresher produce to Indian consumers.

◆ Small shops employ workers without proper contracts, making them work long hours. Many unorganized small shops depend on child labor. A well-regulated retail sector will help curtail some of these abuses.

◆ Organized retail has enabled a wide range of companies to start and flourish in other countries. For example, in the United States, the retailer Whole Foods has rapidly grown to annual revenues of $9 billion by working closely with farmers, delighting customers, and caring about the communities where its stores are located.

◆ The claims that there is no consensus within the Indian government is without merit. About ten years ago, when opposition formed the central government, they had proposed retail reforms and suggested India consider FDI in retail. Retail reform discussions are not new. More recently, announced retail reforms evolved after a process of intense consultation and consensus building. In 2010, the Indian government circulated a discussion paper on FDI retail reforms. On July 6, 2011, another version of the paper was circulated by the central government of India. Comments from a wide cross-section of Indian society, including farmers' associations, industry bodies, consumer forums, academics, traders' associations, investors, and economists were analyzed in depth before the matter was discussed by the Committee of Secretaries. By early August 2011, the consensus from various segments of Indian society was overwhelmingly in favor of retail reforms. The reform outline was presented in India's Rajya Sabha in August 2011. The announced reforms are the result of this consensus process. The current opposition is not helping the consensus process, since consensus is not built by threats and disruption. Those who oppose current retail reforms should help build consensus with ideas and proposals. The opposition parties currently disrupting the Indian Parliament on retail reforms have not offered even one idea or a single proposal on how India can eliminate food spoilage, reduce inflation, improve food security, feed the poor, or improve the incomes of small farmers.

♦ A study by Global Insights research found that modern retailers such as Walmart create jobs directly, indirectly, and by induced effects. In the Dallas–Fort Worth area of the United States, where there is a population of about 2 million people, Global Insights found that Walmart alone had helped create about 6,300 net new jobs with an average salary of over $21,000 each. For India's urban population of over 400 million, with an average salary of less than $2,100 per year, this scales to over 12 million new jobs. Other multibrand retailers, such as Mitsukoshi of Japan, employ a much higher number of sales support and employees per store than Walmart to suit local consumer culture. The Global Insights study also found that modern retailers such as Walmart were key contributors in creating new net jobs and maintaining low consumer price inflation rates from 1985 to 2005.

OPPOSITION TO RETAIL REFORMS

Within a week of the retail reform announcement, the Indian government faced a political backlash against its decision to allow competition and 51 percent ownership of multibrand organized retail in India. Despite the fact that Salman Khurshid, India's law minister, claimed that many opposition parties, including the Bharatiya Janata Party, had privately encouraged the government to push through the retail reform, the intense criticism targeted the Congress Party–led coalition government and its decision to push through one of the biggest economic reforms in years for India. Opposition parties claimed supermarket chains are ill-advised, unilateral, and unwelcome.

Mamata Banerjee, the chief minister of West Bengal and the leader of the Trinamool Congress, announced her opposition to retail reform, claiming, "Some people might support it, but I do not support it. You see America is America . . . and India is India. One has to see what one's capacity is."

The other states whose chief ministers either personally announced opposition or announced reluctance to implement the retail reforms are Tamil Nadu, Uttar Pradesh, Bihar, and Madhya Pradesh. Chief Ministers in many states have not made a personal statement in opposition or support of India needing retail reforms. Gujarat, Kerala, Karnataka, and Rajasthan are examples of these states. Both sides have made conflicting claims about the position of chief ministers from these states.

A *Wall Street Journal* article reports that in Uttar Pradesh, Uma Bharti, a senior leader of the opposition Bharatiya Janata Party (BJP), threatened to "set fire to the first Walmart store whenever it opens" with her colleague Sushma Swaraj busy tweeting up a storm of misinformation about how Walmart allegedly ruined the US economy.

On December 1, 2011, an India-wide "bandh" (closing of all businesses in protest) was called by political parties opposing the retail reform. While many organizations responded, the reach of the protest was mixed. *The Times of India,* a national newspaper in India, claimed people appeared divided over the bandh call, and internal rivalry among trade associations led to a mixed response, leaving many stores open all day long and others opening for business as usual in the second half of the day. Even Purti Group, a network of stores owned and operated by Nitin Gadkari, were open for business, ignoring the call for bandh. Gadkari is the president of BJP, the key party currently organizing opposition to retail reform. Prime Minister Modi belongs to the BJP.

The Hindu, another widely circulated newspaper in India, claimed the opposition's call for a nationwide shutdown on December 1, 2011, in protest of retail reform received a mixed response. Some states had strong support, while most did not. Even in states where opposition political parties are in power, many ignored the call for the shutdown. In Gujarat, Bihar, Delhi, Andhra Pradesh, Haryana, Punjab, and Assam the call evoked a partial response. While a number of wholesale markets observed the shutdown, the newspaper claimed a majority of kirana stores and neighborhood small shops, for whom the trade bandh had been called, remained open, ignoring the shutdown call. Conflicting claims were made by the organizers of the nationwide shutdown. Contrary to eyewitness reports, one trader union's secretary general claimed traders across the country participated whole-heartedly in the strike.

The political parties opposing the retail reforms physically disrupted and forced India's Parliament to adjourn again on December 2, 2011. The Indian government refused to cave in its attempt to convince the opposition that retail reforms are necessary to protect the farmers and consumers. The Indian Parliament was dysfunctional for the entire week of November 28, 2011, over the opposition to retail reforms.

SUPPORT FOR RETAIL REFORMS

In a pan-Indian survey conducted over the weekend of December 3, 2011, the overwhelming majority of consumers and farmers, in and around ten major cities across the country, supported the retail reforms. Over 90 percent of consumers said FDI in retail would bring down prices and offer a wider choice of goods. Nearly 78 percent of farmers said they would get better prices for their produce from multiformat stores. Over 75 percent of the traders claimed their marketing resources would still be needed to push sales through multiple channels, but they might have to accept lower margins for greater volumes.

A study conducted in India, titled *Foreign Direct Investment in the Indian Retail Sector: Drawing Lessons from the International Experience*, concluded that the entry of FDI in multibrand retail in India could be growth enhancing if proper safeguards are in place and the market environment is regulated.

First, resources should be dedicated to a comprehensive study of retail and its related industries. Second, the number of big retail outlets in a particular city should be determined based on population and the employment level of local youth in the retail business. Third, the format of these retail chains should also be regulated, as is done in Malaysia. They should not be in the form of neighborhood convenience stores and there should be a minimum and maximum limit on the size of these stores. Fourth, it is important to ensure that no single retailer monopolizes the procurement operations in an area, district, or state to protect the local suppliers. Last, the predatory pricing and anticompetition practices of these international retailers should be prohibited to create an even playing field for local retailers.

FARMER GROUPS

Various farmer associations in India have announced their support of the retail reforms. For example:

♦ Shriram Gadhve of All India Vegetable Growers Association (AIVGA) says his organization supports retail reform. He claimed that currently it is the middlemen commission agents who benefit at the cost of farmers. He urged that the retail reform focus on rural areas and that farmers receive benefits. Gadhve said, "Better cold storage would help since this could prevent the existing loss of 34 percent of fruits and vegetables due to the inefficient systems in place." AIVGA operates in nine states including Maharashtra, Andhra Pradesh, West Bengal, Bihar, Chhattisgarh, Punjab, and Haryana, with a membership of 2,200 farmer outfits.

♦ Bharat Krishak Samaj, a farmer association with more than 75,000 members says it supports retail reform. Ajay Vir Jakhar, the chairman of Bharat Krishak Samaj, claimed a monopoly exists between the private guilds of middlemen, commission agents at the sabzi mandis (India's wholesale markets for vegetables and farm produce), and the small shopkeepers in the unorganized retail market. Given the perishable nature of foods like fruits and vegetables, without the option of safe and reliable cold storage, the farmer is compelled to sell his crop at whatever price he can get. He cannot wait for a better price and is thus exploited by the current monopoly of middlemen. Jakhar asked that the government make it mandatory for organized retailers to buy 75 percent of their produce directly from farmers, bypassing the middleman monopoly and India's sabzi mandi auction system.

◆ The Consortium of Indian Farmers Associations (CIFA) announced its support for retail reform. Chengal Reddy, secretary general of CIFA, claimed retail reform could do a lot for Indian farmers. Reddy commented, "India has 600 million farmers, 1,200 million consumers, and 5 million traders. I fail to understand why political parties are taking an antifarmer stance and worry about a half a million brokers and small shopkeepers." CIFA mainly operates in Andhra Pradesh, Karnataka, and Tamil Nadu, but has a growing membership from the rest of India, including Shetkari Sanghatana in Maharashtra, the Rajasthan Kisan Union, and Himachal Farmer Organizations.

◆ Prakash Thakur, the chairman of the People for Environment Horticulture & Livelihood of Himachal Pradesh, announced his support for retail reforms and said that FDI is expected to roll out produce storage centers that will increase market access, reduce the number of middlemen, and enhance returns to farmers. Highly perishable fruits like cherries, apricots, peaches, and plums are in high demand, but farmers are unable to tap the market fully because of the lack of cold storage and transport infrastructure. Sales will boost with the opening up of FDI in retail. Thakur argued that, even though India is the second-largest producer of fruits and vegetables in the world, its storage infrastructure is grossly inadequate.

◆ Sharad Joshi, founder of Shetkari Sangathana (a farmers' association), has announced his support for retail reforms. Joshi claims FDI will help the farm sector improve critical infrastructure and will create a direct connection between farmers and consumers. Existing retail has been unable to supply fresh vegetables to consumers because retailers have not invested in backward integration. When farmers' produce reaches the end consumer directly, farmers will naturally benefit. Joshi feels that retail reform is only a first step toward needed agricultural reforms in India, and that the government should pursue additional reforms.

Suryamurthy, in an article in the *Telegraph*, states that farmers' groups across India do not support the status quo and seek retail reforms, because in the current retail system the farmer is being exploited. For example, Indian farmers get only one-third of the price consumers pay for food staples; the rest is taken as commissions and markups by middlemen and shopkeepers. For perishable produce, the average price that farmers receive is barely 12 to 15 percent of the final price consumers pay. Potato farmers sell their crop for Rs 2 to 3 per kilogram, while the Indian consumer buys the same potato for Rs 12 to 20 per kilogram.

ECONOMISTS AND ENTREPRENEURS

Many business groups in India are welcoming the transformation of a long-protected sector that has left Indian shoppers bereft of the scale and variety made available by their counterparts in more developed markets, where consumers have a choice among competing retailers. B. Muthuraman, the president of the Confederation of Indian Industry, argues the retail reform would open enormous opportunities and lead to much-needed investment in cold chain, warehousing, and contract farming. The supporters of retail reform claim that fresh investment in organized retail will generate ten million new jobs, about five to six million of them in logistics alone.

Organized retail will offer the small Indian farmer more competing venues to sell his or her products, and increase income by reducing spoilage and waste. A Food and Agricultural Organization report states that the small farmer faces significant losses postharvest because of poor roads, inadequate storage technologies, inefficient supply chains, and the farmer's inability to bring the produce into retail markets dominated by small shopkeepers. These experts claim that India's postharvest losses exceed 25 percent, on average, every year for each farmer.

Not only do these losses reduce food security in India, the study claims that poor farmers and others lose income because of the waste and inefficiency of retail. Over US$50 billion of additional income could become available to Indian farmers by preventing postharvest farm losses, improving transport, and creating proper storage and retail facilities. Organized retail is also expected to initiate infrastructure development, creating millions of rural and urban jobs for India's growing population. One study claims that if these postharvest food staple losses could be eliminated with better infrastructure and a retail network in India, enough food would be saved to feed 70 to 100 million people every year.

Retail reforms would mean that more buyers would compete for farmers' produce, leading to better support of farmers and to better bids. With less spoilage of staples and agricultural produce, global retail companies could find and provide additional markets to Indian farmers. Walmart, since its arrival in India's wholesale retail market, already sources and exports about $1 billion worth of Indian goods for its global customers.

Supporters of retail reform, the *Economist* claims, say it will increase competition and quality while reducing prices, helping to reduce India's rampant inflation, which is close to double digits. These supporters say that unorganized small shopkeepers will continue to exist alongside large organized supermarkets, because for many Indians they will remain the most accessible and convenient places to shop. Amartya Sen, the Indian-born Nobel Prize–winning economist, in a December 2011 interview, claimed that FDI in multibrand retail could be good thing or bad thing, depending on the nature of the investment. Quite often, says Professor Sen, FDI is a good thing for India.

ALLOWED IN SOME STATES, BANNED IN OTHERS

The governments of some states, particularly those ruled by the moderately left-wing party Indian National Congress, have said they will allow foreign supermarkets to open in their states. The following states will allow foreign retailers:

♦ Andhra Pradesh, Assam, Delhi, Haryana, Kashmir, Maharashtra, Manipur, Uttarakhand, Daman and Diu, and Dadra and Nagar Haveli.

Other states, particularly those ruled by the right-wing Bharatiya Janata Party, have said they will not allow foreign supermarkets to open in their states. The following states will not allow foreign retailers:

♦ West Bengal, Gujarat, Bihar, Karnataka, Kerala, Madhya Pradesh, Tripura, Orissa, and Rajasthan.

Supporters of retail reform who have promoted organized retail include the chief ministers of several states of India, several belonging to political parties that have no affiliation with the Congress Party–led central government of India. The list includes the chief ministers of Maharashtra, Andhra Pradesh, Tamil Nadu, and Gujarat. In a report submitted in early 2011, these chief ministers urged the prime minister to prioritize reforms that promote organized retail, shorten the retail path from farm to consumer, allow organized retail to buy directly from farmers at remunerative produce prices, and reduce farm-to-retail costs. Similarly, the chief minister of Delhi has come out in support of the retail reform, because in this urban area citizens prefer large supermarkets. The chief ministers of Haryana and Punjab, two rural farming states in north India, claim that the announced retail reforms will never benefit farmers in their states.

The chief minister of the state of Maharashtra, the state with the biggest GDP in India and home to its financial capital, Mumbai, has also welcomed the retail reform. Tarun Gogoi, the chief minister of Assam, an eastern state in India, announced his support for the retail reform, saying, "This will go a long way in bringing about a sea change in the rural economy. The decision will boost agriculture and allied sectors, manufacturing, logistics, integrated cold chains, refrigerated transportation, and food processing facilities in a big way." Criticizing the BJP-organized opposition, Gogoi claimed that these parties who had, just a few years ago, dubbed opening up retail as good for India, are now singing a different tune. Special interest groups have turned the tide. Farmers are now against retail reforms because they are convinced it will hurt their business. With the current system, farmers' survival depends on local and regional cooperatives to help them regulate prices.

2013 STATE ELECTIONS

In December 2013 elections were held in the state of Delhi and a new party came to power. The new chief minister of Delhi opposes foreign investment in retail and has written to the federal government to withdraw permission given by the previous chief minister that allowed foreign retailers to open shops in the state. The Federal Industry Ministry has responded by saying it does not want foreign investors to think of India as an "unpredictable banana republic"; therefore the rules are such that once a state government allows foreign retailers in that state, it cannot disallow the foreign stores if a new party comes to power in that state.

CURRENT SUPERMARKETS

Existing Indian retail firms such as Spencer's, Foodworld Supermarkets, Ltd., Nilgiri's, and ShopRite support retail reform and consider international competition to be a blessing in disguise. They expect a flurry of joint ventures with global majors for expansion capital and opportunity to gain expertise in supply chain management. Spencer's, with two hundred stores in India and retailing fresh vegetables and fruits, accounting for 55 percent of its business, considers retail reform to be a win-win situation. They already procure farm products directly from the growers without the involvement of middlemen or traders. Spencer's claims that there is scope for them to expand their footprint of store locations as well as procurement of farm products. Foodworld, which operates over sixty stores, plans to ramp up its presence to more than two hundred locations. It has already joined with Hong Kong–based Dairy Farm International. With the relaxation of regulations on international investments in Indian retail, India's Foodworld expects its global relationships will only get stronger. Competition and investment in retail will provide more benefits to consumers through lower prices, wider availability, and significant improvement in supply chain logistics.

GROWTH IN THE INDIAN RETAIL SECTOR

India is one of the world's fastest growing economies and the third-largest country in the world in terms of purchasing power parity (PPP), and the GDP has more than doubled in the last ten years. Retail is estimated to be the largest single sector, after agriculture, both in terms of turnover as well as employment. After leading the IT bandwagon, India is poised to grow as a retail hub.

In 2006, India was named the world's largest unexploited retail market, recognized as the leading destination for retail investment in the 2006 Global Retail Development Index. Organized retail accounted for less than 4 percent of the overall sector. Since 2008, the retail sector has grown by more than 400 percent to US $30 billion, taking 8 percent—9 percent of the retail sector as a whole.

Indian companies operating in the retail sector under a single brand are now permitted FDI up to 51 percent and there has been rapid real estate development in recent years. Overseas retailers and wholesalers are also able to operate in India via franchise and strategic licensing agreements.

India has a huge youth market. One-quarter of the world's youth live in India. More than 50 percent of the Indian population is below 25 years of age. By 2050, India will have overtaken China as the world's most populous nation. This means there is a growing consumer class and a rise in disposable income.

There are 209 million households across the country. Although only six million of these are classified as rich, 32 percent are regarded as the consumer classes. Disposable incomes have risen at an average of 8.5 percent per annum. The availability of cheap credit is also increasing, breaking down another barrier to impulse spending.

SHRINKAGE RATE IN THE RETAIL SECTOR

Rising disposable incomes, cheap consumer credit, highly attractive demographics, a booming economy, and an increasingly liberal regulatory environment. No wonder retailers globally are getting serious about India. Though the prize may be great, the road is still a tough one. From understanding local tastes and tailoring the product offering to securing access to the right real estate, entrants to the world's largest untapped retail market face some difficult challenges.

As one of the leading service providers to the Indian retail industry, Ernst & Young offers existing and new retailers an array of risk, tax, advisory, and transaction services. Ernst & Young has been associated with the industry since its early growth phase in India and has worked with players across categories, formats, and scales of operations.

India has an extremely high shrinkage rate. Shrinkage rate is the loss of inventory due to theft, error, fraud, and damage to goods. This includes employee theft, error, and fraud. It seems that the culprit, again, is a lack of work culture.

Figure 4.10: Total Retail Market Average Shrinkage Rate by Retail Sector (India), 2007

Source: CSO, NSSO and Technopak Advisers Pvt., Ltd.

Figure 4.11: Shrinkage as a Percentage of Sales

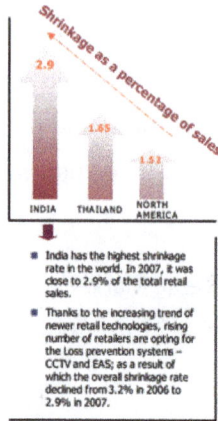

Source: CSO, NSSO and Technopak Advisers Pvt., Ltd.

The Indian retail sector is highly fragmented, with about 15 million retailers. The majority of these sell food items. Since the 1990s, big industrial houses like Rahejas, Piramals, Tatas, and others, began entering the retail industry. In addition, several Indian and foreign companies have been franchising to establish exclusive outlets for their brands, both within the country and overseas. For instance, Bharati Group has entered into a joint venture with the world's largest retail chain, Walmart.

As a result, the Indian retail sector has been undergoing a rapid transformation in the past few years. The traditional formats of kirana stores, hawkers, grocers, etc. are being gradually taken over by the modern formats of department stores, discount stores, malls, supermarkets, convenience stores, fast food outlets, specialty stores, warehouse retailers, hypermarkets, etc. For example, Pantaloon started Big Bazaar discount stores in 2002; Reliance opened its first supermarket named Reliance Fresh Outlet in Hyderabad and has since fanned out to several states; and Subhiksha outlets have been quickly spreading across the nation. Thus, the current face of Indian retail comprising the unorganized small and medium retailers is slowly changing into a more organized form of retailing.

According to the available estimates of the Rs 1,330,000 crore retail market, food and grocery retail is the single largest block estimated to be worth Rs 7,92,000 crore (with a 59.5 percent share), but the organized sector share is miniscule. Clothing, textiles, and fashion accessories constitute the second-largest block, with a 9.9 percent share at Rs 1, 31,300 crore. But the largest segments, as far as organized retailing is concerned, are in the time-wear (48.9 percent share) and footwear (48.4 percent share) sectors. In 2007, the share of organized retail was estimated to be 5.9 percent, which was Rs 78,300 crore. Organized retail touched Rs 2, 30,000 crore (at constant prices) in 2010, constituting roughly 13 percent of the total retail market; by 2020 it is expected to go up to 15 percent. The modern retail segment grew at the rate of 42.4 percent in 2007 and is expected to maintain a faster growth rate, especially considering that major global players and Indian corporate houses are entering into the market in a big way. This growth in modern retailing is linked to several factors, particularly the increasing purchasing power; rapid global interaction and integration, as well as changing consumer needs, lifestyle, and attitude. Furthermore, shopping center business alone became a Rs 40,000 crore business in 2010–2011.

The large organized retail segment, using sophisticated technology and communication networks, offers several benefits to the consumers: the availability of quality products at lower prices; wider selection; shopping with convenience, space, and entertainment; etc. Organized retail is also beneficial for the growth of the economy as a whole because it provides forward linkages for the mass marketing of processed and packaged goods. Its expanded reach and increased volumes translates into more manufacturing, more jobs, better standard of living, and as a result, more prosperity.

Given the current scenario, foreign direct investment into the retail sector would further improve its productivity, competitiveness, and efficiency. Such investments from abroad would supplement and complement domestic efforts to provide opportunities for technological upgrades and access to global managerial skills and practices; provide optimal utilization of human and natural resources; open up export markets; generate backward and forward linkages; provide access to international quality goods and services; and more.

India is also one of the most attractive markets for retail investment. Many national and global players have been investing in the retail segment and have ambitious plans for further expansion. The vast middle class with its rising purchasing power is attracting global retail giants into the almost untapped retail industry. Some of the international players already present in the Indian market include fast food chains like McDonald's, Pizza Hut, Domino's; apparel brands such as Levi, Lee, Nike, Adidas, Benetton; and technology brands such as Sony, Sharp, and Kodak, among others.

The investment opportunities in the domestic retail industry lay in most of the product categories, particularly food and grocery (the largest category); home improvement and consumer durables; apparel and eating out; supply chain infrastructure (cold chain and logistics). India also has significant potential to emerge as a sourcing base for a wide variety of goods for international retail companies.

As of now, there is no policy for FDI in retail. The government allows 100 percent FDI in cash-and-carry through the automatic route and 51 percent FDI in the retail trade of single-brand products. Additionally, the franchise route is available for the big operators. The government also proposes further freedom in the retail sector, allowing 51 percent FDI in consumer electronics, sporting goods, stationery, and building equipment. The current policy regime also bars foreign retailers from selling multiple brands directly to consumers. This policy framework involves numerous licensing formalities for the retailers, so there is a demand for a single-window clearance system, which would make the whole process hassle-free.

The Retailers Association of India is the voice of Indian organized and modern retailers. Launched by the key retailers of the country, its founding membership consists of leading retailers like Aditya Birla Retail, Ltd., Bharat Petroleum Corporation, Ltd; Damas Goldfields Jewelry Pvt., Ltd.;

Globus Stores; Levi Strauss (India) Pvt., Ltd; Lifestyle International Pvt., Ltd; McDonald's India (West & South); Nalli; Pantaloon Retail (India), Ltd; Raymond, Ltd; Reliance Webstore, Ltd; Reliance Retail, Ltd.; Shoppers' Stop; Subiksha Trading Services Pvt., Ltd.; Tata Consultancy Services (TCS) Textile Pvt., Ltd.; Bombay Dyeing & Manufacturing Co., Ltd; Titan Industries, Ltd.; Wadhawan Food Retail (P), Ltd.; and Zodiac Clothing Co., Ltd.; among others.

Several important steps are being taken to give a further a boost to the retail segment of the Indian economy. For the first time, under the aegis of the India Retail Forum, the entire retail industry, F&R Research, and some of the world's top global research and consulting firms (like AT Kearney, Ernst & Young, PwC, Technopak, KPMG, ICICI, AC Nielson-ORG Marg, Synovate, Cushman & Wakefield, etc.) have come together to conduct a detailed study of the Indian retail sector. Other developments in this direction include the launch of the India Retail Report 2007 and 2009 and the portal http://indiaretailing.com/.

Judging by the current growth trends, organized retail in India has indeed gained top speed and is now on the verge of takeoff. Despite the changes, it is believed that the Indian format of retailing is going to retain its own touch with numerous small retailers and other traders located in the city centers and the large organized retailers being established in the suburbs of the metropolitan cities. In other words, small retailers will continue to occupy a niche position as corner-side shops, because with personalized services and convenient walking distance, they are able to provide a special kind of service, which will always be in demand.

5

BANKING

OVERVIEW

The banking sector in India is on a growing trend. Banking has vastly bene-fited from the surge in disposable income. There has also been a noticeable upsurge in transactions through ATMs, the Internet, and mobile banking. Consequently, public, private, and foreign banks have invested consider-ably to increase their banking network and thus, their customer reach.

The banking industry in India has the potential to become the fifth-largest banking industry in the world by 2020 and third-largest by 2025, according to a KPMG-CII report. Over the next decade, the banking sector is projected to create up to two million new jobs, driven by the efforts of the Reserve Bank of India (RBI) and the government of India to integrate financial services into rural areas. Also, the traditional way of operating will slowly give way to modern technology.

HISTORY

Banking in India, in the modern sense, originated in the last decades of the eighteenth century. The first banks were the Bank of Hindustan (1770 – 1829) and the General Bank of India, established in 1786 and since defunct. The largest bank, and the oldest still in existence, is the State Bank of India, which originated as the Bank of Calcutta in June 1806 and became the Bank of Bengal in January 1809. The Bank of Bengal was the first joint-stock bank, sponsored by the government of Bengal and governed by the royal charter of the British Indian government. The Bank of Bombay followed, established in April 1840, and the Bank of Madras was established in July 1843.

These three banks, known as the presidency banks, marked the beginning of the limited liability, joint-stock banking in India and were vested with the right of note issue. Following the introduction of the limited liability banking, a few more banks were established, the notable ones being the Allahabad Bank and the Punjab National Bank. The three presidency banks merged in 1921 to form the Imperial Bank of India, which, upon India's independence, became the State Bank of India in 1955.

For many years the presidency banks acted as quasi-central banks, as did their successors, until the Reserve Bank of India was established in 1935. At that point, the central banking responsibilities of the Imperial Bank of India came to an end, making it a commercial bank. Banking at that time was predominantly based in urban areas.

COLONIAL ERA

The Allahabad Bank, established in 1865 and still functioning today, is the oldest Joint Stock bank in India. It was not the first, though; that honor belongs to the Bank of Upper India, which was established in 1863 and survived until 1913. When it failed, some of its assets and liabilities were transferred to the Alliance Bank of Simla.

Foreign banks too started to appear in the 1860s, particularly in Calcutta. The Comptoir d'Escompte de Paris opened a branch in Calcutta in 1860 and another in Bombay in 1862; branches in Madras and Pondicherry, then a French possession, followed. HSBC established itself in Bengal in 1869. Calcutta was the most active trading port in India, mainly due to the trade of the British Empire, and so it became a banking center.

The first entirely Indian joint-stock bank was the Oudh Commercial Bank, established in 1881 in Faizabad. It failed in 1958. The next was the Punjab National Bank, established in Lahore in 1894, which has survived to the present and is now one of the largest banks in India.

Around the turn of the twentieth century, the Indian economy was passing through a period of relative stability. Around five decades had elapsed since the Indian Mutiny, and social, industrial, and other infrastructure had improved. Indians had established small banks, most of which served particular ethnic and religious communities.

The presidency banks dominated banking in India, but there were also some exchange banks and a number of Indian joint-stock banks. All these banks operated in different segments of the economy. The exchange banks, mostly owned by Europeans, concentrated on financing foreign trade. Indian joint-stock banks were generally undercapitalized and lacked the experience and maturity to compete with the presidency and exchange banks. This segmentation led Lord Curzon, a British statesman who was the viceroy of India, to observe, "In respect of banking it seems we are behind the times. We are like some old fashioned sailing ship, divided by solid wooden bulkheads into separate and cumbersome compartments."

The period between 1906 and 1911 saw the establishment of banks inspired by the Swadeshi movement. The Swadeshi movement inspired local businessmen and political figures to found banks by and for the Indian community. A number of the banks established then have survived to the present, such as Bank of India, Corporation Bank, Indian Bank, Bank of Baroda, Canara Bank, and Central Bank of India.

The fervor of the Swadeshi movement led to the establishment of many private banks in the Dakshina Kannada and Udupi districts, which were unified earlier and known by the name South Canara (South Kanara) district. Four national banks started in this district and a leading private-sector bank. Hence the undivided Dakshina Kannada district is known as the cradle of Indian banking.

The period from the First World War (1914–1918) through the end of the Second World War (1939–1945) and two years thereafter, until the independence of India, was a challenging time for Indian banking. The years of the First World War were turbulent and took their toll, with banks simply collapsing despite the Indian economy gaining an indirect boost from war-related economic activities. At least ninety-four banks in India failed between 1913 and 1918.

POST-INDEPENDENCE

The partition of India in 1947 adversely impacted the economies of Punjab and West Bengal, paralyzing banking activities for months. India's independence marked the end of a laissez-faire regime in Indian banking. The government of India initiated measures to play an active role in the economic life of the nation, and the Industrial Policy Resolution adopted by the government in 1948 envisaged a mixed economy. This resulted in the state's greater involvement in different segments of the economy, including banking and finance. The major steps to regulate banking included the following:

♦ The Reserve Bank of India, India's central banking authority, was established in April 1935 and nationalized on January 1, 1949, under the terms of the Reserve Bank of India (Transfer to Public Ownership) Act of 1948 (RBI, 2005b).

♦ In 1949, the Banking Regulation Act was enacted, which empowered the RBI "to regulate, control, and inspect the banks in India."

♦ The Banking Regulation Act also provided that no new bank or branch of an existing bank could be opened without a license from the RBI, and no two banks could have common directors.

NATIONALIZATION IN THE 1960s

Despite the provisions, controls, and regulations of the Reserve Bank of India, all banks in India, except the State Bank of India (SBI), continued to be owned and operated by private persons. By the 1960s, the Indian banking industry had become an important tool to facilitate the development of the Indian economy. At the same time, it had emerged as a large employer, and a debate had ensued about the nationalization of the banking industry. Indira Gandhi, the prime minister of India at the time, expressed the intention of the government of India in the annual conference of the All India Congress Meeting in a paper entitled "Stray Thoughts on Bank Nationalization." The meeting received the paper with enthusiasm.

Thereafter, her move was swift and sudden. The government of India issued the Banking Companies (Acquisition and Transfer of Undertakings) Ordinance in 1969 and nationalized the fourteen largest commercial banks starting at midnight on July 19, 1969. These banks held 85 percent of all bank deposits in the country. Jayaprakash Narayan, a national leader of India, described the step as a "masterstroke of political sagacity." Within two weeks of the ordinance being issued, the Parliament passed the Banking Companies Acquisition and Transfer of Undertaking Bill. The bill received presidential approval on August 9, 1969.

In 1980, six more commercial banks were nationalized. The stated reason for the nationalization was to give the government more control of credit delivery. With the second dose of nationalization, the government of India controlled around 91 percent of the banking business of India. In 1993, the government merged the New Bank of India with the Punjab National Bank. It was the only merger between nationalized banks, taking the number of nationalized banks to 19. The nationalized banks grew at a pace of around 4 percent, closer to the average growth rate of the Indian economy.

Following the nationalization of major banks in 1969 and 1980, the banking network spread significantly, particularly in the rural and semi-urban areas, with the aim of improving economically disadvantaged areas. Economic reforms, followed by the banking sector reforms of 1991, changed the functioning of Indian banks, making them more stable and stronger.

All the major banks have remained under government ownership since 1969. They are run under a structure known as a "profit-making public-sector undertaking" (PSU) and are allowed to compete and operate as commercial banks. The Indian banking sector is now made up of four types of banks. Since the 1990s, the PSUs and the state banks have been joined by new private commercial banks and a number of foreign banks.

Generally, banking in India was fairly mature in terms of supply, product range, and reach, even though reaching rural India and the poor still remains a challenge. The government has developed initiatives to address this, by expanding the branch network of the State Bank of India and by introducing microfinance through the National Bank for Agriculture and Rural Development, as well as the prime minister's 2014 plan to bring bank accounts to the estimated 40 percent of the population that were still unbanked.

LIBERALIZATION IN THE 1990S

In the early 1990s, the government embarked on a policy of liberalization, licensing a small number of private banks. These came to be known as New Generation tech-savvy banks and included the Global Trust Bank (the first of such new generation banks to be set up), which later amalgamated with Oriental Bank of Commerce, UTI Bank (since renamed Axis Bank), ICICI Bank, and Housing Development Finance Corporation (HDFC) Bank. This move, along with the rapid growth in the economy of India, revitalized the banking sector in India, which has seen rapid growth with strong contribution from all the three sectors of banks, namely government banks, private banks, and foreign banks.

The next stage for Indian banking was the relaxation of norms for FDI, where all foreign investors in banks were given voting rights, which could exceed the cap of 10 percent. The cap has presently been raised to 74 percent with some restrictions. The new policy shook the banking sector in India. Before now, bankers were used to the 4–6–4 method (borrow at 4 percent; lend at 6 percent; go home at 4). The new wave ushered in a modern outlook and tech-savvy methods for traditional banks. All this led to the retail boom in India. People demanded more from their banks and they received more.

CURRENT PERIOD

By 2010, banking in India was fairly mature in terms of supply, product range, and reach, even though reach in rural India still remains a challenge for the private sector and foreign banks. In terms of quality of assets and capital adequacy, Indian banks are considered to have clean, strong, and transparent balance sheets relative to other banks in comparable economies in its region. The Reserve Bank of India is an autonomous body with minimal pressure from the government.

With the growth in the Indian economy expected to be strong for quite some time—especially in its service sector—the demand for banking services (particularly retail banking), mortgage, and investment services are also expected to be strong. One may also expect mergers and acquisitions (M&As), takeovers, and asset sales.

In March 2006, the Reserve Bank of India allowed Warburg Pincus to increase its stake in Kotak Mahindra Bank (a private-sector bank) to 10 percent. This is the first time an investor has been allowed to hold more than 5 percent in a private-sector bank since 2005, when the RBI announced norms stating that it would first vet any stake in the private-sector banks exceeding 5 percent.

In recent years, critics have charged that the nongovernment-owned banks are too aggressive in their recovery efforts for housing, vehicle, and personal loans. Press reports indicate that the banks' loan recovery efforts have driven defaulting borrowers to suicide due to the aggressive tactics of loan recovery agents. This shows a downside to the lack of government interference in the banking sector.

By 2013 the Indian banking industry employed over one million people, had a total of 109,811 branches in India, 171 branches abroad, and managed an aggregate deposit of ₹67504.54 billion (US$1.1 trillion) and a bank credit of ₹52604.59 billion (US$850 billion). The net profit of the banks operating in India was ₹1027.51 billion (US$17 billion) against a turnover of ₹9148.59 billion (US$150 billion) for the financial year 2012–2013.

ADOPTION OF BANKING TECHNOLOGY

The IT revolution has had a great impact on the Indian banking system. After the economic liberalization of 1991, the use of computers in the banking sector and the introduction of online banking in India increased greatly as the country's banking sector has been exposed to the world's market. Before the use of IT, Indian banks were finding it difficult to compete with the customer service available at international banks.

By the end of June 2012, a total number of 99,218 automated teller machines (ATMs) were installed in India by various banks. The new private-sector banks in India have the most ATMs, followed by off-site ATMs belonging to SBI and its subsidiaries, and then by nationalized banks and foreign banks. The nationalized banks of India have the highest number of on-site ATMs.

EXPANSION OF BANKING INFRASTRUCTURE

In the last decade, the physical as well as the virtual expansion of banking through mobile banking, Internet banking, telebanking, biometric, and mobile ATMs has taken place, gaining the most momentum in last few years. According to the census of 2011, 58.7 percent of households are using banking services. There are 102,343 branches of scheduled commercial banks (SCBs) in the country, of which 37,953 (37 percent) are in rural areas and 27,219 (26 percent) are in semi urban areas. SCBs constitute 63 percent of the total number of branches in semi urban and rural areas of the country. However, a significant proportion of the households, especially in rural areas, are still outside the formal fold of the banking system. The Government and Reserve Bank of India is introducing initiatives to extend the reach of banking to those outside the formal banking system. Some of these indicatives are enumerated below.

In October 2011, the government issued a detailed strategy and guidelines on financial inclusion, advising banks to open branches in under-banked districts with populations of 5,000 or more and in other districts with populations of 10,000 or more. By the end of April 2013, out of 3,925 villages or habitations, branches had been opened in 3,402 (including 2,121 ultra-small branches).

Each household is to have at least one bank account; in specific wards in urban areas, banks have been assigned the responsibility of ensuring that every household has at least one bank account.

In 2006, the RBI permitted banks to use the services of intermediaries in providing financial and banking services, such as business facilitators and business correspondents (BCs) with the objective of ensuring greater financial inclusion and increasing the outreach of the banking sector. BCs are retail agents employed by banks to provide banking services at locations other than a bank branch or ATM. BCs and the BC agents (BCAs) represent the bank, enabling the bank to expand its outreach and offer a limited range of banking services at a low cost, particularly when setting up a brick-and-mortar branch is not a viable option. BCs are an integral part of the business strategy for achieving greater financial inclusion.

Banks were permitted to engage individuals or entities as BCs, such as retired bank employees, retired teachers, retired government employees, ex-servicemen, individual owners of kirana/medical/fair price shops, individual public call office operators, agents of Small Savings Schemes of the government of India, insurance companies, etc. In September 2010, the RBI permitted banks to engage as BC for-profit companies registered under the Indian Companies Act, 1956, excluding Nonbanking financial companies. According to the data maintained by RBI, as of December 2012, there were over 152,000 BCs deployed by banks. During 2012–2013, over 183.8 million transactions valued at ₹165 billion (US$2.7 billion) had been undertaken by BCs.

A financial inclusion campaign called Swabhimaan was launched in February 2011. By March 2012, banks had provided banking facilities to over 74,000 areas with populations in excess of 2,000 people using various models and technologies, including branchless banking through BCAs. According to the finance minister's budget speech of 2012–2013, the Swabhimaan campaign was extended to areas with population of more than 1,000 in the northeastern and hilly states and to areas with populations over 1,600 as per the 2001 census. About 40,000 of such habitations are covered under the extended "Swabhimaan" campaign.

Considering banks need to closely supervise and monitor BCAs to ensure that a range of banking services are available to the residents of small villages, ultra-small branches (USBs) are being set up in all villages covered through BCAs under financial inclusion. A USB comprises a small room of 100 square feet (9.3 m²) to 200 square feet (19 m²) where the officer designated by the bank is available with a laptop on predetermined days. While the cash services are offered by the BCAs, the bank officer can provide other services, undertake field verification, and follow up on the banking transactions. The regularity and duration of visits is increased depending upon business potential in the area. Over 60,000 USBs were set up as of 2017.

All the 129 unbanked blocks (91 in northeast states and 38 in other states) identified in July 2009 were provided with banking facilities by March 2012, either through brick-and-mortar branches, business correspondents, or mobile vans. As a next step, all the blocks where there is only a mobile van will be covered by BCAs and USBs.

The National Payments Corporation of India (NPCI) worked on a common unstructured supplementary service data (USSD) platform for all banks and telcos who wish to offer mobile banking using USSD-based mobile banking. USSD is a system that allows cellular phones to communicate with the bank's computer system. The department helped NPCI get a common USSD code, *99#, for all telcos. More than twenty banks have joined the national uniform platform of NPCI and the product has been launched by NPCI with Bharat Sanchar Nigam, Ltd., and Mahanagar Telephone Nigam, Ltd. Other telcos are likely to join in the near future. USSD-based mobile banking offers basic banking facilities like money transfer, bill payments, balance inquiries, merchant payments, etc., on a simple global system for mobile communication–based mobile phone without the need to download an application, as is currently required in the immediate payment service–based mobile banking.

MOBILE BANKING

The use of smartphones throughout the world has skyrocketed over the last few years, and with it has come a substantial increase in mobile banking. More and more of the Indian population are forgoing trips to the bank in favor of conveniently using their smartphones to conduct basic transactions. ICICI Bank, the country's largest private-sector lender, has reported a threefold rise in mobile banking transactions, clocking in more than Rs 1,000 worth of transactions in a month, the highest of any a bank in India

(Anand, 2014). Mobile banking has become a core strategy for many Indian banks, to stay relevant among today's generation of tech-savvy consumers.

Figure 5.1 shows the steady growth of mobile banking since 2011. With the increased use of smartphones and more than 30 percent of the population between the ages of twenty and thirty, we can expect future growth as well.

Figure 5.1: Mobile Banking in India

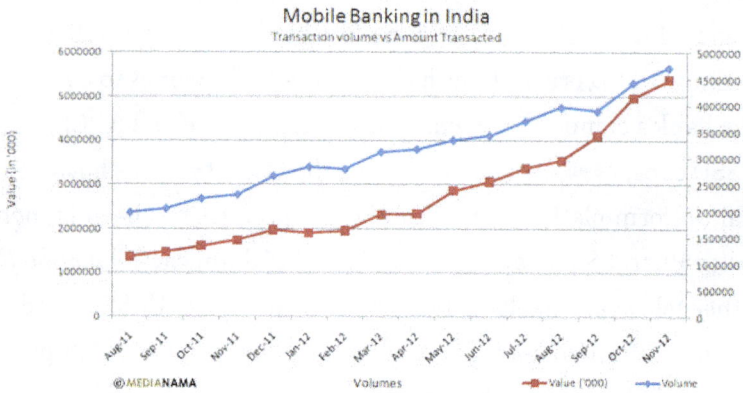

Source: Medianama (2013)

In Figure 5.2 below, we can see the average penetration levels of e-commerce and online banking activities of some of the biggest countries around the world. India seems to be experiencing a relatively low level of penetration compared to more developed countries like Japan and the US. Although India's number was 15 percent in 2014, there is no doubt that this number will continue to grow, as Indian consumers are becoming more comfortable with online payments and banking transactions.

Figure 5.2: Average Penetration Levels of E-Commerce and Online Banking Activities

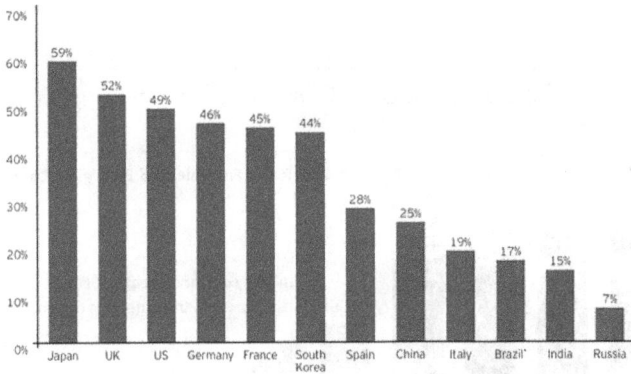

*Brazil figure excludes online banking

Source: Ernst & Young (2014)

Figure 5.3 shows the banking and financial services penetration in India. These data clearly show that industry penetration is low, and India may have yet to experience any significant growth in banking and financial services. The population is over 1.2 billion, and yet only 13 percent have a debit card and 2 percent have a credit card. Since debit and credit cards are important means of facilitating online banking and e-commerce transactions, these numbers have to grow for these industries to flourish. Making information available to consumers can aid in expanding the portion of the population who perform regular banking transactions online using a debit or credit card.

Figure 5.3: Banking and Financial Services Penetration in India

Percentage of Population Having	
Bank Account (Savings)	57.0%
Life Insurance	10.0%
Non-Life Insurance	0.6%
Debit Card	13.0%
Credit Card	2.0%
Data Source : Reserve Bank of India www.economicsfanatic.com	

Source: Reserve Bank of India, Economics, and Finance Fanatic (2012)

Figure 5.4: Consumer Debt to GDP Ratio for Emerging Countries

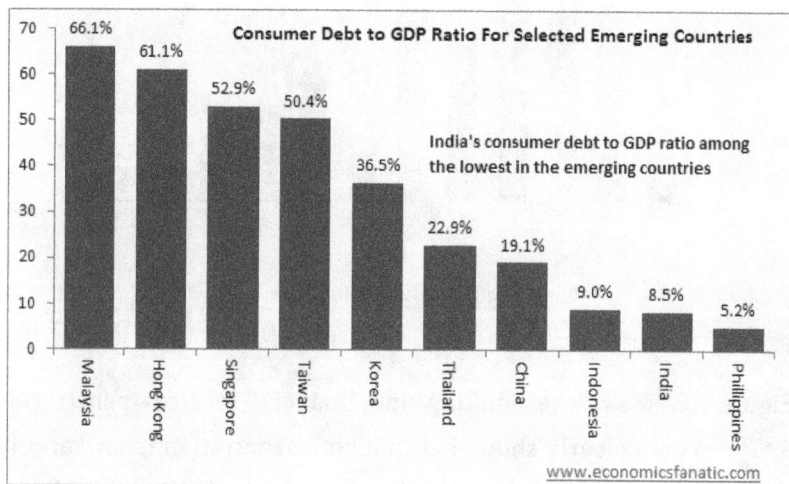

Consumer Debt to GDP Ratio For Selected Emerging Countries

India's consumer debt to GDP ratio among the lowest in the emerging countries

Malaysia 66.1%, Hong Kong 61.1%, Singapore 52.9%, Taiwan 50.4%, Korea 36.5%, Thailand 22.9%, China 19.1%, Indonesia 9.0%, India 8.5%, Phillipines 5.2%

www.economicsfanatic.com

Source: Economics and Finance Fanatic (2012)

The consumer debt to GDP ratio for a few select emerging markets is displayed in Figure 5.4 above. It shows that India has one of the lowest ratios among these emerging countries. This seems consistent with the data from Figure 5.3, since having a low penetration of banking and financial services and a small percentage of the population owning a credit card would result in a small percentage of consumer debt to GDP. Since India can be considered a fast-growing economy with great potential, having higher levels of penetration in these industries can be key to achieving economic success.

India's bank loan growth, as displayed in Figure 5.5, has been experiencing a continuous decline over the last decade. From 2005 to 2014, the percentage of bank loans issued to the Indian population has gone from over 30 percent to under 10 percent. This shows that even though the number of bank loans issued has been growing, it is growing by smaller and smaller amounts. There are many factors that could cause this slow growth, such as higher income levels earned by consumers and a decrease in the need for external funding. It is also possible that the growing use of credit cards is a factor, even though, as previously mentioned, credit card ownership is quite low.

Figure 5.5: India Bank Loan Growth, 2005–2014

INDIA BANK LOAN GROWTH

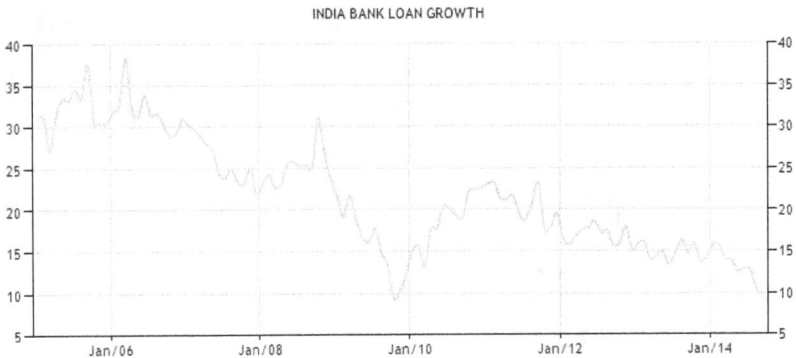

SOURCE: WWW.TRADINGECONOMICS.COM | RESERVE BANK OF INDIA

Source: Trading Economics (2014)

Figure 5.6 shows the ratio of bank credit to GDP in 2007. The global banking industry has been growing rapidly in the recent period. The United States holds a major share in global banking. In the 2007 survey, the United States accounted for 19.1 percent of the aggregate capital of the world's top 1,000 banks, 13.2 percent of the aggregate assets, 23.6 percent of the profits, and posted an average return on capital of 28.9 percent—much higher than the world average of 23.4 percent. Japan accounted for 10 percent of each of the aggregate tier I capital and total assets respectively and 7 percent of overall profits with a return on capital of 16.2 percent. Emerging economies, which have been showing rapid growth in the global financial markets, also made a mark in banking. The banking industry in Asia, most notably in China, India, and South Korea, witnessed rapid growth in business, and their aggregate assets went up by 16.2 percent. India had a total of approximately 80 percent bank credit with respect to GDP, which is a promising number considering the economy's continuous growth.

Figure 5.6: Bank Credit as Percentage of GDP

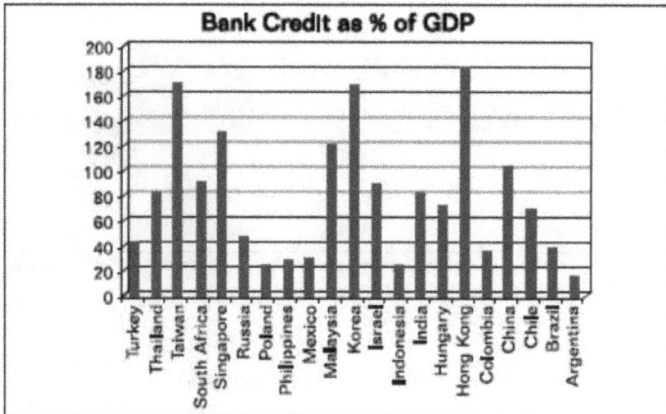

Source: IMF, World Bank, IBES Estimates, Credit Suisse Research

Figure 5.7 shows the basic structure of the Indian banking system from 2002 to 2007. One of the major outcomes of the banking sector reforms was a strong and sound system. The reforms required banks adopt prudential norms with respect to capital, income recognition, disclosure and transparency standards, and profitability and productivity. While technological advancements enabled efficient distribution, competition brought in product innovation and quality customer service. Today, Indian banking displays robust prospects for growth and compares favorably with other major banks.

Figure 5.7: Structure of Indian Banking

Structure of Indian Banking	2002	2003	2004	2005	2006	2007
Number of Commercial Banks	297	292	290	289	222	183
a. Scheduled Commercial Banks	293	288	286	285	218	179
Public Sector	27	27	27	28	28	28
Private Sector	30	29	30	29	28	25
Foreign Banks	40	36	33	31	29	29
b.Non-Scheduled Commercial Banks	4	4	5	4	4	4
No of Regional Rural Banks	196	196	196	196	133	96
Number of Bank Offices	68195	68500	69170	70373	71177	73836
Of which Rural	32503	32283	32227	30790	30436	30560
Semi Urban	14962	15135	15288	15325	15811	16434
Urban	11328	11566	11806	12419	13034	13840
Metropolitan	9402	9516	9750	11839	12404	12952
Population Per Office (thousands)	15	16	16	16	16	16

Source: Reserve Bank of India

Figure 5.8, 5.9, and 5.10 show the breakup, advances, and income growth in Indian banks through the fiscal years 2006 and 2007. In FY 2007, the Bharat Overseas Bank was merged with the Indian Overseas Bank, the Ganesh Bank of Kurundwad was amalgamated with the Federal Bank, Ltd., and the United Western Bank was amalgamated with the Industrial Development Bank of India, Ltd. Consequently, by March 2007, the number of SCBs was reduced from eighty-two in the previous year to eighty. Moreover, UTI Bank was renamed Axis Bank, while Chohung Bank was renamed Shinhan Bank. The Sangli Bank, Ltd., was amalgamated with ICICI Bank, Ltd., and Lord Krishna Bank was merged with Centurion Bank of Punjab in August 2007.

The aggregated balance sheet of the SCBs in FY 2007 increased by 24.3 percent, compared to 18.2 percent in FY 2006. The detailed rate of deposit growth is shown in figure 5.8.

Figure 5.8: Breakdown of Bank Deposits by Group

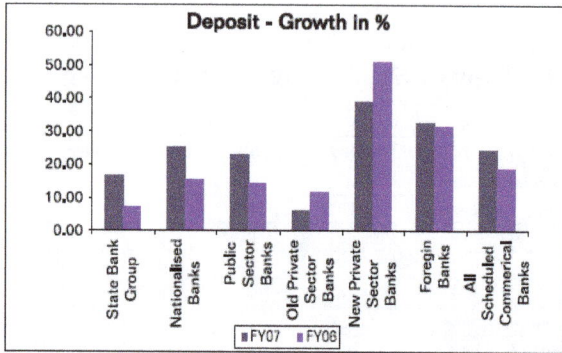

Source: Reserve Bank of India

The percentages of growth in advances are shown in Figure 5.9 below.

Figure 5.9: Breakdown of Banks' Advances by Group

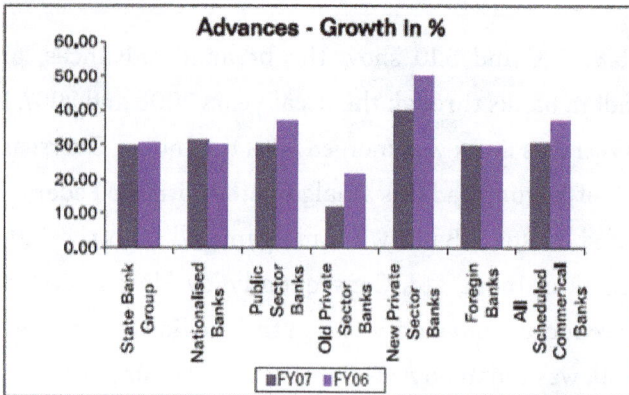

Source: Reserve Bank of India

Figure 5.10 shows the growth of net profit.

Figure 5.10: Breakdown of Banks' Net Profit by Group

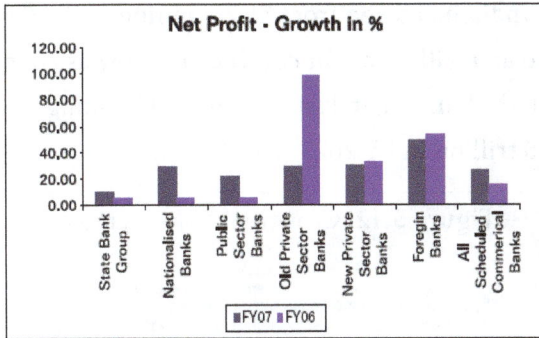

Source: Reserve Bank of India

The loan growth in Indian banking was characterized by the high growth of retail loans in the recent period. In FY 2005 retail loans grew at 41.2 percent and the pace remained the same in FY 2006. However in FY 2007, there is a slowdown, with the retail loans showing a growth of 29.9 percent. Retail loans as a percent of total loans and advances increased from 21.9 percent in FY 2004 to 25.8 percent in FY 2007. Similarly, credit outstanding in the sensitive sectors comprising the capital market, real estate market, and commodities grew 22.5 percent in FY 2004, 35.2 percent in FY 2005, 74.4 percent in FY 2006, and they slowed down to 41.2 percent in FY 2007.

Figure 5.11: Total Assets of Indian Banking Sector

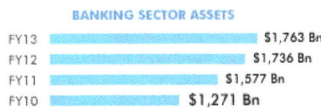

Source: IBEF (2014)

India's banking sector is constantly growing. Since the new millennium, there has been a noticeable upsurge in transactions through ATMs, Internet, and mobile banking. From FY 2010 to FY 2013, the value of banking sector assets in India increased from $1,271 billion to $1,763 billion. This is a major increase and will no doubt continue to grow as consumers become more invested in the banking industry. The total banking assets are expected to cross $28.5 trillion in FY 2025 (IBEF, 2014).

Figure 5.12: Growth of ATMs in India

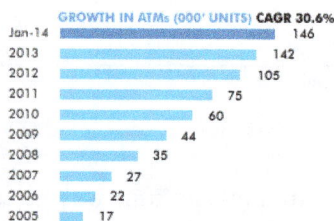

Source: IBEF (2014)

Figure 5.12 shows that ATM numbers have sharply increased from 2005 and they now stand at 146,000. Considering that the population is larger than one billion, this is still a comparatively small number; however, this number will grow alongside the increase in banking activity and investment in the banking and financial services industry.

GOVERNMENT INITIATIVES

There have been a number of developments in the Indian banking sector:

◆ To help micro, small, and medium enterprises, Reserve Bank of India has permitted an exchange-based trading platform to facilitate corporate and other buyers to finance bills raised by small entities, including government departments and PSUs.

♦ The government of India plans to reduce its stake in public-sector banks to 52 percent. The reduced stake fetched the government Rs 89,120 crore (US$14.46 billion) on the basis of the share prices as on November 21, 2014.

♦ The government of India has cleared a proposal by HDFC Bank, Ltd., to increase the foreign investment limit of the lender while taking the view that the stake held by its parent, Housing Development Finance Corporation, Ltd., amounts to overseas investment. The Foreign Investment Promotion Board has approved HDFC Bank's proposal to increase foreign investment in the bank to 74 percent.

♦ The Reserve Bank of India has created four verticals, which will be looked after by each of the deputy governors, as part of an organizational restructuring move.

♦ To give a boost to shipbuilding in the country, the Export-Import Bank of India (Exim Bank) is planning to set up a dedicated Rs 1,500 crore (US$243.37 million) fund with government support.

THE ROAD AHEAD

With the advancements in technology, mobile and Internet banking services have come to the fore. Banks in India are focusing more and more on providing better services to their clients and have also started upgrading their technology infrastructure, which can help improve customer experience as well as give banks a competitive edge.

Many banks, including the likes of HDFC, ICICI, and AXIS, are exploring the option of soon launching contactless credit and debit cards in the market. The cards, which use a near field communication mechanism, will allow customers to transact without having to insert or swipe the card.

Other industries in India can learn from the banking sector, which has experienced excellent growth in recent years. The success of this sector can be traced back to the government policy of liberalization in the 1990s. The lack of government interference in banking has led to healthy competition in the banking sector. The result has been improved service and increased use of technology, leading to greater efficiency. The government has further supported the growth of the banking sector by improving infrastructure in rural areas. There is room for greater development, however, by increasing access to credit cards, allowing for growth in online banking and e-commerce.

6

ENGINEERING, MACHINERY, AND TECHNOLOGY

ENGINEERING INDUSTRY

OVERVIEW

Engineering is a diverse industry with various segments. It is also the largest of all industrial sectors in India. A company in this sector can be a power equipment manufacturer; or an execution specialist for engineering, procurement, and construction (EPC); or even a niche player. The engineering sector has seen tremendous growth in recent years owing to significant investments in power generation projects and the infrastructure sector. The power sector itself contributes about 70-75 percent of engineering companies' revenues.

On its quest to become a global superpower, India has made significant strides towards the development of its engineering sector. The Indian government has appointed the Engineering Export Promotion Council to be the apex body in charge of promotion of engineering goods, products, and services from India. India exports transport equipment, capital goods, other machinery and equipment, and light engineering products, such as castings, forgings, and fasteners to various countries of the world.

Encouraged by favorable regulatory policies and growth in the manufacturing sector, many foreign players have started to invest in the country. On June 13, 2014, India became a permanent member of the Washington Accord (WA). This means India is now a part of an exclusive group of seventeen countries that are permanent signatories of the WA, an elite international agreement on engineering studies and the mobility of engineers.

Figure 6.1 below shows the structure of the Indian engineering industry.

Figure 6.1: Structure of the Indian Engineering Sector

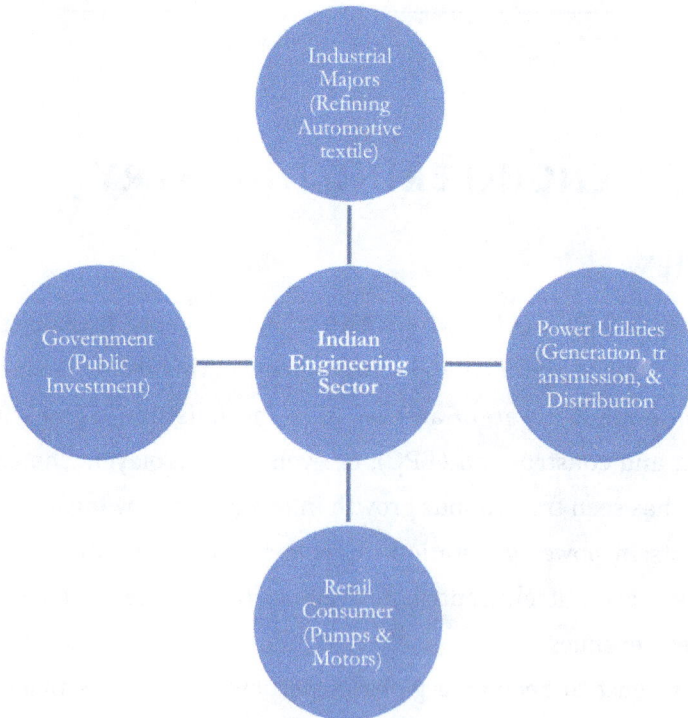

Source: Corporate Catalyst India (2013)

HEAVY ENGINEERING INDUSTRY

TEXTILE MACHINERY

The Indian textile machinery industry is a significant component of the capital goods industry. This industry comprises of over 1,446 machinery and components manufacturing units with over six hundred units producing complete machinery and the remaining producing parts and accessories. The range includes textile machinery required for the sorting, cording, and processing of yarns, fabrics, and weaving. The industry is gearing itself toward supplying machines for the export target of garment manufacturers since the Multi-Fiber Arrangement, an international trade agreement that limited the amount of textiles developing countries could export to developed countries. The industry is also delicensed, has FDI up to 100 percent under the automatic route, and technology collaboration is allowed freely. Old and new machinery is also is allowed to be imported freely.

CEMENT MACHINERY

Cement plants based on raw mill grinding, pyro-processing, and cement-grinding process technology for capacities up to 10,000 tons per day, are being manufactured in collaboration with foreign technology providers. Modern cement plants are designed for zero downtime, high product quality, and better output, with minimum energy consumed per unit of cement production, etc.

At present, there are six major suppliers of complete cement plant machinery, with an installed capacity of around Rs 600 crore/annum. The industry is fully capable of meeting the domestic demand. This industry is also delicensed and allows FDI up to 100 percent under automatic route, and technological collaboration is allowed freely. Import of old and new machinery is also allowed freely.

SUGAR MACHINERY

Domestic manufacturers of sugar plants dominate the global market and are capable of building manufacturing plants, from concept to commissioning stage, with a capacity up to 10,000 tons crushed per day.

RUBBER MACHINERY

At present, there are ten units in the organized sector for the manufacture of rubber machinery, which is mainly needed in the tire and tube industry. The range of equipment manufactured in the country includes intermixers, tire-curing presses, tube splicers, bladder-curing presses, tire molds, tire-building machines, turnet servicers, bias cutters, rubber-injection molding machines, bead wires, and so on.

MATERIAL HANDLING EQUIPMENT

The range of material handling equipment manufactured includes crushing and screening plants, coal/ore/ash handling plants, and associated equipment such as stackers, reclaimers, ship loaders and unloaders, wagon tipplers, feeders, etc. Manufacture of this equipment caters to the growing and rapidly changing needs of the core industries in India, such as coal, cement, power, port, mining, fertilizer, and steel plants.

There are fifty units in the organized sector for the manufacture of material handling equipment. In addition, there are a number of units operating in the small-scale sector. The industry is self-sufficient in meeting the domestic demand and is also capable of competing in the global market.

OIL FIELD EQUIPMENT

The petroleum industry in India is undergoing a major change. With the ongoing process of liberalization, the industry has been thrown open to the private sector in all major areas of exploration, production, refinement, and marketing, and this has resulted in increased demand for the oil field and related equipment.

Domestic production mainly covers onshore drilling equipment. Under offshore drilling, only offshore platforms and some other technological structures are being produced locally. The major producers of this equipment are Bharat Heavy Electricals, Ltd., Hindustan Shipyard, Mazagon Dock, and Larsen & Toubro.

METALLURGICAL MACHINERY

Metallurgical machinery includes equipment for mineral beneficiation, ore dressing, size reduction, steel plant equipment, foundry equipment, and furnaces. At present, there are thirty-nine units in the organized sector engaged in the manufacture of various types of metallurgical machinery. The existing production capacity is sufficient to meet the demand for this equipment in India.

Domestic manufacturers are in the position to supply the majority of the equipment for steel plants (e.g., blast furnaces, sinter plants, coke oven steel melting shop equipment, continuous casting equipment, rolling mills, and finishing line).

MINING MACHINERY

At present, there are thirty-two manufacturers in the organized sector, both public and private, for underground and surface mining equipment of various types. Out of these, seventeen units manufacture underground mining equipment. Domestic manufacturers are meeting most of the needs of the mining industry.

DAIRY MACHINERY

At present, there are around twenty units, both public and private, manufacturing dairy machinery in the organized sector. They produce equipment such as evaporators, milk refrigerators, storage tanks, milk and cream deodorizers, centrifuges, clarifiers, agitators, homogenizers, spray dryers, and heat exchangers. Small-scale units are also contributing to domestic production, producing spray dryers, heat exchangers, and other core equipment for milk powder plants.

Figure 6.2: Classification of Heavy and Light Engineering Sub segments

Heavy engineering sector	Light engineering sector
Textile machinery	Rolling bearing
Cement machinery	Medical and surgical instruments
Sugar machinery	Process control instruments
Rubber machinery	Industrial fasteners
Material handling equipment	Ferrous castings
Oil field equipment	Steel forgings
Metallurgical	Seamless steel pipes and tubes
Mining machinery	Electrical resistance welded (ERW) steel pipes and tubes
Dairy machinery	Submerged-arc welded (SAW) pipes
Machine tool	Bicycle

Source: Ministry of Heavy Industries and
Department of Industrial Policy and Promotion (2013)

Figure 6.2 above shows the classification of heavy and light engineering sub segments in the Indian engineering industry. Both heavy and light sectors are discussed further below.

The engineering industry in India manufactures a variety of products, with heavy engineering goods accounting for the majority of the production. Most of the leading players manufacture high-value heavy engineering goods using high-end technology. Huge capital investment is required and acts as an entry barrier. Consequently, the small and unorganized firms have a small market presence. The unorganized sector specializes in manufacturing low-technology products, while a few small-scale units are involved only in assembly of imported components. This segment caters to the replacement market for a few products, such as low-quality small bearings.

Figure 6.3 below shows important locations of heavy engineering industries in India, including automobiles, ships and dockyards, railways, and aircraft.

Figure 6.3: Heavy Engineering Industries

Source: Maps of India (2014)

LIGHT ENGINEERING

On the other hand, manufacturers of light engineering goods use medium- to low-end technology. The required capital investment and technology is low, meaning there is less of an entry barrier. This segment is dominated by small and unorganized players, which manufacture low-value-added products. However, a few medium and large-scale firms produce high-value-added products as well. This segment is also character-ized by small capacities and a high level of competition.

The Indian engineering industry is highly competitive, with several companies in each of the segments. Several multinational companies of the likes of ABB, Siemens, Honda, and Cummins have entered the industry.

Figure 6.4 below shows the major players in each of the equipment and machinery industries.

Figure 6.4: Classification of the Engineering Sector in India

Categories	Players
Textile Machinery	Lakshmi Machine Works Ltd, Veejay Lakshmi Engg. Works Ltd, Lakshmi Automatic Loom Works Ltd, Batliboi Ltd
Cement Machinery	Larsen & Toubro Ltd, Walchandnagar Industries Ltd
Sugar Machinery	K C P Ltd
Rubber Machinery	Larsen & Toubro Ltd, Alfred Herbert Ltd
Material Handling Equipment	Andhra Pradesh Heavy Machinery & Engg. Ltd, Bharat Earth Movers Ltd, L & T-Komatsu Ltd., T R F Ltd, Telco Construction Equipment Co. Ltd, W M I Cranes Ltd
Oil Field Equipment	Sagar International Ltd
Metallurgical Machinery	Tata Steel Ltd

Source: D&B (2014)

The engineering sector is a major contributor to the country's total merchandise shipments. The US and Europe together account for over 60 percent of India's total engineering exports. Engineering exports mainly in-clude transport equipment, capital goods, other machinery and equipment, and light engineering products like castings, forgings, and fasteners. The Ministry of Commerce and Industries has set a target of shipping US$125 billion worth of engineering goods by the end of 2013–2014. Indian engi-neering companies are scouting for newer markets (like Latin America, Africa, etc.) for exports as well as to strengthen their base in the US and Eu-rope. Engineering goods represent India's third-biggest export sector, which rose 2 percent in August 2013. Engineering exports cumulatively expanded by 22 percent between September and December 2013 to US$21.5 billion, compared to US$17.1 billion in 2012.

Figure 6.5 below shows the export performance of principle commodities in the engineering sector for FY 2013.

Figure 6.5: Export Performance of Principle Commodities (FY 2013)

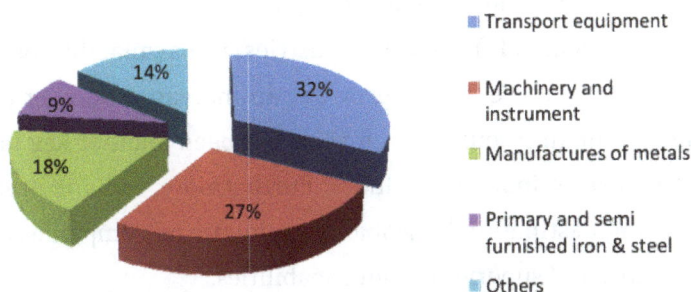

Legend:
- Transport equipment
- Machinery and instrument
- Manufactures of metals
- Primary and semi furnished iron & steel
- Others

Source: Corporate Catalyst India (2013)

ENGINEERING INDUSTRY MARKET SIZE

Driven by strong demand for engineering goods, exports from India registered double-digit growth at 10.22 percent to touch US$26.4 billion in June 2014 from US$24.02 billion in the corresponding month of 2013. This growth can be credited to the robust expansion in shipments of aircraft, spacecraft parts, and automobiles. The second-best-performing sector was nonferrous metals and metal products.

Engineering exports from India surpassed US$70 billion in FY 2015, registering a growth of 15 percent over the previous fiscal year, as demand in key markets such as the US and the UAE was on the rise. Apart from these traditional markets, markets in Eastern and Central European countries such as Poland also hold huge promise. Recently, India's engineering exports to Japan and South Korea have increased, with shipments to these two countries rising by 16 and 60 percent, respectively.

Growth in the domestic engineering industry has been fueled by growth in the key end-user industries and by the many new projects undertaken in core industries, such as railway, power, and infrastructure. Capacity creation in sectors such as infrastructure, oil and gas, power, mining, automobiles, auto components, steel, refinery, and consumer durables has driven growth in this sector. For example, the domestic sales of automobiles have grown at a CAGR of around 18 percent over the past several years, thereby increasing the demand for engineering goods.

Apart from demand from user industries, the availability of technical education infrastructure, which provides an increased number of technically trained human resources each year, has been another key factor aiding the engineering industry in India. Furthermore, India is preferred as an outsourcing destination by global manufacturing companies due to its lower labor cost and superior design capabilities.

Figure 6.6 below shows an overview of India's engineering exports in 2014.

Figure 6.6: India's Engineering Exports

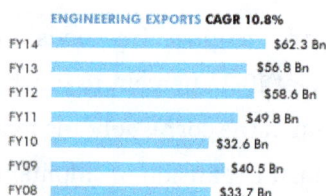

ENGINEERING EXPORTS **CAGR 10.8%**

FY14	$62.3 Bn
FY13	$56.8 Bn
FY12	$58.6 Bn
FY11	$49.8 Bn
FY10	$32.6 Bn
FY09	$40.5 Bn
FY08	$33.7 Bn

Source: India Brand Equity Foundation (2014)

INVESTMENTS

The FDI inflows into India's miscellaneous mechanical and engineering industries during April 2000 to July 2014 stood at around Rs 12,413.44 crore (US$2.02 billion), according to data released by the Department of Industries Policy and Promotion.

The following are some of the major investments and developments in the Indian engineering and design sector:

- Rolta has been awarded an additional scope of work by Sadara Chemical Company, Saudi Arabia, to implement a comprehensive engineering information system within Sadara's Jubail integrated chemical complex.

- Engineers India, Ltd. (EIL), has inked a US$139 million consultancy deal for a 20- MT refinery and polypropylene plant being built in Nigeria by Dangote Group.

- Jakson Group has won EPC orders aggregating US$34.21 million for its electrical contracting and solar businesses for FY 14.

- Maharashtra-based engine and engine components maker Cooper Corporation Private, Ltd., is planning to enter into the light commercial vehicles segment with its four-wheeler and six-wheeler offerings in the range of 1.5 to 3.5 tons.

- Crompton Greaves has opened its first global design center in Bhopal to address the evolving market needs of its clientele. The product portfolio would cover commercial motors and highly engineered medium voltage motors and generators.

- Tech Mahindra has inked a deal with Wichita State University (WSU) in the US and will collaborate with WSU and its National Institute for Aviation Research on multiple areas of engineering, including composites, advanced materials, and structural testing.

Figure 6.7 shows the investments in the Indian electrical and nonelectrical machinery industries from 2000 to 2007.

Figure 6.7: Investments in Electrical and Nonelectrical Machinery Industry

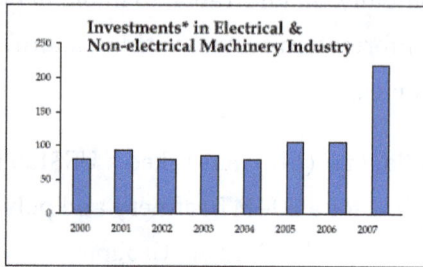

Investments* in Electrical &
Non-electrical Machinery Industry

*Outstanding Investments as of January each year (Rs bn)
Source: CapEx (CMIE) and D&B Research

Most of India's car manufacturing industry is based around three clusters in the south, west, and north. The southern cluster in Chennai is the biggest, with 35 percent of the revenue share. The western hub, near Mumbai and Pune, contributes 33 percent of the market, and the northern cluster, around the national capital region, contributes 32 percent. Chennai houses the India operations of Ford, Hyundai, Renault, Mitsubishi, Nissan, BMW, Hindustan Motors, Daimler, Caparo, Mini, and Datsun. Chennai accounts for 60 percent of the country's automotive exports. Gurgaon and Manesar in Haryana form the northern cluster, where the country's largest car manufacturer, Maruti Suzuki, is based. The Chakan corridor near Pune, Maharashtra, is the western cluster, where companies like General Motors, Volkswagen, Skoda, Mahindra and Mahindra, Tata Motors, Mercedes Benz, Land Rover, Jaguar Cars, Fiat, and Force Motors have assembly plants. Nashik has a major base of Mahindra and Mahindra with an SUV assembly unit and an engine assembly unit. Aurangabad, with Audi, Skoda, and Volkswagen, also forms part of the western cluster. Another emerging cluster is in the state of Gujarat, with a manufacturing facility for General Motors in Halol and further plans for Tata Nano at their plant in Sanand. Ford, Maruti Suzuki, and Peugeot-Citroen plants are also set to open in Gujarat. Other automotive manufacturing regions around the country include Kolkata with Hindustan Motors, Noida with Honda, and Bangalore with Toyota.

Figure 6.8: Indian Exports of Electrical Machinery

INDIA EXPORTS OF ELECTRICAL MACHINERY ETC

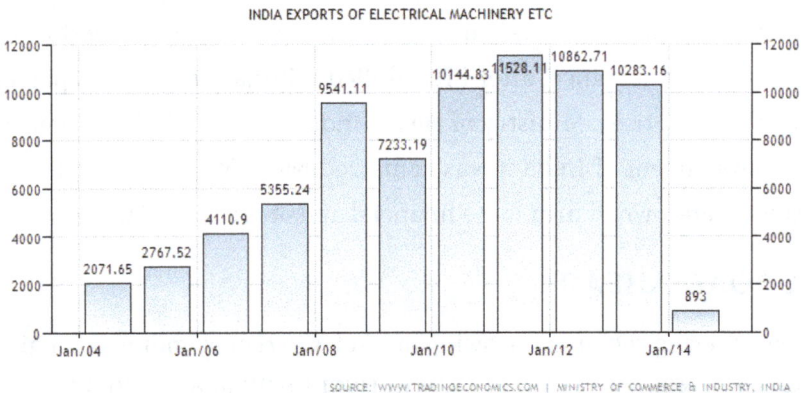

Source: Ministry of Commerce and Industry, India (2014)

Figure 6.8 shows the exports of electrical machinery in the span of a decade (2004–2014) with information provided by India's Ministry of Commerce and Industry.

GOVERNMENT INITIATIVES

The Indian engineering sector is of strategic importance to the economy, owing to its intense integration with other industry segments. The sector has been delicensed and enjoys 100 percent FDI. With the aim to boost the manufacturing sector, the government has relaxed the excise duties on factory gate tax, capital goods, consumer durables, and vehicles. It has also reduced the basic customs duty from 10 percent to 5 percent on forged steel rings used in the manufacture of bearings for wind-operated electricity generators.

The government of India in its Union Budget, 2014–2015, provided investment allowance at the rate of 15 percent to a manufacturing company that invests more than US$4.17 million in any year in a new plant and machinery. The government has also taken steps to improve the quality of technical education in the engineering sector by allocating a sum of Rs 500 crore (US$81.69 million) for setting up five more Indian Institutes of

Technology in the states of Jammu, Chhattisgarh, Goa, Andhra Pradesh, and Kerala.

Steps have also been taken to encourage companies to perform and grow better. For instance, after EIL fulfilled criteria set by the Department of Public Enterprises, Ministry of Heavy Industries, and Public Enterprises of the government of India it was conferred Navaratna status. This status gives the state-owned firm more financial and operational autonomy.

THE ROAD AHEAD

The engineering sector is a growing market. Current spending on engineering services is projected to increase to US$1.1 trillion by 2020. With development in associated sectors, such as automotive, industrial goods, and infrastructure, coupled with a well-developed technical human resources pool, engineering exports touched US$120 billion in 2015.

The Union Budget for 2014–2015 allocated funds for several infrastructure projects that are expected to provide a further boost to the engineering sector. The industry can also look forward to deriving revenues from newer services and from newer geographies with Big Data, Cloud, machine-to-machine, and Internet of Things becoming a reality.

THE AUTO INDUSTRY

OVERVIEW

The automobile industry is one of India's most vibrant and growing industries. This industry accounts for 22 percent of the country's manufacturing GDP. The auto sector is one of the biggest job creators, both directly and indirectly. It is estimated that every job created in an auto company leads to three to five indirect ancillary jobs. India's domestic market and its growth potential have been a big attraction for many global automakers. India is presently the world's third-largest exporter of two-wheelers after China and Japan. According to a report by Standard Chartered Bank, India is likely to overtake Thailand in global auto-export market share by the year 2020. The next few years are projected to show solid but cautious growth due to improved affordability, rising incomes, and untapped markets. With the government's backing and international trends, such as the decline in price of natural rubber, the Indian automobile industry is slated to witness some major growth.

Figure 6.9: Passenger Vehicle Production in India

Passenger vehicle production in India
Passenger vehicles was the fastest growing segment, representing a CAGR of 12.9 per cent.

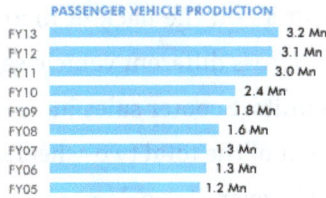

PASSENGER VEHICLE PRODUCTION

Year	Value
FY13	3.2 Mn
FY12	3.1 Mn
FY11	3.0 Mn
FY10	2.4 Mn
FY09	1.8 Mn
FY08	1.6 Mn
FY07	1.3 Mn
FY06	1.3 Mn
FY05	1.2 Mn

Source: IBEF (2014)

Figure 6.10: Passenger Vehicle Exports from India

Passenger vehicle exports from India
Passenger vehicle exports from India stood at 0.5 million during FY13.

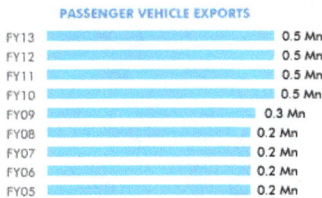

PASSENGER VEHICLE EXPORTS

Year	Value
FY13	0.5 Mn
FY12	0.5 Mn
FY11	0.5 Mn
FY10	0.5 Mn
FY09	0.3 Mn
FY08	0.2 Mn
FY07	0.2 Mn
FY06	0.2 Mn
FY05	0.2 Mn

Source: IBEF (2014)

MARKET SIZE

The cumulative FDI inflows into the Indian automobile industry during the period April 2000–August 2014 was recorded at US$ 10,119.68 million, according to data from the Department of Industrial Policy and Promotion. Data from the industry body Society of Indian Automobile Manufacturers (SIAM) showed that 137,873 passenger cars were sold in July 2014, compared to 131,257 units during the corresponding month of 2013. Among the automakers, Maruti Suzuki, Hyundai Motor India, and Honda Cars India emerged the top three gainers, with sales growth of 15.45 percent, 12 percent, and 11 percent, respectively. The three-wheeler segment posted 24 percent growth to 51,461 units on the back of increased demand from the urban market. Total sales across different vehicle segments grew 12 percent year on year to 1,586,123 units. Scooter sales jumped by 29 percent in 2014 and now make up 27 percent of the total two-wheeler market, up from just 8 percent a decade earlier. The ever-rising demand for scooters, which has far outstripped supply, has prompted Honda to set up its first dedicated scooter plant in Ahmedabad. Tractor sales in the country are expected to grow at a CAGR of 8 to 9 percent in the next five years, making India a high-potential market for many international brands.

Figure 6.11: Market Share of Indian Automobile Industry by Volume

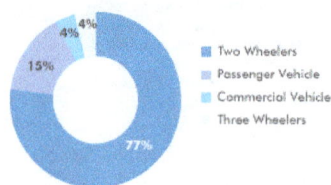

Market share of Indian automobile industry by volume
Two wheelers dominate production volumes; in FY13, the segment accounted for 77 per cent of the total automotive production in India.

- Two Wheelers
- Passenger Vehicle
- Commercial Vehicle
- Three Wheelers

Source: IBEF (2014)

INVESTMENTS

To match production with demand, many automakers started to invest heavily in various segments of the industry in the last few years. Some of the major investments and developments in India's automobile sector are as follows:

- ◆ Ashok Leyland invested Rs 450–500 crore (US$73.54–81.71 million) in India, by way of capital expenditure and investment during FY 2015. The company was required to manage Rs 6,000 crore (US$ 980.56 million) of assets in seven locations across the world, which required maintenance capital expenditure.

- ◆ Honda Motors set up the world's largest scooter plant in Gujarat and has rolled out 1.2 million units annually to achieve a leadership position in the Indian two-wheeler market. The company spent around Rs 1,100 crore (US$179.76 million) on the new plant in Ahmedabad and expanded its range with a few more offerings.

- ◆ Yamaha Motor Company restructured its business in India. Now, Yamaha Motor India takes care of its India operations. "The restructuring is part of Yamaha's mid-term plan aimed at improving organizational efficiency," said Mr. Hiroyuki Suzuki, chief executive and managing director. YMI is responsible for corporate planning and strategy, business planning and business expansion, quality control, and regional control of Yamaha's India business.

- ◆ Tata Motors put in place the hub-and-spoke model, for which India became the key manufacturing base with mini hubs in overseas markets, like Africa, the Middle East, and Southeast Asia.

GOVERNMENT INITIATIVES

The government of India encourages foreign investment in the automobile sector and allows 100 percent FDI under the automatic route. To boost manufacturing, the government lowered excise duty on small cars, motorcycles, scooters, and commercial vehicles from 12 percent to 8 percent, on sports utility vehicles from 30 percent to 24 percent, on mid-segment cars from 24 percent to 20 percent, and on large-segment cars from 27 percent to 24 percent. The government's decision to resolve value-added tax disputes has also resulted in the top Indian automakers, namely, Volkswagen, Bajaj Auto, Mahindra & Mahindra, and Tata Motors, announcing an investment of around Rs 11,500 crore (US$1.87 billion) in Maharashtra. The Automobile Mission Plan designed by the government for the period 2006–2016 is aimed at accelerating and sustaining growth in this sector. Also, the well-established regulatory framework under the Ministry of Shipping, Road Transport, and Highways plays a part in providing a boost to this sector. SIAM and the Automotive Components Manufacturers Association were appointed by the government of India to be responsible for developing the Indian automobile industry.

Figure 6.12: FDI in Indian Automobile Industry

FDI in Indian automobile industry
FDI inflows in the Indian automotives sector aggregated to US$ 9.6 billion during April 2000-February 2014.

FDI TRENDS

FY14*	$1.3 Bn
FY13	$1.5 Bn
FY12	$0.9 Bn
FY11	$1.3 Bn
FY10	$1.2 Bn
FY09	$1.2 Bn

FY14* - April to February

Source: IBEF (2014)

THE ROAD AHEAD

The future of the auto industry depends on the positive sentiments of consumers and the demand for vehicles in the market. The festival seasons at the start of spring in April and during Diwali, between October and November, is a popular time to buy luxury items as a way of celebrating. The Indian auto sector tends to see a rise in demand during this period, which brings major growth. An auto dealer survey by the firm UBS suggested that the Indian auto industry, riding on trends like the festival season and declines in fuel prices, experienced 12 percent growth in 2015. Also, keeping up with international trends, a surge is expected in the number of hybrid vehicles in the Indian auto sector in the years to come due to a rise in fuel prices and concerns about pollution.

CHEMICAL INDUSTRY

OVERVIEW

India's specialty chemicals industry has consistently grown in recent years and the industry is valued at $25 billion dollars in 2017. As a main supplier for India's domestic industries and agricultural development, the chemical industry is widely regarded as an engine of growth for the country. Figure 6.13 below shows the structure of the Indian chemical industry.

Figure 6.13: Structure of the Indian Chemical Market

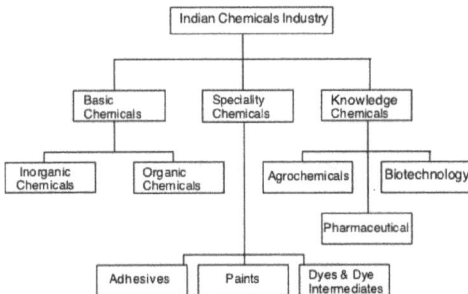

Source: Business Monitor International (2009)

The specialty chemicals segment grew at 11 to 13 percent per year over the period of the government's eleventh Five-Year Plan (FY 2007 to FY 2011). Since India's independence, the government has created plan for the economy every five years. The country's specialty chemical industry (excluding agrochemicals and dyes and pigments) is currently valued at US$17.7 billion. Industry insiders believe this segment has the potential to reach US$38 billion by the end of 2017, with estimated growth rates of 13–14 percent per year.

Figure 6.14: Volume of the Indian Chemical Industries (FY 2011)

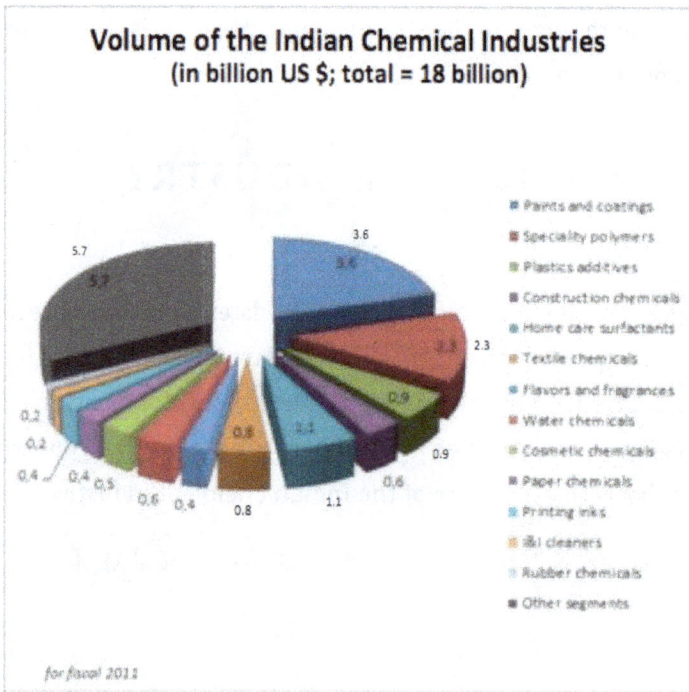

Source: Stephan (2012)

The scale of chemical manufacturing tends to decline from largest to smallest, with Petrochemicals and commodity chemicals being the largest segment, then specialty chemicals, and the smallest, fine chemicals. The commodity and petrochemical-manufacturing units are, on the whole, single-product continuous processing plants. Specialty chemical and fine chemical manufacturing is mostly done in discrete batch processes.

Chemicals made on the largest scale are manufactured in very few locations around the world, for example in Louisiana, USA, Teesside in the Northeast of England, and Rotterdam in the Netherlands. Not all of the petrochemical or commodity chemical materials are made in a single location; instead groups of related materials are produced in one facility for industrial symbiosis as well as material, energy, and utility efficiency, and other economies of scale. Specialty and fine chemical companies are often found in similar locations, but in many cases they are to be found in multisector business parks.

Figure 6.15: Map of Chemical Industries in India

Source: Maps of India (2014)

EXPORTS

Exports of miscellaneous chemical products are reported by the Ministry of Commerce and Industry. Exports decreased to US$733.51 million in 2014 from US$3088.55 million in 2013. Exports of miscellaneous chemical products averaged US$1197.68 million from 1996 to 2014, reaching an all-time high of US$3088.55 million in 2013 and a record low of US$261.31 million in 1996.

Figure 6.16: Indian Exports of Miscellaneous Chemical Products

INDIA EXPORTS OF MISCELLANEOUS CHEMICAL PRODUCTS

Source: Ministry of Commerce and Industry (2014)

The combined exports of the chemical and petrochemical sector registered a CAGR of 13.8 percent during FY 2007 to FY 2012, whereas the collective imports registered a superior CAGR of 18.2 percent during the same period. In FY 2012 imports grew by 4.1 percent, whereas exports declined by 9.2 percent. Growth of combined export and import of chemicals and petrochemicals was in line with the import and export of chemicals. Import of chemicals in FY 2012 grew 12.3 percent whereas export declined 14.3 percent. Petrochemicals followed a reverse trend wherein their imports declined 12.7 percent and exports grew 1.5 percent year on year in FY 2012. Figure 6.17 shows the international trade scenario of the chemical and petrochemical sector:

Figure 6.17: Exports and Imports in the Chemical and Petroleum Sectors

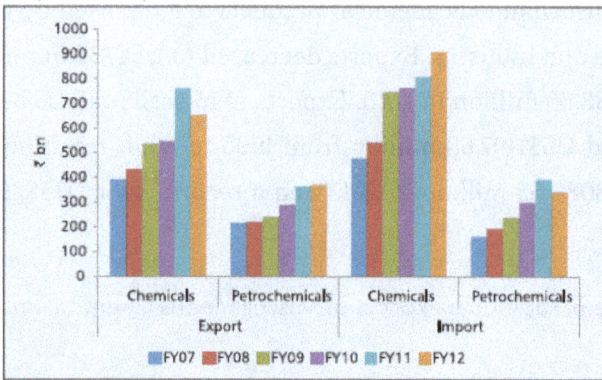

Source: Department of Chemicals and Petrochemicals, D&B India (2014)

The Indian chemical industry is widespread across the country; however it is most concentrated along the west coast, primarily due to proximity and availability of raw materials, fuel, and ports. Figures 6.18 and 6.19 below show the share of production of major chemicals and petrochemicals by state.

Figure 6.18: Share in the Production of Major Chemicals by State, FY 2007 (percent)

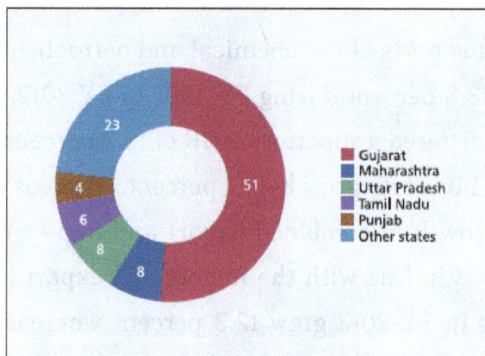

Source: Department of Chemicals and Petrochemicals, D&B India (2014)

Figure 6.19: Share in Production of Petrochemicals
by State, FY 2007 (percent)

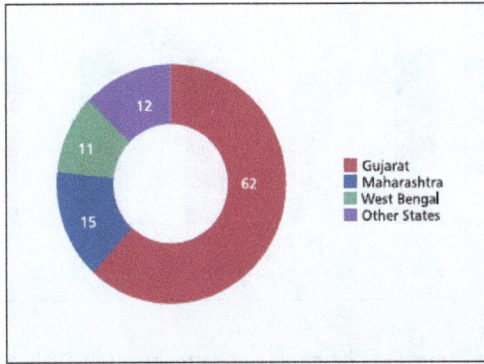

Source: Department of Chemicals and Petrochemicals, D&B India (2014)

Gujarat alone dominates the major chemical and petrochemical production, with about 52 percent and 62 percent shares of all India production, respectively. Maharashtra is the second-leading state in terms of production of both major chemicals and petrochemicals, which contributes 7.5 percent and 15 percent, respectively, to India's total production. The other major chemical and petrochemical producing states include Uttar Pradesh, Tamil Nadu, Punjab, and West Bengal.

PRODUCTION TREND: CHEMICALS AND PETROCHEMICALS

The chemical industry is among the most diversified industrial sectors and produces more than 70,000 commercial products. The chart below highlights the major segments of chemicals produced in the organized sector from FY 2007 to FY 2011:

Figure 6.20: Segments of Major Chemicals Produced in the Organized Sector

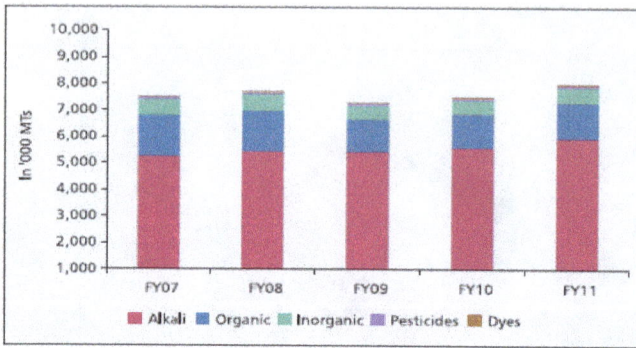

Source: Department of Chemicals and Petrochemicals, D&B India (2014)

KEY TRENDS AND DEVELOPMENTS

Players in the Indian chemical industry have been focusing on sustainable development. Some of the issues the industry is grappling with are water usage, environmental impact, raw materials, safety over lifecycle, and energy use. Indian chemical companies are largely investing in innovative solutions to find the answers to these challenges. Some successful examples from the industry are as follows:

◆ Kanoria Chemicals & Industries, Ltd. (KCI), launched a "waste to wealth" program at its Ankleshwar plant with the objective of recovery of recyclable water from distillery effluents. KCI went for reverse osmosis technology to achieve maximum recycle and minimum possible disposal.

◆ The Arulpuram common effluent treatment plant in Tirupur adopted technology to recycle more than 98 percent of the water and reuse of more than 90 percent of the salt needed for production by implementing a pretreatment system followed by water recovery system using reverse osmosis.

♦ Bristol-Myers Squibb integrated pervaporation technology with its constant volume distillation operation. Pervaporation is a process for separating liquids using partial vaporization. With the integrated approach Bristol-Myers achieved a 56 percent reduction in tetrahydrofuran (100 percent reduction in entrainer) and a 93 percent reduction in wastes generated.

Apart from investing in innovative solutions, companies have also made major investments in the upcoming petroleum chemicals and petrochemical investment region (PCPIRs). OPaL has committed an investment of US$3.2 billion for 1.1 million metric tons per annum multifeed petrochemical cracker and US$560 million for C2/C3 extraction unit at Dahej PCPIR. Other chemical units who have invested in PCPIR are Reliance Petrochemicals Complex, Gujarat Alkalies and Chemicals, Ltd., BASF, Birla Copper, Gujarat Chemical Port Terminal Company, Ltd., Petronet LNG, and Welspun. As of January 2013, a total of US$21 billion has been committed for investment.

The chemical industry is also offering new products according to the changing requirements of the market. The industry has developed microbial decolorization and degradation procedures for textiles and has begun exploring biodiversity for natural dyes and developing eco-friendly methodology for synthetic dyes. Hindustan Petroleum Corporation, Ltd., a public-sector refiner, intends to bring to market green lubricants developed from renewable feedstock. DuPont, as part of its research and development (R&D) strategy, has set up a knowledge center in India focusing on areas like green technologies for refinery processes. Tata Chemicals has established an Innovation center to focus on green technologies in emerging areas such as nanotechnology, fermentation, and biofuels.

According to reports, the chemical industry foresees the following trends:

- Western companies will look to expand their presence in Asia as Asian markets emerge as a major consumption hub.

- Commodity chemical companies will look for entry into specialty chemicals for growth and profitability. M&A would be the preferred route for cash-rich global companies to expand in specialty chemicals in Asia.

- After the EU, registration, evaluation, authorization, and restriction of chemicals regulations are expected to come up in other nations, such as China and the USA. This will increase the cost of production and may make certain companies uncompetitive.

- With the availability of shale gas as cheaper feedstock, the US could become a major processing hub. To remain competitive, Asian producers will have to look toward innovation, such as alternative sources of feedstock and the right product mix.

- The petrochemicals industry will face reduced margins due to oversupply in the global petrochemicals market. Between 2012 and 2016 ethylene capacity is expected to grow by 25 million tons. Major capacity buildup is happening in the USA, the Middle East, and China. Global capacity utilization levels were observed to be at all-time lows of 80 percent in 2011. This may continue until the global demand picks up.

- With the increasing availability of natural gas and new gas finds, the dependency on naphtha as major feedstock for petrochemicals complexes will go down. In the Middle East, substantial capacity additions will be based on ethane as a feedstock.

FUTURE PROSPECTS AND INVESTMENT OPPORTUNITIES

The Indian chemical industry is expected to register a growth of 8–9 percent in the next decade and is expected to double its share in global chemical industry to 5–6 percent by 2021. The Indian chemical industry has the potential to grow significantly, provided some of the key growth imperatives are addressed. Securing feedstock, the right product mix, and M&A opportunities are currently the key imperatives for the chemical industry in India. The following are some highlighted investment opportunities:

♦ Chemical companies in India can either explore alternate feedstock or invest in setting up plants in other resource rich nations to secure feedstock.

♦ Companies need to invest in exploring the right product mix to be competitive and profitable using the available feedstock in India (i.e., Naphtha and its derivatives).

♦ Indian companies can explore possible mergers, JV opportunities for technology, capital, or access to the international market by taking advantage of the increasing expansion of western companies in India.

♦ Chemical companies can invest in exploring strategic energy management and strategic water management to cut down their energy costs and contain water availability concerns.

♦ Companies can invest in upcoming PCPIRs in India and overcome challenges related to infrastructure, power, and water availability.

♦ There are good opportunities in segments such as specialty chemicals and specialty polymers as manufacturing hubs to cater to huge emerging domestic demand.

BIOTECHNOLOGY

OVERVIEW

Biotechnology is one of the most significant sectors for enhancing India's global profile and contributing to the growth of the economy. This sector is directly and indirectly related to the health and agricultural sectors of India. India is among the top twelve centers for biotechnology in the world and is the largest producer of the recombinant hepatitis B vaccine. Of the top ten biotech companies in India (based on revenue), six focus their expertise in biopharmaceuticals, and four specialize in agri-biotech— using scientific techniques to develop agriculture. India recently overtook Canada to emerge as the fourth-largest producer to biotech or genetically modified crops, as farmers in the country planted about 11 million hectares of Bt cotton. The global acreages of genetically modified crops increased to 175.2 million hectares in 2013, about 5 million more hectares than in the previous year.

India has no dearth of talent in this sector, as a number of institutions, both government and autonomous, provide the necessary opportunities for students seeking to obtain a degree in this sector. The government of India has also provided adequate scope to this sector by providing facilities for R&D in the field of biotechnology.

Figure 6.21: Market Break-Up of Indian Biotechnology Industry

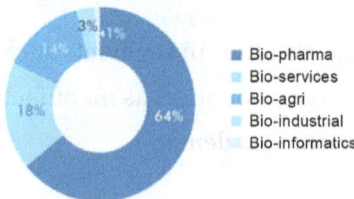

Market break-up of Indian biotechnology industry
The bio-pharmaceutical segment accounted for the largest share of the biotech industry, with 64 per cent of total revenues in FY13.

- Bio-pharma
- Bio-services
- Bio-agri
- Bio-industrial
- Bio-informatics

Source: IBEF (2014)

MARKET SIZE

India holds about a 2 percent share of the global biotech industry. With the growth in the customer base and more investments taking place in the biotech sector, the biotech industry is expected to grow to around US$73.73 billion by the year 2020. The high demand for different biotech products has also opened up scope for the foreign companies to set up bases in India and reap great profits.

Comprising about four hundred companies, the Indian biotech industry has grown threefold in the five years from 2008 to 2013 to reach US$4 billion in FY 2013. Growing at an average rate of about 20 percent per year, India's biotech industry comprising bio pharmaceuticals, bio services, bio agriculture, bio industry, and bioinformatics reached US$7 billion by 2015 and in 2017 it crossed the US$15 billion mark.

Biopharma is the largest sector, contributing about 62 percent of the total revenue, followed by bio services (18 percent), bio agriculture (15 percent), bio industry (4 percent), and bioinformatics (1 percent).

India has emerged as a leading destination for clinical trials, contract research, and manufacturing activities owing to the growth in the bio services sector, which accounts for revenue generation worth about US$636.73 million.

Figure 6.22: Market Size of Indian Biotechnology Sector

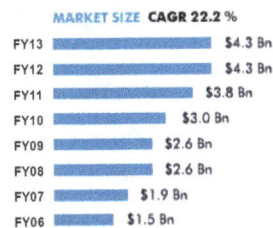

Market size of Indian biotechnology sector
The total industry size was US$ 4.3 billion at the end of FY13.

MARKET SIZE CAGR 22.2 %

FY13 $4.3 Bn
FY12 $4.3 Bn
FY11 $3.8 Bn
FY10 $3.0 Bn
FY09 $2.6 Bn
FY08 $2.6 Bn
FY07 $1.9 Bn
FY06 $1.5 Bn

Source: IBEF (2014)

Figure 6.23: Market Size of Bioinformatics in India

Market size of bioinformatics in India
Bioinformatics in India is estimated to grow at a CAGR of 35 per
cent to reach US$ 2.7 billion during FY12-25.

MARKET SIZE **CAGR 35.0%**

FY25E $2,700 Bn
FY15E $140 Bn
FY12 $55 Bn

E - Estimates

Source: IBEF (2014)

INVESTMENTS

India's biotech sector has attracted a significant amount of attention over the past two decades. Several global companies have aggressively joined hands with Indian companies due to India's strong biotechnology potential. Some of the recent investments in this sector are as follows:

♦ Bristol-Myers Squibb and Syngene International, the contract research subsidiary of Biocon, announced a five-year extension of their drug discovery and development collaboration with India.

♦ The representatives of five IT companies from Kerala attended the first Innovation Conference of Israel (MIXiii), an international event that focuses on biomedical sciences and high technology. The event was aimed at bringing together the world's biomed and hi-tech companies to create networking opportunities.

♦ The Bhabha Atomic Research Centre through its Center for Incubation of Technologies signed a memorandum of understanding with M/s Veena Industries, Nagpur, to incubate technology for biodegradable and edible films for food and pharmaceutical packaging.

♦ Cancer Genetics, Inc. (CGI), acquired Hyderabad-based genomics services provider BioServe India for US$1.9 million. This will enable CGI to better position itself globally in personalized cancer care.

♦ The Shanghai Jiading Advanced Technology Innovation and Business Incubator invited Indian technology innovators and small and medium enterprises, especially in renewable energy, biomedical devices, and advanced manufacturing to set up their businesses in Jiading.

♦ Suven Life Sciences, Ltd., obtained two patents, one each from Hong Kong and Canada, for its new chemical entities for the treatment of disorders associated with neurodegenerative diseases.

GOVERNMENT INITIATIVES

The government of India has taken a number of initiatives to improve the biotechnology sector in the country and to offer enough scope for research in this field. The Department of Biotechnology (DBT), along with other government-funded institutions, such as the National Biotechnology Board, and many autonomous bodies representing the biotechnology sector are actively working together to make India a global hub for biotech research and business excellence. Some recent initiatives are as follows:

♦ CSIR Institute of Himalayan Bioresource Technology signed a memorandum of understanding with Phyto Biotech to formalize the transfer of technology for production of unique autoclavable super oxide dismutase enzyme, used in cosmetics, food, and pharmaceutical industries for end applications.

♦ DBT announced the Indo-Australian Career Boosting Gold Fellowships, supporting researchers to undertake a collaborative research project at a leading science institute or university in Australia for a period of up to twenty-four months.

♦ DBT allocated Rs 4.6 crore (US$757,721.9) to the University of Agricultural Sciences to support a national multi-institutional project called A Value Chain on Jackfruit and Its Products. Jackfruit grows plentifully in India. The fruit contains bioactive compounds that may support the prevention of certain diseases.

♦ Under the twelfth Five-Year Plan, the government of India plans to strengthen regulatory science and infrastructure, which includes setting up the Biotechnology Regulatory Authority of India and a central agency for regulatory testing and certification laboratories.

Figure 6.24: Funds Allocated for Biotechnology under Twelfth Five-Year Plan

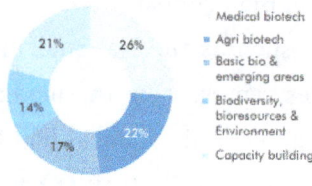

Funds allocated for biotechnology under 12th Five Year Plan
The 12th Five-Year Plan aims to accelerate the pace of research, innovation and development to improve biotechnology in India.

- Medical biotech
- Agri biotech
- Basic bio & emerging areas
- Biodiversity, bioresources & Environment
- Capacity building

Source: IBEF (2014)

THE ROAD AHEAD

The growth in GDP over the next decade will expand the domestic market, Indians will be able to afford healthcare products, and demand for food commodities and energy will grow too. Presently, many countries are looking forward to invest in the Indian biotechnology sector. If there is an annual investment of US$4.019 billion to US$5.024 billion in the next five years, the biotech industry can grow to US$100 billion by 2025, with a 25 percent return on investment, and set a growth rate of 30 percent year on year.

With the support of investments, government initiatives, and the determination to excel, India can soon attain global leadership in providing affordable healthcare, innovative medicines, and increased agricultural production.

PHARMACEUTICALS

OVERVIEW

Globally, the Indian pharmaceutical industry is ranked third-largest in volume and tenth-largest in value. The sector is highly knowledge-based and its steady growth is positively affecting the Indian economy. The organized nature of the Indian pharmaceutical industry is attracting several companies that are finding it viable to increase their operations in the country. The Indian pharmaceutical industry is highly fragmented, with about 24,000 players (330 in the organized sector). The top ten companies make up more than a third of the market.

A large chunk of Indian pharma revenues come from exports. While some are focusing on the generics market in the US, Europe, and semi regulated markets, others are turning their attention to custom manufacturing for innovator companies. Biopharmaceuticals are also becoming an area of increased interest, given the complexity of manufacturing and limited competition.

Figure 6.25: Revenue of Indian Pharmaceutical Industry

Revenue of Indian pharmaceutical industry
The Indian pharmaceuticals market is expected to expand at a CAGR of 23.9 per cent to reach US$ 55 billion by 2020.

REVENUE OF INDIAN PHARMACEUTICAL SECTOR

- 2020F — $55 Bn
- 2013 — $12 Bn
- 2005 — $6 Bn

Source: IBEF (2014)

Figure 6.26: Revenue Share of Indian Pharmaceutical Sub segments

Revenue share of Indian pharmaceutical sub-segments
With 72 per cent of market share (in terms of revenues), generic drugs form the largest segment of the Indian pharmaceutical sector.

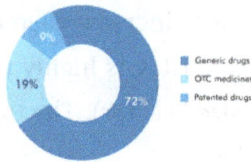

- Generic drugs — 72%
- OTC medicines — 19%
- Patented drugs — 9%

Source: IBEF (2014)

MARKET SIZE

India's pharmaceuticals industry is expected to grow at a CAGR of 14 percent to reach a turnover of Rs 2.91 trillion (US$47.06 billion) by 2018. The domestic drug industry, which is valued at Rs 1.6 trillion (US$ 25.87 billion) at present, according to CARE ratings, is also expected to grow in the local market with aggressive rural penetration by drug makers, increased government spending on health, and growing health awareness.

Figure 6.27: Export Data of Indian Pharma Industry

Export data of Indian pharma industry
In terms of value, exports of Indian pharmaceutical products increased at a CAGR of 26.1 per cent to touch US$ 10.1 billion during FY06-13.

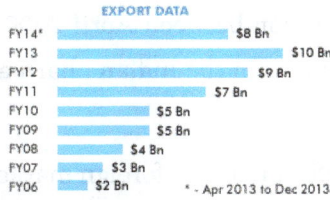

EXPORT DATA

FY14*	$8 Bn
FY13	$10 Bn
FY12	$9 Bn
FY11	$7 Bn
FY10	$5 Bn
FY09	$5 Bn
FY08	$4 Bn
FY07	$3 Bn
FY06	$2 Bn

* - Apr 2013 to Dec 2013

Source: IBEF (2014)

India exports pharmaceutical products to more than two hundred countries. Pharmaceutical exports are expected to reach US$20 billion by 2020. "The growth would be around 15 percent and is driven by formulation exports," said Dr. P. V. Appaji, director-general of the Pharmaceutical Export Promotion Council. During 2013–2014, pharma exports stood at Rs 90,000 crore (US$14.55 billion). Out of this total, the share of formulations was 71 percent.

India currently exports drug intermediates, active pharmaceutical ingredients, Finished Dosage Formulations, biopharmaceuticals, and clinical services across the globe.

Figure 6.28: Indian Pharmaceutical Market Segments by Value

Indian pharmaceutical market segments by value
Anti-infective drugs command the largest share (16 per cent) in the Indian pharma market.

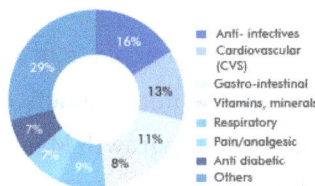

- Anti- infectives 16%
- Cardiovascular (CVS) 13%
- Gastro-intestinal 11%
- Vitamins, minerals 8%
- Respiratory 9%
- Pain/analgesic 7%
- Anti diabetic 7%
- Others 29%

Source: IBEF (2014)

INVESTMENTS

The allowance for FDI in India's pharma sector has been well received by foreign investors. According to data released by the Department of Industrial Policy and Promotion, the drugs and pharmaceutical sector attracted FDI worth US$12,688.71 million between April 2000 and September 2014. Some of the major investments in the Indian pharmaceutical sector are as follows:

♦ Cipla, Ltd., in an effort to reach foreign markets, plans to set up a manufacturing plant in Iran as part of its strategy to boost its presence in the country's US$4 billion pharmaceutical market, which is growing at about 13 percent annually. It has also entered into collaboration with Teva Pharmaceutical Industries, Ltd., for the South African market. "This collaboration is highly complementary and aligns strongly with our philosophy of providing South Africans with access to a broader range of affordable medicines," said Mr. Paul Miller, chief executive officer of Cipla Medpro.

♦ Strides Arcolab plans to acquire Chennai-based Shasun Pharmaceutical in an all-stock transaction that will create a combined entity with a turnover of Rs 2,500 crore (US$404.29 million).

♦ Lupin, Ltd., has signed a strategic partnership with Merck Serono to support the company to expand its generic drug portfolio in emerging markets by developing and supplying finished products.

♦ Lupin has completed the acquisition of Mexico's Laboratories Grin, a leading player in ophthalmic products. The acquisition marks Lupin's foray into the high-growth Mexican and larger Latin American pharmaceutical market. Lupin has also entered into a long-term partnership with Merck Serono, the biopharmaceutical division of Merck, for the emerging markets.

♦ The UN-backed Medicines Patents Pool has signed six sublicenses with Aurobindo, Cipla, Desano, Emcure, Hetero Labs, and Laurus Labs, allowing them to make the generic anti-AIDS medicine tenofovir alafenamide for 112 developing countries.

GOVERNMENT INITIATIVES

The government of India has unveiled Pharma Vision 2020, aimed at making India a global leader in end-to-end drug manufacture. It has reduced approval time for new facilities to boost investments. Further, the government has also put in place mechanisms such as the Drug Price Control Order and the National Pharmaceutical Pricing Authority to address the issue of affordability and availability of medicines. Some of the major initiatives taken by the government to promote the pharmaceutical sector in India are as follows:

♦ The Andhra Pradesh government will provide necessary infrastructure, incentives, and skill-upgrading facilities for the pharma industry. The captains of the industry should come forward to invest on a large scale in the state, according to Chief Minister N. Chandrababu Naidu.

♦ The government of India and the pharmaceutical industry will jointly float a trust to promote the brand image of Indian pharma globally and fight malicious campaigns.

♦ India plans to set up industrial parks in the pharmaceutical and IT sectors in China to strengthen India-China trade and investment ties.

♦ The Union Cabinet of India has cleared a foreign investment proposal worth US$400 million by Kohlberg Kravis Roberts to acquire stakes in two pharmaceutical companies, Gland Pharma and Gland Celsus Bio Chemicals.

WHAT'S AHEAD?

Indian generic drug makers are exploring all options to get a foot in the door of Japan's lucrative but difficult-to-crack US$111 billion drug industry. The penetration of generic drugs in Japan, the world's largest drug market after the US and Europe, is a little more than 30 percent.

According to CARE analysis, in the next three years the domestic market will see a significant growth in sales on the back of increasing affluence and changing lifestyles, resulting in a higher incidence of lifestyle-related diseases, as well as increasing government expenditure on healthcare through schemes like the Central Government Health Scheme, National Program for the Healthcare of the Elderly, Rashtriya Arogya Nidhi, and Janani Suraksha Yojana.

The market is expected to grow, driven by the rise of pharmaceutical outsourcing and investment by MNCs, allied with the country's growing economy, committed health insurance segment, and improved healthcare facilities. The area of pharmaceuticals is one where Indian development shows great promise.

OIL AND GAS

OVERVIEW

In 1997–1998, the New Exploration Licensing Policy was envisioned to deal with the ever-growing gap between supply and demand for gas in India. According to a recent report, the oil and gas industry is expected to be worth US$150,000 million by 2020. With India's economic growth closely linked to energy demand, the need for oil and gas is projected to grow further, rendering the sector a fertile ground for investment.

To cater to the increasing demand, the government of India has adopted several policies, including allowing 100 percent FDI in many segments of the sector, such as natural gas, petroleum products, and refineries, among others. The government's participation has made the oil and gas sector a better target of investment. Today it attracts both domestic and foreign investment, as attested by the presence of Reliance Industries, Ltd. (RIL) and Cairn India.

Figure 6.29: Imports and Domestic Oil Production in India

Imports and domestic oil production in India
Backed by new oil fields, domestic oil output is anticipated to grow to 1 mbpd by FY16.

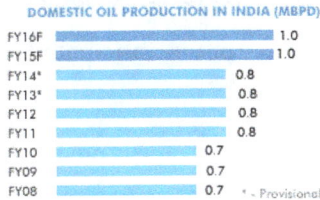

DOMESTIC OIL PRODUCTION IN INDIA (MBPD)

FY	MBPD
FY16F	1.0
FY15F	1.0
FY14*	0.8
FY13*	0.8
FY12	0.8
FY11	0.8
FY10	0.7
FY09	0.7
FY08	0.7

* - Provisional

Source: IBEF (2014)

MARKET SIZE

During FY 2014, the total consumption of petroleum products in India was 158.2 million tons. The share of fuels in the country's exports surged from 5.59 percent in 2003–2004 to 20.05 percent in 2013–2014. Total exports of fuel products amounted to US$62.69 billion in value terms during FY 2014.

India is the fourth-largest consumer of oil and petroleum products in the world. Its energy demand is projected to reach 1,464 million tons of oil equivalent (Mtoe) by 2035, up from 559 Mtoe in 2011. Furthermore, the country's share in global primary energy consumption is anticipated to double by 2035.

Figure 6.30: Oil Consumption in India

Oil consumption in India
Oil consumption in India is estimated to expand at a CAGR of
3.3 per cent during FY2008-16 to reach 4 mbpd.

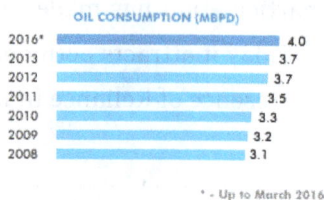

OIL CONSUMPTION (MBPD)

Year	Value
2016*	4.0
2013	3.7
2012	3.7
2011	3.5
2010	3.3
2009	3.2
2008	3.1

* - Up to March 2016

Source: IBEF (2014)

Oil consumption reached 4 million barrels per day (MMbpd) in 2016, expanding at a CAGR of 3.2 percent from FY 2008 to FY 2016. Also, backed by new oil fields, domestic oil output is anticipated to grow to 1 MMbpd by FY 2016.

INVESTMENTS

According to data released by the Department of Industrial Policy and Promotion, the petroleum and natural gas sector attracted FDI worth Rs 31,501.55 crore (US$5.13 billion) between April 2000 and July 2014.

Figure 6.31: Shares in India's Total Refining Capacity

Shares in India's total refining capacity
In FY14, IOC emerged as the largest domestic refiner with a
capacity of 54.2 MMT.

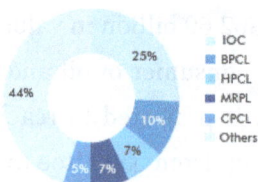

- 44%
- 25%
- 10%
- 7%
- 5%
- 7%

- IOC
- BPCL
- HPCL
- MRPL
- CPCL
- Others

Source: IBEF (2014)

The following are some of the major investments and developments in the oil and gas sector:

- RIL plans to invest US$2 billion in its three shale assets in the US. RIL has already invested US$7.3 billion since 2010 toward development of shale gas and oil in the US market. The company, along with its partner British Petroleum (BP), also plans to invest about Rs 800 crore (US$130.35 million) in exploratory drilling in an offshore block in the Bay of Bengal. RIL is the operator of the offshore block CY-DWN-2001/2, also known as CY-III-D5, with 70 percent equity, with BP holding the remaining stake. BP's contribution to the investment would be Rs 240 crore (US$39.11 million).

- ONGC Videsh, Ltd. (OVL), has signed production sharing contracts for two blocks in Myanmar. The contracts were signed between OVL, Myanmar Oil & Gas Enterprises, Ltd., National Oil Company of Myanmar, and Machine & Solutions Co., Ltd. ONGC will also invest over Rs 5,700 crore (US$928.73 million) to increase production by 6.9 MT of crude oil and 5 billion cubic meters of gas by 2030 from its Mumbai High (North) oil and gas field.

- Steel-to-BPO conglomerate Essar is in talks with Germany's BASF, the biggest chemical company in the world, for a petrochemicals JV, according to sources.

- Larsen & Toubro has won an order worth Kuwaiti Dinar 239.7 million from the Kuwait Oil Company (KOC). L&T Hydrocarbon will carry out the order, which entails engineer-procured construction work for a gathering center of KOC, a subsidiary of Kuwait Petroleum Corporation.

- Indian Oil Corporation, Ltd. (IOCL), through its wholly owned affiliate IndOil Montney, Ltd., Canada, has signed transaction agreements with Progress Energy Canada, Ltd., and PETRONAS Carigali Canada BV for acquiring a 10 percent interest in Progress

Energy Canada's LNG-destined natural gas reserves in northeast British Columbia and the proposed Pacific Northwest LNG, Ltd., export facility on Canada's west coast.

♦ GAIL (India), Ltd., has entered into an agreement with Japan-based Chubu Electric Power Company to collaborate in the area of joint liquefied natural gas (LNG) procurement. Additionally, the two companies will look at working together on shipping optimization.

♦ India and Azerbaijan have proposed to form a joint working group in the field of hydrocarbon. The two countries have agreed to explore opportunities for partnership in the renewable energy sector, energy efficiency, and numerous upcoming projects in petrochemicals, oil and gas, pipelines, etc., in India, Azerbaijan, or other countries, in collaboration or as a joint venture.

Figure 6.32: Shares in Crude Pipeline Network by Length

Shares in crude pipeline network by length
In terms of length, IOCL accounts for 45.5 per cent (4,448 km) of India's crude pipeline network.

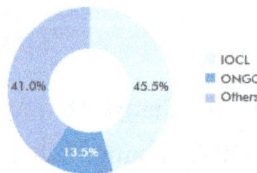

- IOCL
- ONGC
- Others

41.0% 45.5% 13.5%

Source: IBEF (2014)

GOVERNMENT INITIATIVES

Kazuyoshi Akaba, Japan's state minister of Economy, Trade, and Industry, met Dharmendra Pradhan, India's minister of state (independent chargé) for Petroleum and Natural Gas. Mr. Pradhan suggested taking the strong

Indo-Japan bond to a higher level, stating that Japan has inspired India in manufacturing, technology, and philosophy of governance.

The expert appraisal committee of the Indian Ministry of Environment and Forests has given the go-ahead to IOCL's Rs 4,320 crore (US$703.81 million) LNG terminal project at Ennore, near Chennai. The proposed facility's capacity will be 5 MTPA. The terminal is expandable to 10–15 MTPA. This is part of the corporation's Rs 56,000 crore (US$9.12 billion) investment plan for the Twelfth Five-Year Plan (2012–2017).

WHAT'S AHEAD?

By 2015–2016, India's demand for gas touched 124 MTPA against a domestic supply of 33 MTPA and higher imports of 47.2 MTPA, leaving a shortage of 44 MTPA, according to projections by the Petroleum and Natural Gas Ministry of India. Moreover, Business Monitor International (BMI) predicts that India will account for 12.4 percent of Asia-Pacific regional oil demand by 2015, while satisfying 11.2 percent of the supply. This is not to say that the gap cannot be met.

ONGC plans to explore thirty additional shale gas wells in the country at an investment of about Rs 600 crore (US$97.7 million) for the project. The use of shale gas could be the first step toward economic freedom, according M. Veerappa Moily, India's former oil minister. He feels that the country could follow a path similar to the US, which was initially a net importer of energy before becoming a net exporter of energy, driven by shale gas and oil. The oil and gas sector is an example of the success an industry can achieve when the government allows 100 percent FDI. Collaboration with foreign and international companies has allowed India to become a major player in the industry.

STEEL

OVERVIEW

Steel is crucial to the development of any modern economy and is considered to be one of the backbones of human civilization. Per-capita steel consumption is treated as an important index of socioeconomic development in a country. Starting with only three steel plants, a few electric arc furnace-based plants, and a mere one million ton capacity status at the time of independence, India is now the fourth-largest crude steel producer in the world and the largest producer of sponge iron.

Figure 6.33: Value of India's Metals and Mining Industry

Value of India's metals and mining industry
India's metals and mining industry recorded a strong 19.8 per cent expansion in 2011 to touch US$ 141.9 billion.

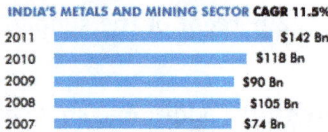

INDIA'S METALS AND MINING SECTOR **CAGR 11.5%**

Year	Value
2011	$142 Bn
2010	$118 Bn
2009	$90 Bn
2008	$105 Bn
2007	$74 Bn

Source: IBEF (2014)

Figure 6.34: Share in India's Metals and Mining Sector

Shares in India's metals and mining sector
Iron and steel is the largest segment of the Indian metals and mining industry, accounting for 73.8 per cent of the overall industry value.

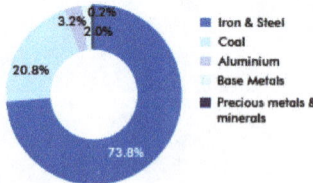

- Iron & Steel — 73.8%
- Coal — 20.8%
- Aluminium — 3.2%
- Base Metals — 2.0%
- Precious metals & minerals — 0.2%

Source: IBEF (2014)

Presently, steel contributes to nearly 2 percent of the GDP and employs over 500,000 people. The total market value of the Indian steel sector stood at US$57.8 billion in 2011, reached US$95.3 billion in 2016, and continues to grow. India's per-capita steel consumption stood at 57.8 kilograms in 2013, according to a World Steel Association report, and is expected to rise with increased industrialization throughout the country.

Figure 6.35: Market Value of the Indian Steel Sector

Market value of the Indian steel sector
In 2011, the Indian steel sector's total market value was US$ 57.8 billion.

STEEL MKT VALUE **CAGR 17.7%** (FY07-11)

2016E	$95.3 Bn
2011	$57.8 Bn
2010	$46.8 Bn
2009	$36.5 Bn
2008	$43 Bn
2007	$30.1 Bn

Source: IBEF (2014)

MARKET SIZE

India is slated to become the second-largest steel producer in the world by 2018. Steel production in the country increased at a compound annual growth rate of 6.9 percent from 2008 to 2012. India's real consumption of total finished steel grew by 0.6 percent year on year from April 2013 to March 2014, to 73.93 MT, according to the Joint Plant Committee, Ministry of Steel.

Increasing demand by sectors such as infrastructure, real estate, and automakers at home and abroad has put India on the world map. The construction sector accounts for around 60 percent of the country's total steel demand, while the automobile industry accounts for 15 percent.

Figure 6.36: Steel Exports from India

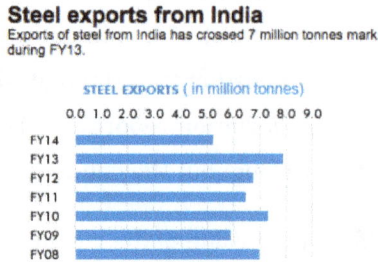

Steel exports from India
Exports of steel from India has crossed 7 million tonnes mark during FY13.

Source: IBEF (2014)

INVESTMENTS

The steel industry and its related metallurgy and mining industries have witnessed quite a few investments and developments in the recent past. Some of the notable investments are as follows:

♦ L&T Special Steels and Heavy Forgings entered into a five-year technology transfer agreement with Japan Steel Works. This agreement covers transfer of critical technology for steel melting and heavy forgings made from ingots weighing up to 200 tons and for the hydrocarbon and thermal power sectors.

♦ Jindal Steel and Power, Ltd., Group commissioned a greenfield 2-MT steel plant in Sohar, Oman, at an investment of US$800 million. The greenfield unit will be one of the largest steel plants in the gulf region.

♦ Steel Authority of India, Ltd. (SAIL), has secured contracts to supply over 117,000 tons of rails after successful bids for two global tenders floated by Rail Vikas Nigam, Ltd., for major upcoming passenger rail line projects in India.

♦ Jindal South West Holding, Ltd., (JSW) Steel plans to commission a Rs 4,500 crore (US$748.55 million) cold rolling mill at its integrated steel plant in Torangal, Karnataka. The unit, which will produce high-strength auto-grade steel, has an installed capacity of 2.3 million tons per annum.

♦ JSW Steel is also set to acquire WelspunMaxsteel for about Rs 1,100 crore (US$182.98 million) in a move aimed at sourcing cheaper raw material, bringing down production costs, and enhancing its presence in the northern and western markets.

♦ Canada has invited Coal India, Ltd., to explore mining opportunities in British Columbia, according to Stewart Beck, Canadian high commissioner in India.

GOVERNMENT INITIATIVES

India's Ministry of Steel is considering setting up a strong R&D mission/center, virtual or otherwise, to step up innovative research and technology development in the country's steel industry.

The center's Steel Development Fund (SDF) and Plan Scheme presently provide financial assistance for R&D in the sector. Under the SDF scheme, 82 R&D projects have been approved, with total project cost of Rs 677 crore (US$112.61 million) wherein SDF assistance is Rs 370 crore (US$61.54 million). Under the Plan Scheme, eight projects have been approved, at a total cost of Rs 123.27 crore (US$20.51 million) wherein government assistance is Rs 87.28 crore (US$14.51 million).

To increase industrial activity, the government of India, through the Ministry of Steel, has signed memoranda of understanding with all the major steel-producing PSU companies such as SAIL and Rashtriya Ispat Nigam, Ltd. These will help to direct the companies to achieve targets and benefit the sector as a whole.

THE ROAD AHEAD

The liberalization of the industrial policy and other initiatives taken by the government has spurred the growth of the private sector in the steel industry. While the existing units are being modernized or expanded, a large number of new steel plants have also come up in different parts of the country, based on cost-effective and state of-the-art technologies. In the last few years, the rapid and stable growth of the demand side has also prompted domestic entrepreneurs to set up fresh greenfield projects in different states of India.

With the increase in the global population, there is a greater need for steel to build public-transport infrastructure. Emerging economies will continue to drive demand, as these countries require a significant amount of steel for urbanization and industrialization purposes. India's steel sector is anticipated to witness investment of about Rs 2 trillion (US$33.26 billion) in the coming years, according to Tata Steel.

7

TRANSPORTATION

OVERVIEW

Transportation is an important part of India's economy. Since the economic liberalization of the 1990s, infrastructure development has progressed rapidly, and today there is a variety of transportation available by land, water, and air. However, India's relatively low GDP per capita means that access to transportation varies throughout the country.

Figure 7.1: Population vs. Public Transport in Twenty Indian Cities (2009)

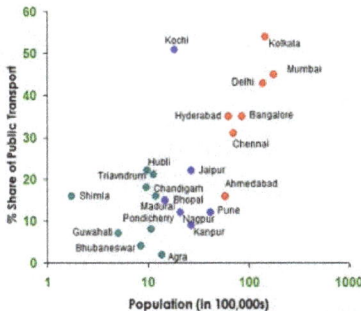

Source: Ministry of Urban Development (2009)

Public transportation, including railways, buses, and rapid mass transit, remains the primary mode of transport for most of the population, and India's public transport systems are among the most heavily used in the world. India's rail network is the fourth-longest and the most heavily used system in the world as of 2012, transporting 8.2 billion passengers and over 969 million tons of freight annually.

Motor vehicle penetration is low by international standards, with only 10.3 million cars on the nation's roads, compared to 253 million cars and trucks in the United States. Motorcycles and scooters are prevalent but not ubiquitous. Only around 10 percent of Indian households own a motorcycle. Regardless, the number of deaths caused by traffic is among the highest in the world and is increasing. The automobile industry in India is rapidly growing, with an annual production of over 4.6 million vehicles, and vehicle volume is expected to rise greatly in the future. Figure 7.2 below shows the percentage of Indian households owning some mode of transportation in 2011.

Figure 7.2: Percentage of Indian Households
Owning a Mode of Transportation (2011)

Percentage of Indian Households Owning a Mode of Transportation

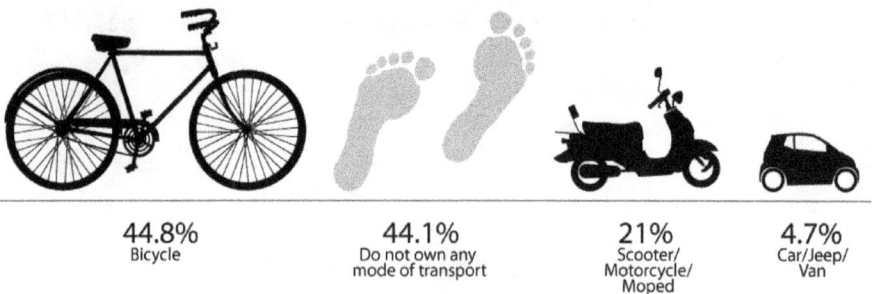

| 44.8%
Bicycle | 44.1%
Do not own any
mode of transport | 21%
Scooter/
Motorcycle/
Moped | 4.7%
Car/Jeep/
Van |

Source: India Charts—Wordpress, Ministry of Home Affairs

PUBLIC TRANSPORT BY ROAD

Public transportation is the predominant mode of motorized local travel in cities. Buses are the main form of public transportation. Commuter rail services are available only in the seven metropolitan cities of Mumbai, Delhi, Chennai, Kolkata, Bangalore, Hyderabad, and Pune, while dedicated city bus services are known to operate in at least twenty-five cities with a population of over one million. Intermediate public transport modes, such as scooters and cycle rickshaws, assume importance in medium-size cities. However, the share of buses is negligible in most Indian cities as compared to personalized vehicles, two-wheelers, and cars, which account for more than 80 percent of vehicles in most large cities.

BUSES

Buses account for over 90 percent of public transportation in Indian cities and they serve as a cheap and convenient mode of transport for all classes of society. Bus services are mostly run by state-government-owned transport corporations. Since the economic liberalization, many state transport corporations have introduced improved facilities like low-floor buses for the disabled and air-conditioned buses to attract private car owners and help decongest roads. Bengaluru was the first city in India to introduce Volvo B7RLE intracity buses in January 2006. It was also the first Indian city to have an air-conditioned bus stop, built by Airtel, and located near Cubbon Park. Tamil Nadu State Transport Corporation has been identified as the single corporation with the largest bus fleet in the world. The city of Chennai houses one of Asia's largest bus terminuses, the Chennai Mofussil Bus Terminus.

Figure 7.3: City Buses per 100,000 People (2009)

City Buses per Lakh Population

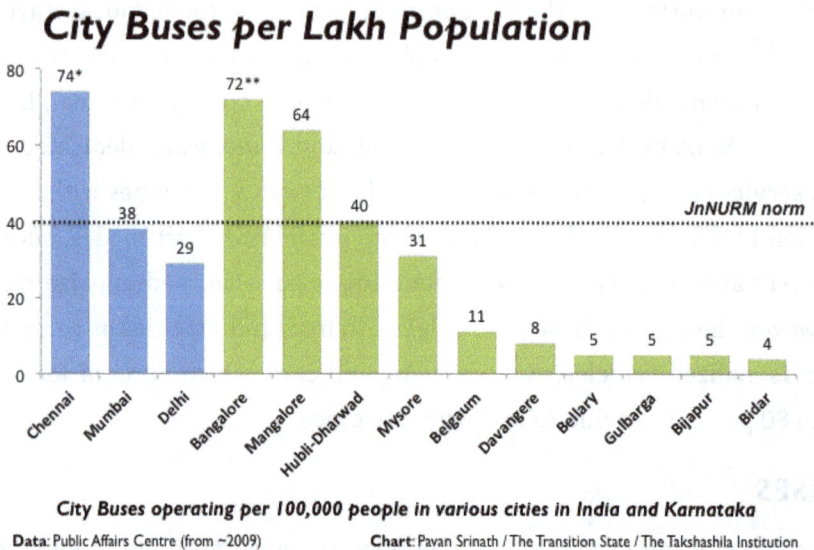

City Buses operating per 100,000 people in various cities in India and Karnataka

Data: Public Affairs Centre (from ~2009)　　**Chart**: Pavan Srinath / The Transition State / The Takshashila Institution

Source: Public Affairs Centre, Srinath (2013)

TAXIS

Most of the traditional taxicabs in India are either Premier Padmini or Hindustan Ambassador cars. Depending on the city and state, taxis can either be hailed from the curb or hired from taxi stands. In cities such as Bangalore, Hyderabad, and Ahmedabad, taxis must be hired over phone, whereas in cities like Kolkata and Mumbai, taxis can be hailed on the street. According to the government of India regulations, all taxis are required to have a fare meter installed. There are additional surcharges to be paid by the passenger for luggage, late-night rides, and toll taxes. Since 2006, radio taxis have become increasingly popular with the public because of safety and convenience. Citizens use share taxis in cities and localities where taxis are expensive or do not comply with government- or municipal-regulated fares. These are taxis that carry multiple passengers with destinations close to one another. The passengers are charged according to the number of people with different destinations. A similar system exists for auto rickshaws, known as share autos. In Kolkata there are many no-refusal taxis available, which are white and blue in color. These are taxis that cannot refuse a passenger for any reason. They continue to work during strikes and holidays.

AUTO RICKSHAW

An auto rickshaw is a three-wheel vehicle for hire that has two side doors and is generally characterized by a small cabin for the driver in the front and a seat for passengers in the rear. Generally, it is painted in yellow, green, or black and has a black, yellow, or green canopy on the top, but designs vary considerably from place to place. The color of the auto rickshaw is also determined by the fuel that powers it; for example Agartala, Ahmedabad, and Delhi have green autos, indicating the use of compressed natural gas, whereas the rickshaws of Mumbai, Kolkata, and Bangalore are green or black, indicating the use of LPG.

In Mumbai and other metropolitan cities, "autos," or "ricks," as they are popularly known, have regulated metered fares. A recent law prohibits auto rickshaw drivers from charging more than the specified fare or charging night fare before midnight. It also prohibits the driver from refusing to go to a particular location, unless auto rickshaws are prohibited in that location. Mumbai and Kolkata are the only two cities that prohibit auto rickshaws from entering sections of the city—South Mumbai and certain parts of Downtown Kolkata. In these areas the auto rickshaws create too much congestion among car and truck traffic. In cities like Chennai, it is common to see auto rickshaw drivers demand more than the specified fare and refuse to use the fare meter.

Airports and railway stations in many cities, such as Howrah, Chennai, and Bengaluru, provide a facility of prepaid auto booths, where the passenger pays a fixed fare as set by the authorities for various locations.

LONG DISTANCE TRANSPORT

SUBURBAN RAILWAY

The suburban railway services in India are limited and are operate only in Mumbai, Kolkata, Pune, Chennai, Delhi, and Hyderabad. The Mumbai Suburban Railway was the first rail system in India, beginning service in 1867. It transports 6.3 million passengers daily and has the highest passenger density in the world. The first rapid transit system in India, the Kolkata Suburban Railway, was established in Kolkata in 1854. Its first service ran between Howrah and Hooghly, covering a distance of 38.6 km (24 miles).

URBAN RAPID MASS TRANSIT

India has one of the largest railway systems in the world, particularly as gauged by the number of passengers. The first modern rapid transit in India was the Kolkata Metro, which started its operations in 1984. The Kolkata Metro is also the 17th Zone, the largest railway network in India. The Delhi Metro in New Delhi began operations in 2002 and the Namma Metro in Bangalore began operations in 2011. More rapid transit systems are under construction or in planning in several major cities of India.

Figure 7.4: Indian Railway Map

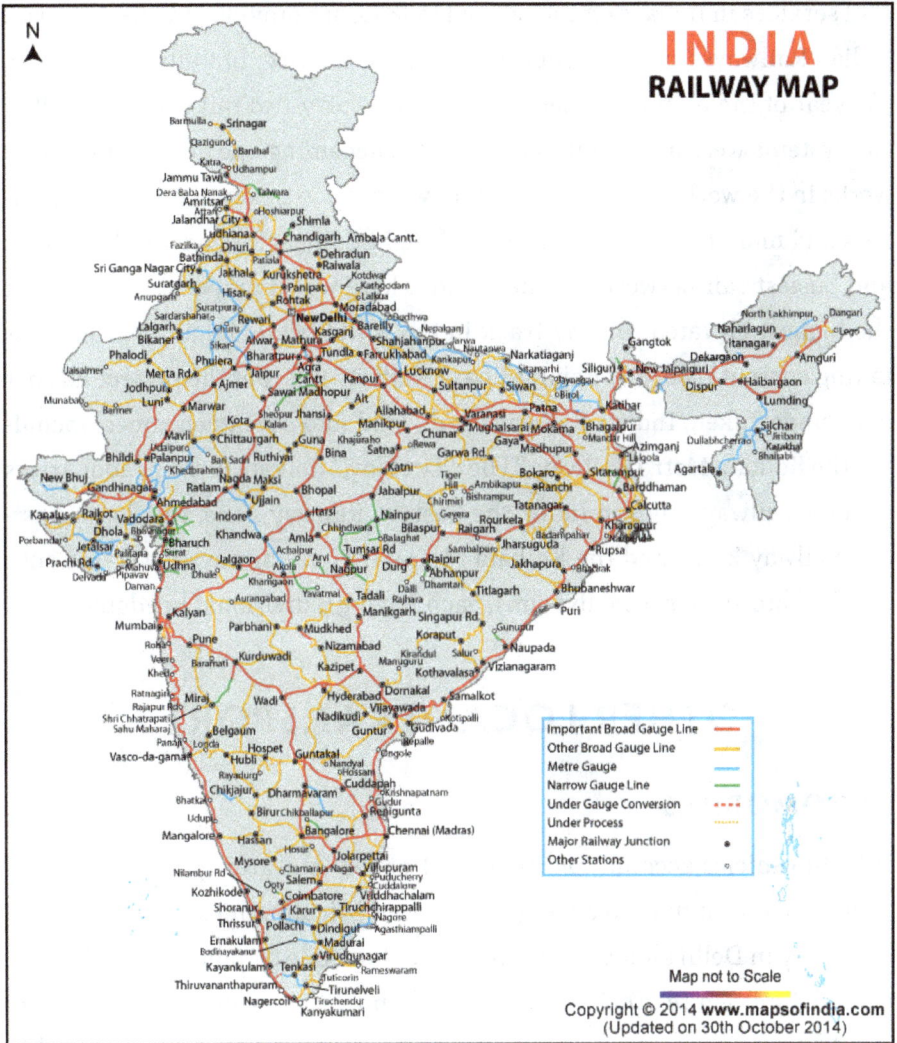

Source: Maps of India

RAILWAY

Rail services in India, first introduced in 1853, are provided by the state-run Indian Railways under the supervision of the Ministry of Railways. By 1947, the year of India's independence, there were forty-two rail systems. In 1951 the systems were nationalized as one unit, becoming one of the largest networks in the world. Indian Railways now transports over 18 million passengers and more than 2 million tons of freight daily across one of the largest and busiest rail networks in the world. There was a proposal to construct the highest elevated railway track in the world from Manali to Leh, overtaking current record of Beijing-Lhasa Railway line, but the project has not been undertaken. Indian Railways is divided into seventeen zones, including the Kolkata Metro Railway. "The city of joy," Kolkata is the headquarters of three railway zones in India: the Eastern Railway Zone, the South Eastern Railway Zone, and the Kolkata Metro. Indian Railways is further subdivided into sixty-seven divisions, each having a divisional headquarters.

OTHER LOCAL TRANSPORT

AUTOMOBILES

Private vehicles account for 30 percent of the total transport demands in urban areas of India. An average of 963 new private vehicles are registered every day in Delhi alone. The number of automobiles produced in India rose from 6.3 million in 2002–2003 to 11 million in 2008–2009. However, India still has a very low rate of car ownership for its population. Car ownership in India is on a par with China and exceeded by Brazil and Russia.

Figure 7.5: Projected Percentage Change in Passenger Transport by Mode and Car Ownership Rate from 2000 to 2050

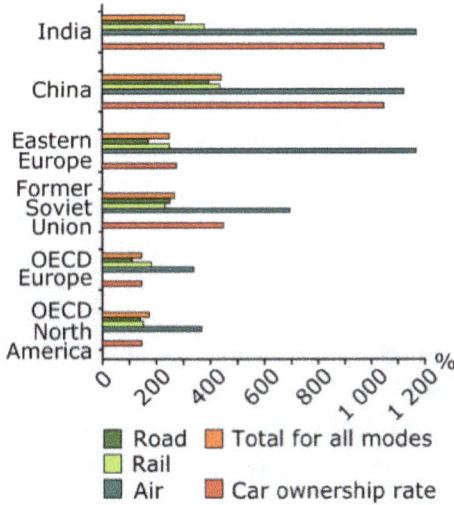

Legend:
- Road
- Rail
- Air
- Total for all modes
- Car ownership rate

Categories (top to bottom): India, China, Eastern Europe, Former Soviet Union, OECD Europe, OECD North America

X-axis: 0, 200, 400, 600, 800, 1 000, 1 200 %

Source: European Environment Agency

Compact cars, especially hatchbacks, predominate due to affordability, fuel efficiency, mobility in traffic, and small parking spaces in most cities. Chennai is known as the "Detroit of India" for its automobile industry. Maruti, Hyundai, and Tata Motors are the most popular brands in the order of their market share. The Ambassador, a brand of automobile, once had a monopoly but is now an icon of preliberalization in India, and it is still used by taxi companies. Maruti 800, launched in 1984, created the first revolution in the Indian auto sector because of its low pricing. It had the highest market share until 2004, when it was overtaken by other low-cost models from Maruti, such as the Alto and the Wagon R, the Indica from Tata Motors, and the Santro from Hyundai. Over the twenty-year period since its introduction, about 2.4 million units of the Maruti 800 have been sold. However, with the launch of the Tata Nano, the least expensive car in the world, Maruti 800 has lost its popularity.

Figure 7.6: Vehicles Growth in India

Vehicles Growth in India, 1998-2006
(Figures in Millions)

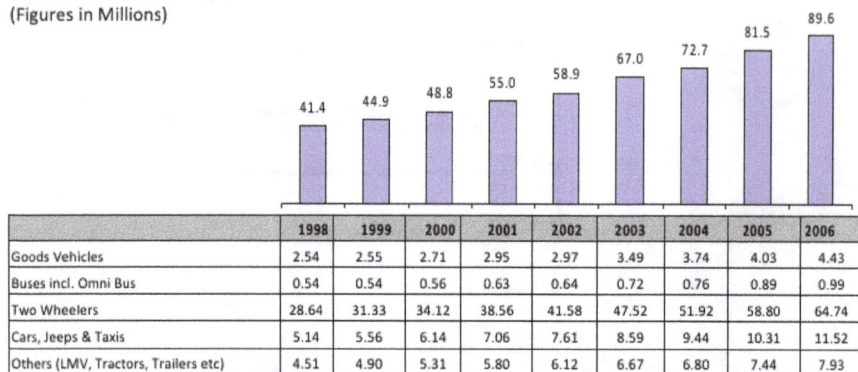

	1998	1999	2000	2001	2002	2003	2004	2005	2006
Goods Vehicles	2.54	2.55	2.71	2.95	2.97	3.49	3.74	4.03	4.43
Buses incl. Omni Bus	0.54	0.54	0.56	0.63	0.64	0.72	0.76	0.89	0.99
Two Wheelers	28.64	31.33	34.12	38.56	41.58	47.52	51.92	58.80	64.74
Cars, Jeeps & Taxis	5.14	5.56	6.14	7.06	7.61	8.59	9.44	10.31	11.52
Others (LMV, Tractors, Trailers etc)	4.51	4.90	5.31	5.80	6.12	6.67	6.80	7.44	7.93

Source: Road Transport Year Book 2006-2007 (March 2009), Ministry of Shipping,
Road Transport and Highways, government of India

Given the lack of infrastructure, with few roads connecting small towns with big cities, urban areas are congested by excessive car and truck traffic. In the city of Bengaluru, Radio One and the Bangalore Traffic Police launched a campaign featuring celebrities, such as Robin Uthappa and Rahul Dravid, encouraging the public to carpool. The initiative got a good response and by the end of May 2009, Ten thousand people are said to have carpooled in the city. Carpooling, however, is not expected to slow the market's increasing demand for automobiles.

PORTS AND SHIPPING

There are many major ports in India. Maritime transportation is managed by the Shipping Corporation of India, a government-owned company that also manages offshore and other marine transport infrastructure in the country. It owns and operates about 35 percent of Indian tonnage and operates in practically all areas of shipping business, servicing both national and international trades.

It has a fleet of seventy-nine ships of 275,000 gross tonnage (GT) (4.8 million deadweight tons [DWT]) and also manages fifty-three research, survey, and support vessels of 120,000 GT (60,000 DWT) on behalf of various government departments and other organizations. Personnel are trained at the Maritime Training Institute in Mumbai, a branch of the World Maritime University, which was set up in 1987. The corporation also operates in Malta and Iran through joint ventures.

Visakhapatnam seaport is one of the busiest ports on the East Coast of India. The ports are the main centers of trade. In India about 95 percent of foreign trade by quantity and 70 percent by value passes through the ports. Mumbai Port and Jawaharlal Nehru Port (Navi Mumbai) handles 70 percent of maritime trade in India. There are twelve major ports: Navi Mumbai, Mumbai, Kochi, Kolkata (including Haldia), Paradip, Visakhapatnam, Ennore, Chennai, Tuticorin, New Mangalore, Mormugao, and Kandla. Other than these, there are 187 minor and intermediate ports, 43 of which handle cargo.

The distinction between major and minor port is not based on the amount of cargo handled. The major ports are managed by port trusts, which are regulated by the central government. They come under the purview of the Major Port Trusts Act of 1963. The respective state governments regulate the minor ports and many are private ports or captive ports. The total amount of traffic handled at the major ports in 2005–2006 was 382.33 MT.

Figure 7.7 below shows the outlook for traffic at Indian ports in recent years.

Figure 7.7: Outlook on Traffic at Indian Ports

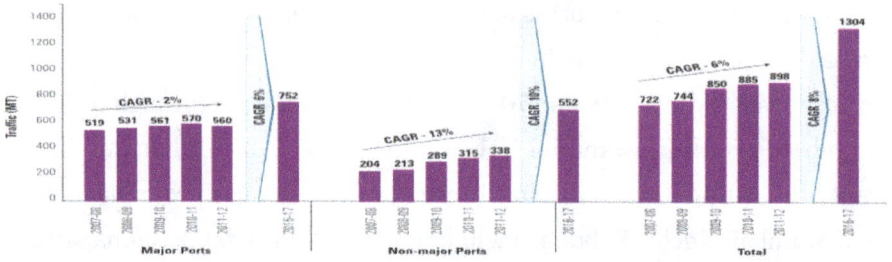

Outlook on traffic at Indian Ports

Source: KPMG in India analysis

Given the pivotal role it plays in the economy, the Indian ports sector appears to be well poised for a long-term growth wave. Looking ahead, the key game changers expected to drive growth in the port sector include fulfillment of Maritime Agenda 2010–2020, growth of nonmajor ports, increased containerization, and east coast ports.

AVIATION

Air cargo serves as a vital link between domestic and international markets. Air cargo needs adequate and appropriate focus to facilitate, integrate, and expand India's fast-growing international and domestic trade by air. While the total volume of air cargo traffic currently constitutes about 1 percent of total trade, it accounts for close to 29 percent of total trade value.

In the early 1990s, the government of India adopted the Open Sky policy for the air cargo sector, under which Indian or foreign carriers were allowed to operate both scheduled and nonscheduled cargo services between all airports in India. Since then, the sector has witnessed significant growth from 0.7 million metric tons (MMT) in 1995–96 to 2.7 MMT in 2011–2012.

Figure 7.8: Map of Domestic Airports

Source: Maps of India

Between 2006 and 2012, air cargo traffic handled at Indian airports increased at a CAGR of 11.5 percent, with domestic cargo growing at 12.3 percent, which was faster than international cargo (11.2 percent). Over the next decade, total air cargo traffic is expected to grow at a CAGR of 10.3 percent to reach 5.9 MMT, with domestic and international cargo expected to grow at CAGRs of 11.6 percent and 9.5 percent, respectively, contributing 2.4 MMT and 3.5 MMT, respectively, by 2020.

International cargo, which accounts for two-thirds of total cargo, is largely concentrated in the metro airports of Mumbai, Delhi, Chennai, Bengaluru, and Hyderabad. The Delhi and Mumbai airports collectively handle around 50 percent of India's domestic and international cargo.

Figure 7.9: Air Cargo Throughput for All Indian Airports

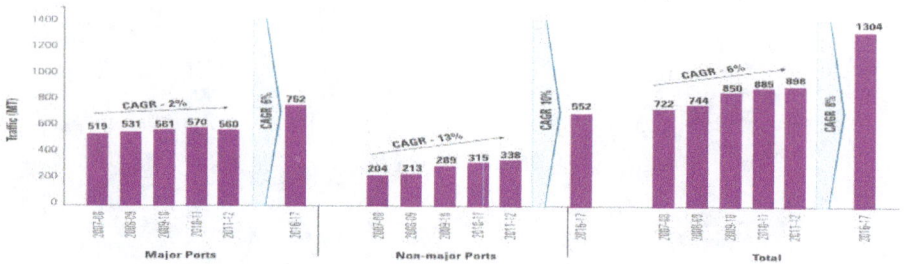

Source: KPMG in India analysis

While there are 346 civilian airfields in India—253 with paved runways and 93 with unpaved runways—only 132 were classified as "airports" as of November 2014. Of these, the state-owned Airports Authority of India operates forty-six domestic and fifteen international airports. Additionally, airports in Delhi, Mumbai, Bangalore, and Hyderabad were developed under the PPP model with private companies. Thirty airports are civil enclaves in defense or customs airports and thirty-one were not in operation. State Governments and union territory governments or the private sector operate a total of six airports. Sixty-six airports are licensed in the public-use category by the Directorate General of Civil Aviation, while twenty-one are licensed for private use.

Figure 7.10: India's Top Fifteen Airports (2013)

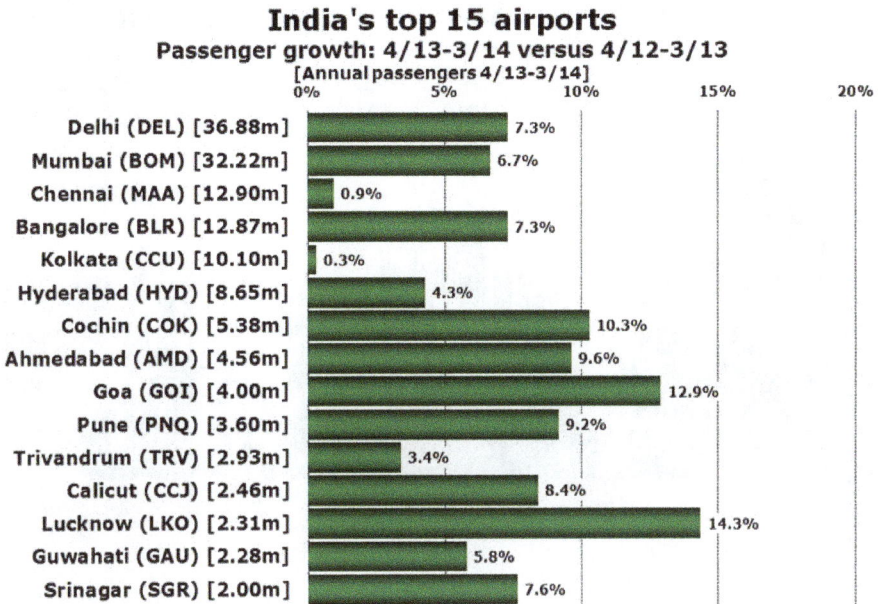

India's top 15 airports
Passenger growth: 4/13-3/14 versus 4/12-3/13
[Annual passengers 4/13-3/14]

Delhi (DEL) [36.88m]	7.3%
Mumbai (BOM) [32.22m]	6.7%
Chennai (MAA) [12.90m]	0.9%
Bangalore (BLR) [12.87m]	7.3%
Kolkata (CCU) [10.10m]	0.3%
Hyderabad (HYD) [8.65m]	4.3%
Cochin (COK) [5.38m]	10.3%
Ahmedabad (AMD) [4.56m]	9.6%
Goa (GOI) [4.00m]	12.9%
Pune (PNQ) [3.60m]	9.2%
Trivandrum (TRV) [2.93m]	3.4%
Calicut (CCJ) [2.46m]	8.4%
Lucknow (LKO) [2.31m]	14.3%
Guwahati (GAU) [2.28m]	5.8%
Srinagar (SGR) [2.00m]	7.6%

Source: Airports Authority of India

The operations of the major airports in India have been privatized over the past five years and this has resulted in better-equipped and cleaner airports. The terminals have either been refurbished or expanded.

For the year ending in March 2014, international traffic was up 8.3 percent to 46.6 million passengers, though for the last five months growth was less than 6 percent. Delhi (up 9.6 percent to 12.7 million) and Mumbai (up 4.1 percent to 10.3 million) handle almost half of all international passengers passing through the country's airports, with Chennai (up 1.7 percent to 4.5 million) in a distant third place. Among the airports handling at least 500,000 international passengers, the fastest-growing airports were Ahmedabad (+21.9 percent), Trichy (+15.9 percent), Hyderabad (+13.8 percent), and Goa (+12.2 percent).

Figure 7.11: International Air Traffic Development

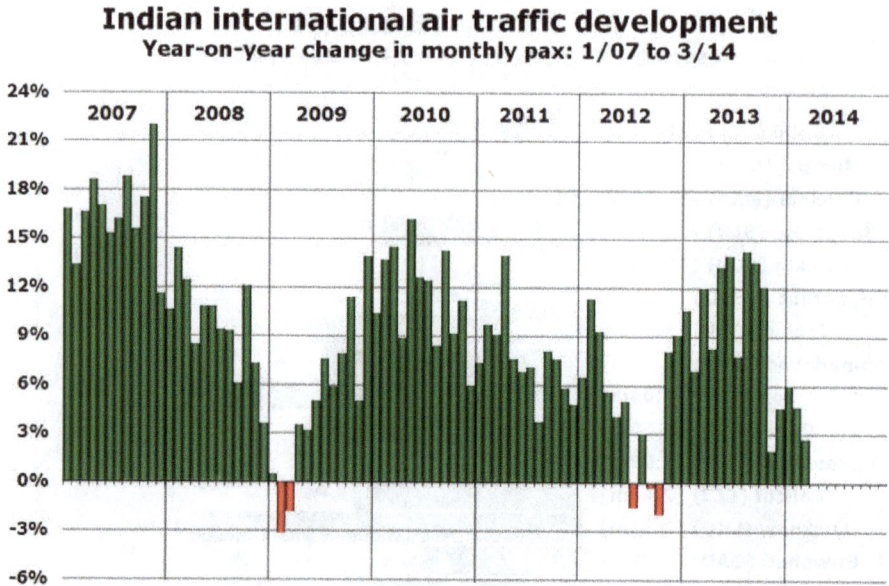

Indian international air traffic development
Year-on-year change in monthly pax: 1/07 to 3/14

Source: Airports Authority of India

JNNURM PROJECT

Jawaharlal Nehru National Urban Renewal Mission (JnNURM) is a large-scale city-modernization scheme. It was launched by the government of India (2005–2012) with an aim to provide financial help for cities to upgrade their infrastructure and governance. The government is aiming to invest over $20 billion over a seven-year period.

The Ministry of Urban Development is the nodal agency under the Urban Development Department, which sanctions the proposals received from Indian cities and directs the funds. For the funding procedure, cities were categorized based on their population and the economic situation. More than sixty-three plus cities were identified as being eligible for National Urban Renewal Mission funding.

Almost all the states of India actively participated in the funding mission for various components like storm water management, sanitation, water supply, housing for the urban poor, transportation, and so on. A special program for funding buses was also launched under this mission. The funding was not limited to city buses but was extended to State Transport Undertakings to procure buses. A total of 15,260 city buses have since been sanctioned and many states received funding for bus procurement.

Figure 7.12: Buses Procured under JnNURM by State

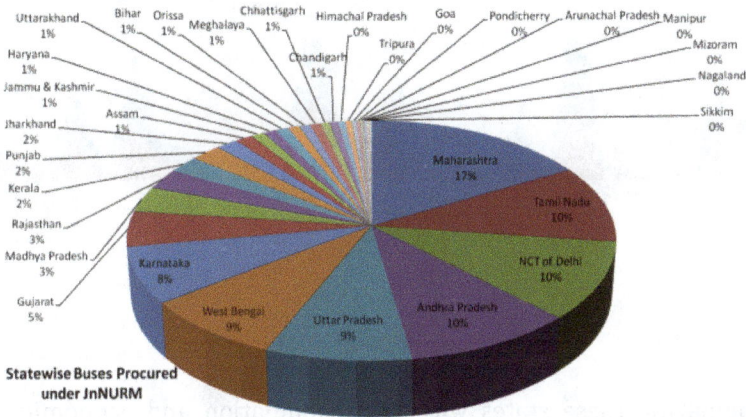

Source: Dave (2013)

A closer look at the statistics of states' participation in procuring buses gives an overall picture. The above chart (Figure 7.12) shows which Indian states are serious about public transportation and have benefited from the mission by obtaining funds and procuring large fleets of city buses, whether they are normal buses with left side doors or bus rapid transit buses with right side doors. Maharashtra is a leader in procuring city buses, followed by Delhi, Andhra Pradesh, Tamilnadu, West Bengal, Uttar Pradesh, and Karnataka (these states procured more than 1,000 buses). Other states have an almost negligible contribution toward city bus procurement, especially eastern and northeastern states like Tripura, Sikkim, and Nagaland.

Figure 7.13 shows investments made by different states in procuring city buses and the government of India's contribution. Delhi is the lead city in investing in public transport, followed by the states of Maharashtra, Tamilnadu, Andhra Pradesh, West Bengal, Karnataka, and Uttar Pradesh.

Figure 7.13: Investments by States in Procuring City Buses under JnNURM and Share of Government of India

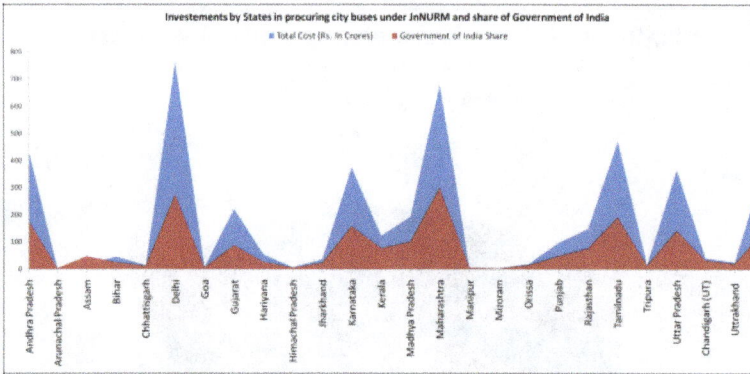

Investements by States in procuring city buses under JnNURM and share of Government of India

Source: Dave (2013)

Comparing these states with their population and economic profile (percentage share in the national GDP, GDP growth rate) with the percentage of city buses they have procured, forms the picture shown in Figure 7.14. GDP growth rates in states do not reflect procurement of buses, which provide public transportation to masses; however, in some states, GDP growth correlates with bus procurement and infrastructure improvements—thus, the dilemma between development, bureaucracy, and productivity is in evidence here.

Figure 7.14: City Buses Procured by States Compared to
Respective Population and Economic Profile

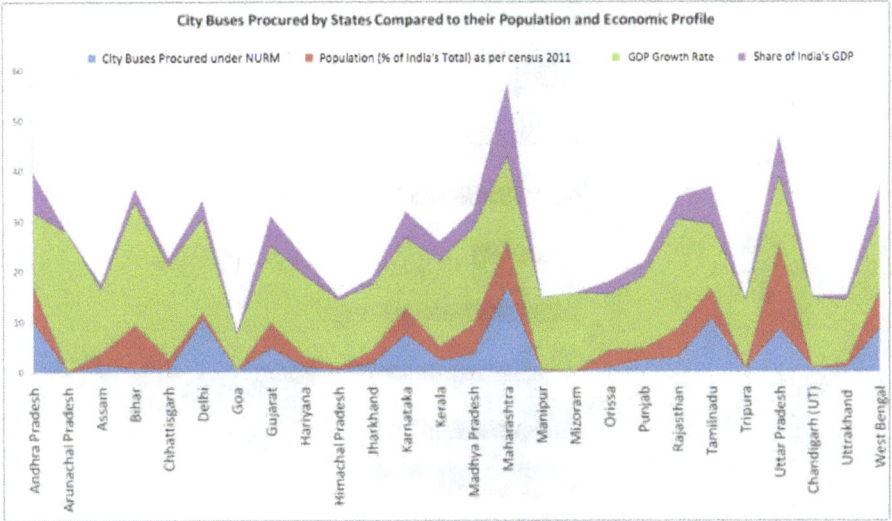

City Buses Procured by States Compared to their Population and Economic Profile

- City Buses Procured under NURM
- Population (% of India's Total) as per census 2011
- GDP Growth Rate
- Share of India's GDP

Source: Dave (2013)

TRANSPORT SERVICES TRADE

In 2011, Asian economies saw their growth rate halved compared to 2010, while European nations showed signs of recovery after the global financial crisis. Asia slowed down mainly due to slower growth in transportation services and other commercial services. India saw a large growth in the export of transportation services, moving from a 21 percent change in 2010 to 32 percent annual change in 2011.

Figure 7.15: Exports of Transportation Services, 2010–2011

Exports of transportation services, 2010-11

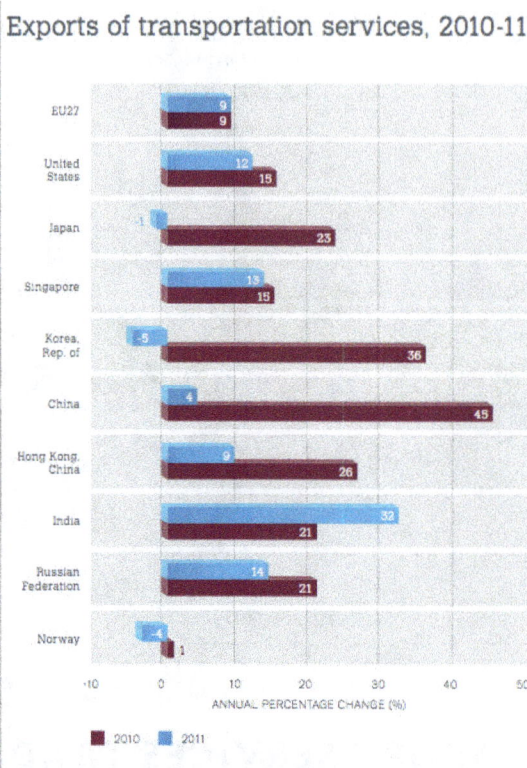

Source: WTO International Trade Statistics (2012)

CONTRIBUTION TO GDP

Between 2009 and 2011 there was an influx of tourists visiting India, result-ing in a sharp increase in the GDP contributions from the trade, hotel, and transportation industries. The increase in tourism occurred during a period when economic policies became more liberal, leading to increased FDI. As a result international businesses were traveling to India at a higher rate.

Figure 7.16: Contribution to GDP from Various Industries

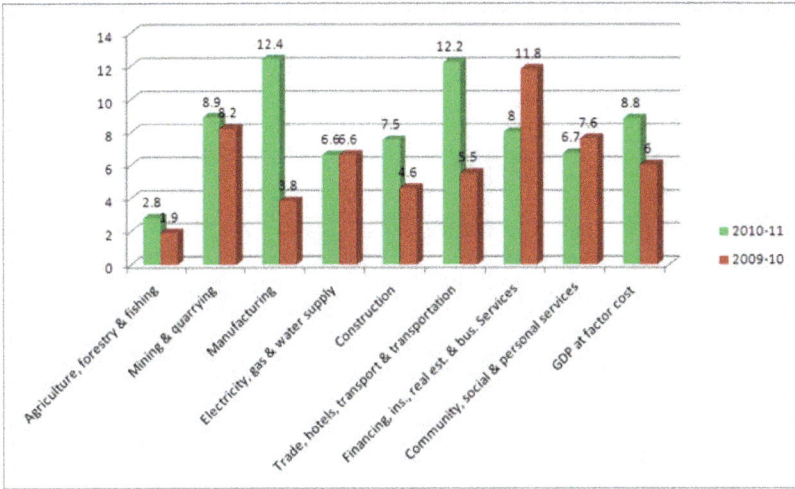

Source: Ministry of Statistics and Program Implementation

CHALLENGES

Despite ongoing improvements in the sector, several aspects of the transportation sector are still riddled with problems due to outdated infrastructure and lack of investment in less economically active parts of the country. The demand for transportation infrastructure and services has been rising by around 10 percent each year with the current infrastructure unable to meet these growing demands. According to Goldman Sachs, India will need to spend US$1.7 trillion on infrastructure projects over the next decade to boost economic growth, of which US$500 billion is budgeted in the government's Eleventh Five-Year Plan.

8

INFORMATION TECHNOLOGY AND INFORMATION TECHNOLOGY ENGINEERING SERVICES

OVERVIEW

India has the highest human resources reserve of any country, according to a study called "Leadership Development" conducted by, Harvard Human Resources, and a leader in human resources development. Certainly this is an advantage over other nations, though the same study raises concerns about unemployment in the IT industry. The Indian IT industry has emerged as one of the most promising industries over the years and provides employment to a large pool of talent. However, due to the lack of quality of education available for students, the industry is facing challenges in hiring a skilled work force that is employable per industry requirements. This shows how shortcomings in the education sector can hamper the growth of industries such as IT. There is a huge employability gap in the industry that must be reduced for the betterment of the Indian economy.

Figure 8.1: Major Segments in the IT and ITES Industry

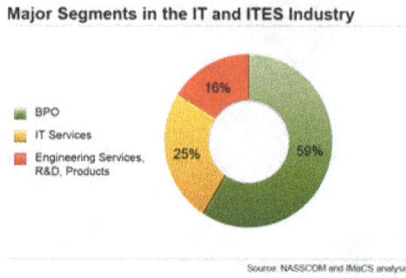

Major Segments in the IT and ITES Industry

BPO
IT Services
Engineering Services, R&D, Products

16%
25%
59%

Source: NASSCOM and iMaCS analysis

Source: NASSCOM and iMaCS analysis

The IT–business process outsourcing (BPO) industry in India produced aggregate revenues of US$88.1 billion in FY 2011; and the IT software and IT service sector (excluding hardware) contributed US$76.1 billion. The software product segment touched 157 billion in Indian rupees (INR) with a growth rate of 14 percent. The domestic IT-BPO sector grew by 16 percent to reach US$20 billion in FY 2012. According to the National Association of Software and Services Companies (NASSCOM), the IT service sector is one of the fastest-growing segments across the Indian domestic market and has grown by 16.8 percent to reach INR 501 billion. Three-quarters of large Indian enterprises increased IT spending in 2013, with an average IT budget of US$12.2 million, according to a survey by Gartner. This clearly indicates that there is a huge demand for a skilled and employable workforce across the country.

Figure 8.2: Industry Verticals in the IT and ITES Sector

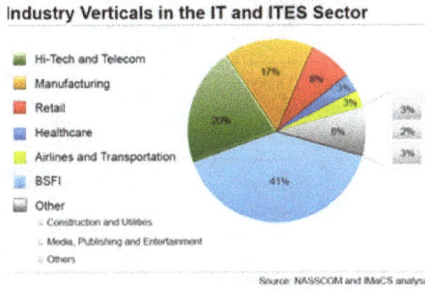

Source: NASSCOM and iMaCS analysis

The availability of human resources with the required skill set will be the key factor in the growth of the IT industry, and India's youth will be one of the primary driving forces of this growth. The industry has much more potential compared to its estimated contribution to the economic growth of the country; however, the shortage of skilled workers is considered a significant challenge. According to research conducted by NASSCOM, every year more than 3 million graduates and postgraduates join India's workforce. Out of these, only 25 percent of IT graduates are considered employable by the fast-growing IT and information technology enabled service (ITES) industry based on their level of education.

The Indian IT-BPO sector, including the domestic and export segments, continues to grow from strength to strength, witnessing high levels of activity both onshore and offshore. The companies continue to move up the value chain to offer higher-end research and analytics services to their clients. India's leadership position in the global IT and BPO industries is based primarily on the advantages described in the following sections.

Figure 8.3: Segments of the Indian IT Sector

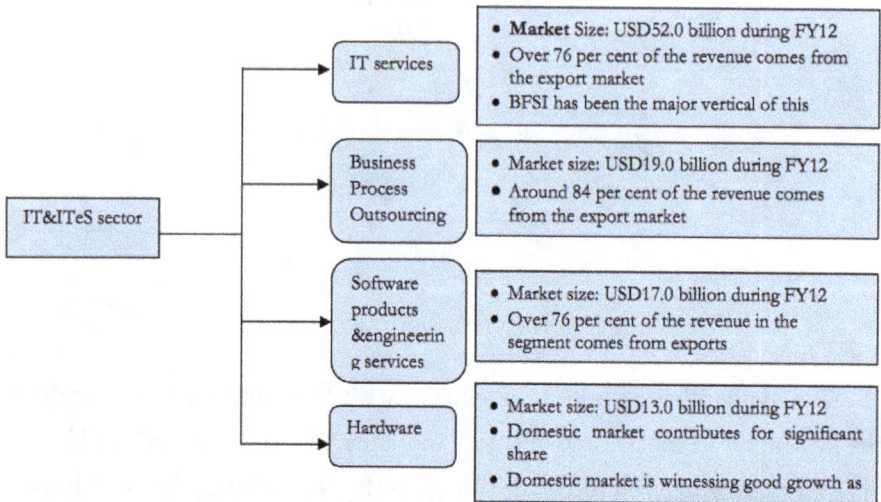

Source: Corporate Catalyst India (2013)

MARKET OVERVIEW

The Indian IT and ITES industry has continued to perform as the most consistent growth driver for the economy. Service, software exports, and BPO remain the mainstay of the sector. Over the last five years, the IT and ITES industry has grown at a remarkable pace. A majority of the Fortune 500 and Global 2000 corporations are sourcing IT and ITES from India, and it is the premier destination for the global sourcing of IT and ITES, accounting for 55 percent of the global market in offshore IT services, garnering 35 percent of the ITES-BPO market.

India's IT and BPO sector exports grew by 14 percent in 2014 to reach US$87 billion. The Indian IT infrastructure market grew by 9.7 percent year on year to reach US$2.1 billion in 2013.

Figure 8.4: Market Size of IT Industry in India (US$ billion)

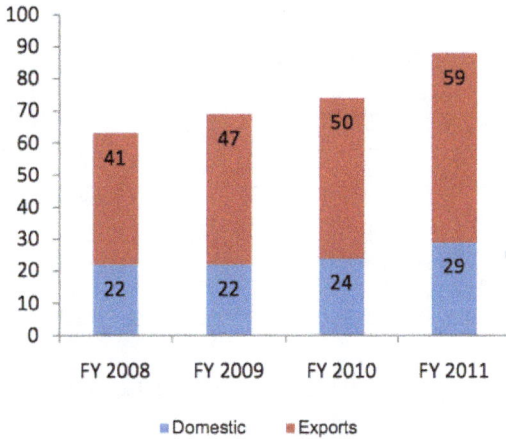

Source: Corporate Catalyst India (2013)

The contribution of the IT sector to India's GDP has registered an impressive growth. According to Reserve Bank of India, IT's contribution to GDP rose from about 2 percent at the start of the new millennium to 4.8 percent at the end of fiscal year 2005–2006 (April–March). According to NASSCOM, India's IT association, the IT industry's share in GDP was estimated at 5.4 percent for 2006-07 (NASSCOM, 2007). The growth is even more impressive considering the fact that India's GDP has itself been growing by well over 6 percent per annum in this period. Figure 8.5 below illustrates the impact of the IT sector on the economy.

Figure 8.5: Growth of the Indian IT Sector

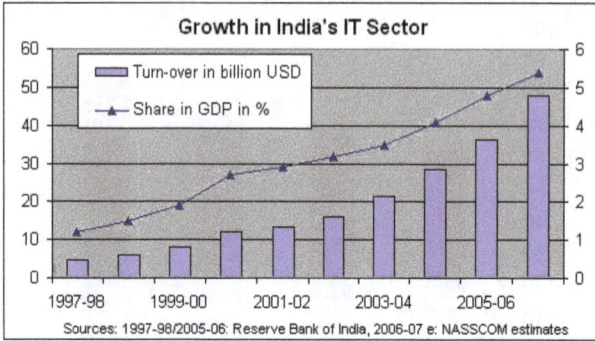

Sources: 199–1998/2005–2006: Reserve Bank of India; 2006–2007 e: NASSCOM estimates

PROJECTED INDUSTRY SIZE

According to estimates, the Indian IT industry is expected to record US$220 billion from exports and US$60 billion on the domestic front by FY 2022, growing at a CAGR of 12.8 percent. There are various reasons why IT is considered the driving force of the domestic market, such as increased public-sector spending, sustainable GDP growth, implementation of IT solutions in different industries, and expansion of the IT industry in tier-2 and tier-3 cities.

To sustain the growth of the IT industry, India needs a rich pool of skilled workers to provide integrated and end-to-end IT solutions with flexible business models and technological expertise. Currently, about 80 percent of the IT workforce in India are software engineers and mathematics and computer associates. The proportion of science and IT graduates who are engaged in software development is expected to see significant increase from about 10 percent currently to 15 percent.

Figure 8.6: Estimated Size of Indian IT and ITES Industry by 2022

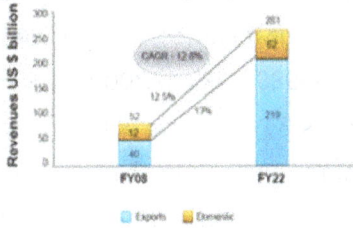

Source: NASSCOM 2020 Perspective and iMaCS analysis

The major cities that account for nearly 90 percent of the sector's exports are Bengaluru, Jammu and Kashmir, Hyderabad, Kolkata, Chennai, Trivandrum, Noida, Mumbai, and Pune. Bengaluru is considered to be the Silicon Valley of India because it is the leading IT exporter. Exports dominate the industry and constitute about 77 percent of the total industry revenue; however, the domestic market is also significant, with a robust revenue growth. The industry's share of total Indian exports (merchandise plus services) increased from less than 4 percent in FY 1998 to about 25 percent in FY 2012. The phenomenal growth rate of India's software exports, with (a ten-year rolling) average annual growth, has never fallen below 30 percent, and overall exports exceeded US$36 billion in 2008–2009.

Figure 8.7: Indian Software Exports (1980–2009)

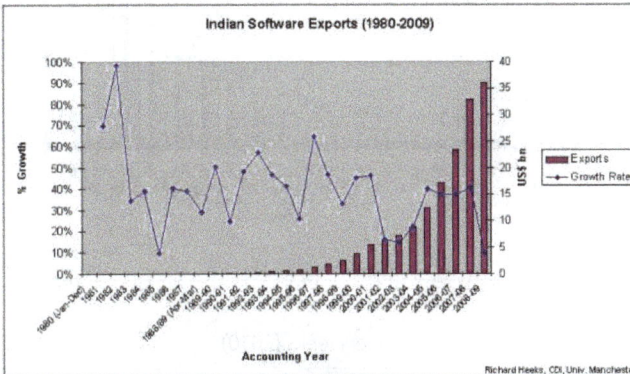

Source: Heeks (2010)

The weak domestic software market is a matter of serious concern for India. While software exports are growing very quickly, domestic software cannot seem to keep pace. For instance, when domestic software increased from Rs 64 crores in 1985–1986 to Rs 47,300 crores in 2007–2008, software exports increased from Rs 34 crores to Rs 163,000 crores in 2007–2008. Also, the share of software exports in the total output, which was 34.69 percent in 1985–1986, leaped to 70.43 percent in 1999–2000 and further to 77.51 percent in 2007–2008. Correspondingly, the domestic market declined from 65 percent to about 22 percent during the same period. This is an indication of a weak domestic market. A strong and vibrant domestic market is essential for the sustained export of software and to insulate India from fluctuations in the international market. Therefore, the government has to implement the appropriate policies to promote the diffusion of IT into various sectors of the economy.

Figure 8.8: Indian IT: Export's Share of Total Outputs (1991–2009)

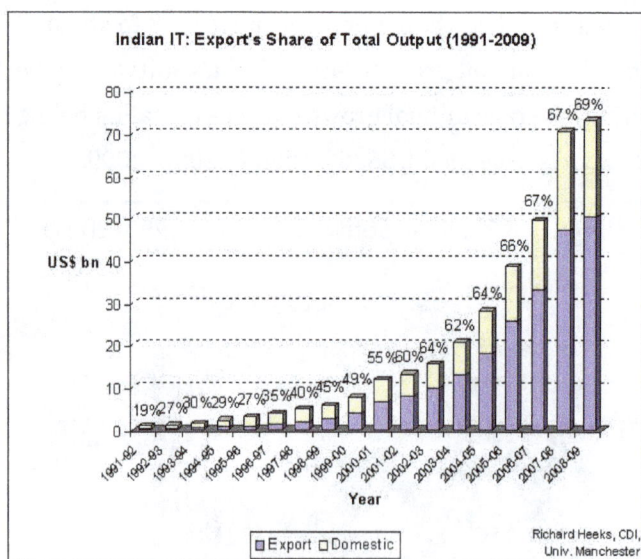

Source: Heeks (2010)

Why does India have a weak domestic market in IT? The reasons are quite clear. The installed base of personal computers (PCs) in India is too small to support a thriving domestic software industry. The total installed base of PCs is close to 20 million. This amounts to less than 15 PCs per 1,000 people. The high costs of hardware and piracy are also a stumbling block for the growth of the domestic software industry. Also, in the software sector profits on exports are considerably higher than domestic sales.

There has been a much higher growth rate of Indian IT exports compared to production for the domestic market. As a result, the share of exports in total IT output has risen from 19 percent in 1991–1992 to 69 percent in 2008–2009 (shown in Figure 8.9).

Figure 8.9: Indian IT Growth Rates: Exports vs. Domestic (1992–2009)

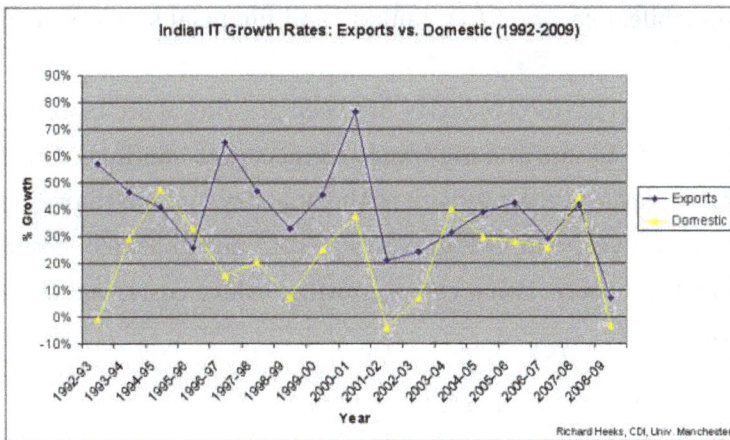

Source: Heeks (2010)

BUSINESS PROCESS OUTSOURCING

Business process outsourcing (BPO) is the contracting of a specific business task, such as payroll, to a third-party service provider. Knowledge process outsourcing (KPO) is the outsourcing of business processes that require significant domain expertise. India has become one of the most sought-after destinations for companies that want to outsource their business, knowledge, research, legal, and related high-end processes. BPO and KPO not only boost exports, increase national income, and create greater employment avenues, they also increase tax revenues and cater to the growth of other related industries.

The companies involved in outsourcing activities tend to earn huge profits, and as a result, are in a position to offer their employees competitive pay packages along with attractive employee benefits. Companies outsourcing work to a KPO vendor can save costs up to 32 percent on revenues, assuming that the profit margin remains constant. The Indian KPO service industry is estimated to be around US$5.7 billion and has grown by 15–17 percent in recent years. Indian KPO providers offer a range of solutions to diverse industry segments, such as fast-moving consumer goods, engineering, automobile, telecom, R&D, banking and financial services, insurance, etc.

The Indian ITES-BPO industry has been growing at an impressive pace over the past few years and the trend is expected to continue. Third-party and captive players expect growth in the industry at more than 20 percent in the next two years. In fact, growth will continue unabated, despite concerns about the appreciating rupee, growing salary costs, and shortage of manpower.

Figure 8.10: IT-BPO Revenues

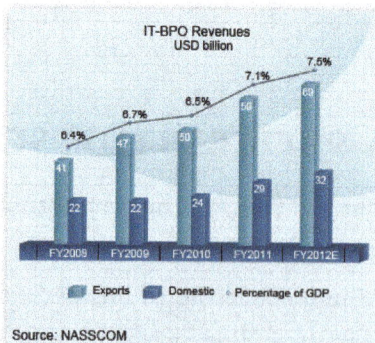

Source: NASSCOM

To promote and boost the software industry, the Indian government has created software technology parks, providing a suitable framework covering licensing processes and providing top quality IT infrastructure in a cost-effective manner.

Software Technology Parks of India is a 100 percent export-oriented scheme to develop software to export using data communication links. This society was set up under the Ministry of Information Technology in 1991. At present there are 23 software technology parks in India.

Figure 8.11: Map of Software Parks of India

Source: Maps of India (2014)

The major contributor to India's software success has been the software services sector. Using highly skilled labor with relatively little capital, Indian firms can satisfy foreign clientele (mainly from the US and other industrialized countries in Western Europe) with cost-effective IT solutions. This accounts for the lion's share (nearly 80 percent) of India's IT sector.

About 80 percent of the software sector's revenues are generated by exporting IT services. Exports were estimated to account for US$31.3 billion out of US$39.7 billion turnover in FY 2006–2007 (NASSCOM, 2007). The software sector has emerged as the primary driver of the overall foreign exchange reserve. Meanwhile, it consists of nearly 80 percent of the IT sector in India. Figure 8.12 shows the impressive export growth of software services by calendar year.

Figure 8.12: India's Trade of Software Services in Billion USD

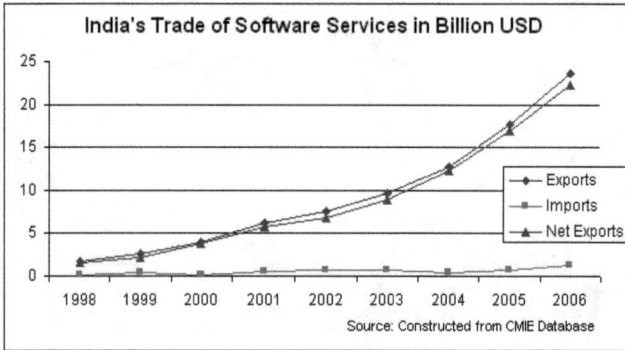

Source: CME Database, Hamburg University of Technology

EXPORTERS

India is also home to some of the most renowned IT firms. While India's own Infosys, TCS, Wipro, and Satyam are growing into the role of "global players," the world's leading players are entering India in a big way. All the major names, such as Microsoft, Oracle, IBM, and Systems Applications and Products maintain a significant presence in India. Some firms have their biggest operations in India, employing more people than even the headquarters. For others, their software development in India is the only operation of its kind outside their own home market.

Figure 8.13: Global Ranking of Top Five Indian IT Companies

Company	Global Ranking 2011	Global Ranking 2012	2011 Revenue	2012 Revenue	2012- 2011 Growth (%)	2011 Market Share (%)	2012 Market Share (%)
TCS	16	16	9,451	10,888	15.2	1.1	1.2
Cognizant	28	23	5,875	7,053	20.1	0.7	0.8
Infosys	27	26	6,279	6,691	6.6	0.7	0.7
Wipro	31	31	5,334	5,737	7.6	0.6	0.6
HCL Technologies	47	41	3,316	3,916	18.1	0.4	0.4
Total			**30,255**	**34,285**	**13.3**	**3.5**	**3.7**

Source: Gartner

Source: Gartner (2013)

The Top two hundred IT Companies in India logged combined revenue of US$84 billion (Rs 384,250 crore) in FY 2011, to grow at 25 percent, the highest rate of growth in the last four years. The revenues of these companies in FY 2010 and FY 2009 were Rs 307,126 crore and Rs 289,093 crore, respectively. The combined revenue of the Top twenty IT companies was US$54 billion (Rs 247,808 crore) in FY 2011, also representing a growth of 25 percent. This is significantly higher than the 8 percent growth recorded in FY 2010, with revenues of Rs 198,017 crore.

The FY 2011 growth surpasses the 24 percent growth witnessed in FY 2008, the year before the slowdown, according to the annual research findings on the Indian IT industry, carried out by *Dataquest,* the flagship journal of Cyber Media in South Asia. Each of the top twenty IT companies was over US$1 billion in FY 2011, together posting revenues of US$54 billion (Rs 247,808 crore), contributing 64 percent to the top two hundred companies' revenue.

According to the findings, the top five Indian IT companies in FY 2011 were TCS, Infosys, Wipro, Hewlett-Packard, and Cognizant, with revenues of Rs 33,112 crore (25 percent growth over last year), Rs 25,997 crore (22 percent), Rs 24,899 crore (13 percent), Rs 23,227 crore (30 percent), and Rs 21,393 crore (37 percent), respectively. Wipro, which recorded the slowest growth in the top five, surrendered the number two slot to Infosys after six years.

Figure 8.14: Top Fifty Indian IT Service Exporters

The Top 50 Indian IT Service Exporters							
	2009-10	2008-09	Growth (%)		2009-10	2008-09	Growth (%)
TCS	24,289	23,922	2 ▲	Sonata Software	983	955	-8 ▼
Infosys	21,141	20,188	5 ▲	iGate	831	826	1 ▲
Wipro	16,681	16,138	3 ▲	Genpact	827	897	-7 ▼
Cognizant	15,581	12,741	22 ▲	Headstrong	824	830	-1 ▼
HCL Technologies	10,104	8,063	25 ▲	Bartronics	803	589	36 ▲
IBM India	6,442	6,265	3 ▲	Tata Technologies	782	927	-16 ▼
Accenture India	4,464	4,092	9 ▲	NIIT Technologies	781	844	-7 ▼
Tech Mahindra	4,297	4,131	4 ▲	Mastek	755	966	-22 ▼
MphasiS	3,874	3,261	19 ▲	Keane India	671	683	-2 ▼
Patni	2,961	2,981	-1 ▼	KPIT Cummins	666	737	-10 ▼
Oracle Financial Services	2,730	2,723	0	Infinite Computer Solutions	637	466	37 ▲
Capgemini	2,410	2,278	6 ▲	Geodesic	625	642	-3 ▼
CSC India	1,937	2,045	-5 ▼	Sapient	624	550	13 ▲
L&T Infotech	1,802	1,746	3 ▲	Intelligroup	595	747	-20 ▼
Syntel	1,694	1,520	11 ▲	Persistent	571	576	-1 ▼
Aricent	1,689	1,848	-9 ▼	Zylog	543	456	19 ▲
Prithvi	1,341	1,774	-24 ▼	Birlasoft	518	597	-13 ▼
Polaris	1,216	1,226	-1 ▼	Geometric	481	574	-16 ▼
Mindtree	1,205	1,164	4 ▲	ITC Infotech	477	588	-19 ▼
Mascon Global	1,084	1,097	-1 ▼	Steria	468	499	-6 ▼
3i Infotech	966	1,089	4 ▲	Subex Azure	461	556	-17 ▼
				Deloitte Consulting	436	349	25 ▲
Infotech Enterprises	924	863	7 ▲	Saksea	419	537	-22 ▼
Hexaware	918	1,072	-14 ▼	Ness Technologies	382	395	-3 ▼
Honeywell India	916	837	9 ▲	SFO Technologies	378	339	12 ▲
Zensar	885	814	9 ▲	Synechron	337	253	33 ▲

Revenues (in Rs crore)
■ Growth ■ Decline

Source: Madaan (2012)

BARRIERS TO INNOVATION

A German study revealed that certain barriers to innovation might be overcome through close cooperation with international partners from industry and academia or by setting up one's own global R&D facilities. The study was conducted by TIM/TUHH on behalf of the Hamburg State Ministry of Economic and Labor Affairs and was a part of the EU Regional Innovation Strategies project. The purpose was to identify and remove barriers to innovation in small and medium-sized enterprises. India might be an attractive location for innovation activities due to its proven base of scientific capabilities, existing and emerging clusters in the high-tech sectors, positive demographic factors, and its political stability with a democratic system and independent judiciary.

Figure 8.15: Largest Barriers to Innovation in the IT Sector

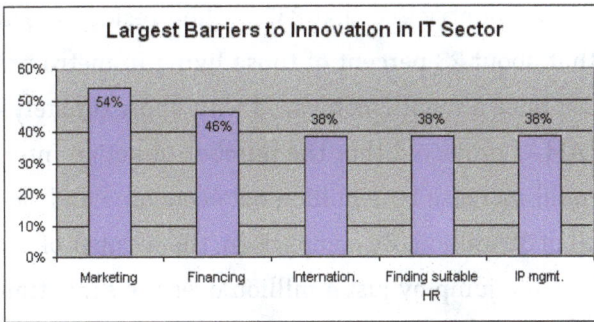

Source: Hamburg University of Technology

INTERNET PENETRATION AND DATA USAGE

India is already undergoing a full-fledged digital transformation, but substantial obstacles to growth still remain. Right now the country can best be described as a place of vast future upside potential. Internet penetration in India remains quite low to date at fewer than 9 percent of the population and actually trails the US and China in terms of the total number of Internet users. This is due to the large population, lack of electricity in rural areas, and issues of cost and infrastructure.

While recent economic growth has helped to develop a larger middle class in the nation, a sharp divide remains between the various groups within the Indian socioeconomic class structure. The economies of the most populous cities, often referred to as the metros, are outpacing those of the more rural areas. Therefore, this gap is reflected in the country's Internet usage.

The Internet and Mobile Association of India (IAMAI) reported that in June 2012, 71 percent of active Internet users—now 80 million people— were in cities, while the remaining 31 million lived in rural areas. Relying on census figures, the IAMAI estimated that 339 million people lived in urban areas of the country and that 833 million resided in rural sections. That means that about 23 percent of those living in metro areas used the Internet at least once a month, compared with approximately 4 percent in rural areas. IAMAI projected that the number of active Internet users in rural areas would increase by 7 million between June and December 2012 to reach a total of 38 million. By comparison, the number of active Internet users in cities would jump by just 4 million over the same time period, reflecting the urban market maturity.

Figure 8.16: Internet Users and Penetration in India, 2011–2016

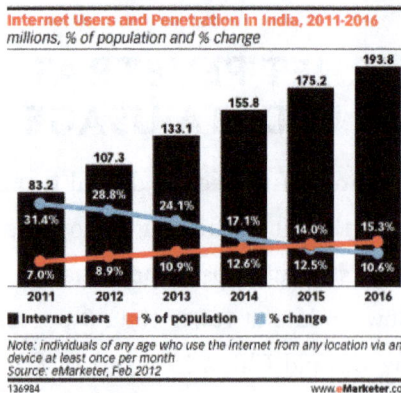

Internet Users and Penetration in India, 2011-2016
millions, % of population and % change

	2011	2012	2013	2014	2015	2016
Internet users	83.2	107.3	133.1	155.8	175.2	193.8
% change	28.8%	24.1%	17.1%	14.0%	15.3%	
% of population	31.4%	8.9%	10.9%	12.6%	12.5%	10.6%

Note: individuals of any age who use the internet from any device at least once per month
Source: eMarketer, Feb 2012
136984   www.eMarketer.com

Source: eMarketer (2012)

IT MARKET SALARIES

A D&B study provides interesting insight into the major concerns facing the ITES industry. The most pressing issue is the continuously rising salary levels, and not the appreciating rupee or the attrition rate. In fact, a majority of the profiled companies ranked rising salary levels as the factor affecting, or likely to affect, the growth of the industry. This is followed by the rising rupee, a shortage of skilled manpower, and the removal of tax sops. Labor attrition is ranked as the fifth-biggest issue. About 51 percent of the profiled companies feel that the attrition rate will continue to be more than 20 percent.

Figure 8.17: Major Concerns Likely to Affect ITES-BPO Industry

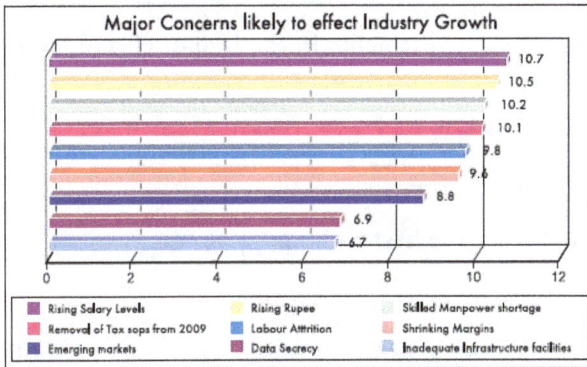

Source: D&B India

INVESTMENTS

Core competencies and strengths in the field of IT have placed India on the international canvas, attracting investments from advanced industrialized countries. According to data released by the Department of Industrial Policy and Promotion, the computer software and hardware sector attracted FDI worth US$13,238.58 million between April 2000 and September

2014. Companies have also spent a large amount on training for the IT-BPO sector.

Figure 8.18: Training Expenditure by Indian IT-BPO Sector

Source: IBEF (2014)

Some of the major investments in the Indian IT and ITeS sector are as follows:

♦ Microsoft began offering its commercial and cloud services—Azure and Office 365—from three local data centers at the end of 2015, making it the first technology company to set up cloud data centers in India.

♦ Infosys plans to invest Rs 1,400 crore (US$228.04 million) in a campus for its workers to be built in Noida, Uttar Pradesh. The project is estimated to generate 35,000 direct and indirect jobs.

♦ Cognizant has acquired US-based digital marketing agency Cadient Group. The latter is expected to boost Cognizant's presence in the healthcare segment.

♦ Visa set up a technology center in India in 2014 and joined a host of global system players who have established technology centers in the country to access its software and engineering talent.

♦ Genpact, Ltd., has signed an agreement with the US-based Automation Anywhere to provide automated business processes for its clients.

♦ Nielsen India has acquired Indicus Analytics. This acquisition will add to Nielsen's capabilities for macro- and microeconomic research for the public and private sectors.

GOVERNMENT INITIATIVES

The government of India has played a key role in publicly funding a vast, well-trained pool of engineers and management personnel to forge the Indian IT industry. Government spending on IT reached US$7.2 billion in 2015, a 5 percent increase over 2014, according to a report by Gartner, Inc. Some of the major initiatives taken by the government to promote the IT and ITES sector in India are as follows:

♦ The government of India, through the Board of Approval under the Union Ministry of Commerce and Industry, has approved a plan by Wipro, Ltd., to set up a special economic zone in Visakhapatnam.

♦ The government of India has launched the .bharat domain name, which will cover eight languages. The domain will help to bridge the digital divide and improve the Internet's reach in remote villages.

♦ The government of Andhra Pradesh and Google India have signed a memorandum of understanding to launch a number of initiatives aimed at bridging the state's digital divide and enabling skill development.

♦ The governments of Karnataka and Nasscom plan to launch a series of new initiatives to help shore up the local startup and technology ecosystem in the state, including plans to build one of

Asia's largest startup warehouses and the country's first "hack-celerator." This is an event where hackers meet entrepreneurs to team up on new business ventures.

♦ The central government and the respective state governments collectively spent US$6.4 billion on IT products and services in 2014, an increase of 4.3 percent over 2013, according to a study by Gartner.

THE ROAD AHEAD

India continues to be the top offshore destination for IT companies, followed by China and Malaysia. Leading IT service firms are expanding their traditional offerings in India to include research and development, product development, and other niche services.

Emerging technologies present a whole gamut of opportunities for IT firms in India. Social, mobility, analytics, and cloud (SMAC) collectively provide a US$1 trillion opportunity. Cloud represents the largest opportunity under SMAC, increasing at a CAGR of approximately 30 percent to around US$650–700 billion by 2020. Social media is the second-most lucrative segment for IT firms, offering a US$250 billion market opportunity by 2020.

9

REAL ESTATE

OVERVIEW

The real estate industry, which is an integral part of the Indian economy, is undergoing challenging times. Traditional methodologies have been put to test, providing an exciting phase for developers to evaluate new growth channels. The sector, riding high on the back of rapid urbanization, positive demographics, and increasing income levels, has attracted significant investment over the past few years. Between 2009 and 2011 real estate grew at about 8 percent but witnessed a deceleration to about 6.5 percent during 2012 to 2013, due to the sluggish growth of the Indian economy, rising input costs, and overall global economic sentiments. Currently, real estate contributes about 5 percent of India's GDP and the total revenue generated in FY 2011 stood at US$66.8 billion.

Figure 9.1: Market Size of Real Estate in India (USD billion)

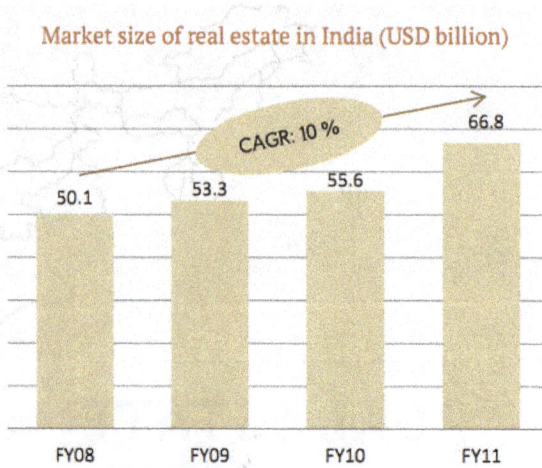

Market size of real estate in India (USD billion)

CAGR: 10 %

	50.1	53.3	55.6	66.8
	FY08	FY09	FY10	FY11

Source: BMI, Aranca Research

The real estate sector assumed greater prominence with the liberalization of the economy, as the consequent increase in business opportunities and labor migration led to rising demand for commercial and housing space. At present, the real estate and construction sectors are playing a crucial role in the overall development of India's core infrastructure. The growth of the real estate industry is linked to developments in the retail, hospitality, and entertainment industries (hotels, resorts, cinemas); economic services (hospitals, schools); and information technology enabled services (call centers).

The Indian real estate sector has traditionally been dominated by a number of small regional players with relatively low levels of expertise and/or financial resources. Historically, the sector has not benefited from institutional capital; instead it has traditionally tapped high net-worth individuals and other informal sources of financing, which has led to a lack of transparency. This scenario underwent a change in line with the sector's growth. Today, the real estate industry's dynamic reflects consumers' expectation for higher quality with India's increasing integration with the global economy.

HOUSING SHORTAGE

The housing shortage in urban India stood at 20.5 million in 2010, while the housing shortage in rural India stood at 26 million in 2010. The housing shortages in both urban and rural India were around 21.7 and 19.7 million units, respectively, in 2014. There has been a significant increase in real estate activity in two-tier cities like Indore, Raipur, Ahmadabad, Jaipur, and others. This has opened new avenues of growth for the sector.

Figure 9.2: Urban-Rural Housing Shortage (million)

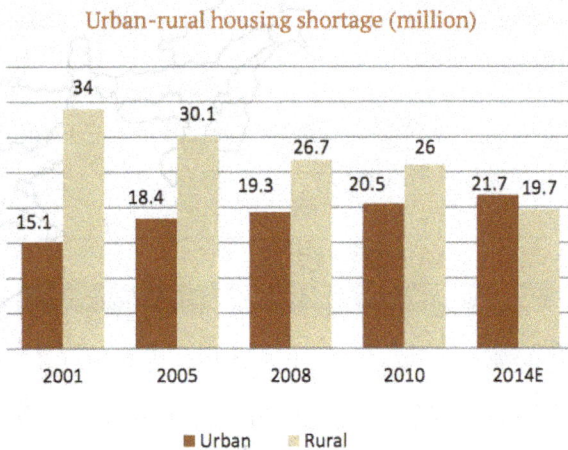

Source: BMI, CRISIL, ARANCA Research

INDIA'S HOUSING BOOM

From 2002 to 2007, housing prices in India rose rapidly. The rise was supported by strong economic growth, urbanization, inadequate infrastructure in city centers, lack of planning, and antiquated land laws. From 2005 to 2007, the economy grew at 8.9 percent per annum, making it one of the world's fastest-growing economies, following on from 7.6 percent per annum growth from 2003 to 2004.

India has witnessed the sharpest appreciation in real estate prices in the last couple of years, according to data from the Global Property Guide, an organization that collates real estate data from across the world. Compared to cities in forty-three other countries, property prices in Delhi witnessed the steepest appreciation, at roughly 60 percent. Interestingly, while this data set only has information for Delhi, official data on Indian cities suggest that Jaipur has seen an even faster rise in residential property prices, at 67 percent over this period.

Figure 9.3: World's Biggest Percentage Change in Property Prices (2011–2013)

BIGGEST GAINERS

% CHANGE IN PROPERTY PRICES (Q-1 2011 to Q-1 2013)			
India-Delhi	60	Jaipur	67
Brazil-Sao Paulo	43	Delhi	60
Hong Kong	33	Pune	49
UAE-Dubai	28	Chennai	42
Turkey	26	Bhopal	38
Estonia	23	Mumbai	27
Phillipines- Makati-CBD	17	Faridabad	25
Norway	13	Bengaluru	24
Iceland	12	Lucknow	17
Indonesia	11	Ahmedabad	16

Source: Residex (2013)

The price increases were accompanied by interest rates that fell as low as 7.5 percent from early 2004 until 2005. By 2006 a small speculative boom had been set off, and residential properties in Mumbai cost one hundred times the average annual income. Developers' capital rapidly grew as their stock prices increased, and they used it to make high bids for huge plots of land, making it relatively easy to sell properties at very high prices.

During the world economic downturn in 2008, demand for luxury housing fell 50 percent. Housing prices in Delhi fell by as much as 13.08 percent during 2009. Developers refocused on building low-income homes, but India's economy quickly rebounded, and housing prices soon started rising again—supported by an accommodating central bank.

Knight Frank's Global House Price Index is published quarterly and tracks the performance of mainstream national housing markets around the world. Even as global housing prices recorded a growth of a mere 0.9 percent in 2011–12, India saw 12 percent growth in the same period, according to the report shown in Figure 9.4.

Figure 9.4: Knight Frank Global House Price Index

KNIGHT FRANK GLOBAL HOUSE PRICE INDEX

Price change in %

Rank	Country	April 2011–March 2012
1	Brazil	23.50
2	Estonia	13.90
3	India	12.00
4	Austria	11.00
5	Germany	9.80
6	Colombia	9.60
7	Turkey	8.70
8	Russia	8.20
9	Iceland	7.30
10	Canada	6.80
11	Malaysia	6.60
12	Switzerland	6.30
13	Norway	6.30
14	Malta	6.20
15	Luxembourg	5.60

Source: Knight Frank Report

Source: Knight Frank report (2012)

Affordable housing is deemed affordable to those with a median household income as rated by the country, state (province), region, or municipality using a recognized Housing Affordability Index. In India, it is estimated that in 2009–2010, approximately 32 percent of the population was living below the poverty line (66) and there is a huge demand for affordable housing. The deficit in urban housing is estimated at 18 million units, most of which are among the economically weaker sections of society. Some developers are building low-cost and affordable housing for this population. The government of India has taken up various initiatives for developing low-cost and affordable properties. They have also looked at a PPP model for development of these properties.

Figure 9.5: Indian Real Estate Affordability Index

IMPROVED AFFORDABILITY

1 Lac = 1,00,000

Representation of property price estimates	Affordability equals property prices by annual income

Source: HDFC, Ltd.

INDIA'S MOST POPULOUS CITIES

MUMBAI

Mumbai experiences urbanization challenges similar to those of other fast-growing cities in developing countries—there are wide disparities in housing among the affluent, middle-income, and low-income segments of the population.

Highly desirable neighborhoods such as Colaba, Malabar Hill, Marine Drive, Bandra, and Juhu house professionals, industrialists, Bollywood movie stars, and expatriates. Upscale flats have three or more bedrooms, ocean views, tasteful interior decoration, parking for luxury cars, and sleeping quarters for maids and cooks. Only a tiny fraction of Mumbai's population lives in these luxury high-rises. In 2007, Mumbai condominiums were the priciest in the developing world at around US$ 9,000 to US$ 10,200 per square meter. In Mumbai there are more than 1,500 high-rise buildings that are in the planning stages, constructed, or under construction.

Despite recent economic growth, a huge segment of the population is still in poverty, unemployed, and living poor housing conditions. With available space at a premium, working-class Mumbai residents often reside in cramped, poor quality, yet relatively expensive housing, usually far from their workplaces. Despite this, Mumbai's economic boom continues to attract migrants in search of opportunities from across the country. The number of migrants from outside Maharashtra was 1.12 million from 1991 to 2001, which amounted to a 54.8 percent net addition to the population of Mumbai.

Over 9 million people, over 60 percent of the population of Mumbai, live in informal housing or slums. The growth rate of slums in Mumbai is greater than the general urban growth rate. Slums are temporary and illegal shelters used by those in extreme poverty. In India, slum dwellers are organized and have political clout. Politicians actively seek their votes during elections. Although more than half the population of Mumbai live in slums, they cover only 6 to 8 percent of the city's land area.

The *Financial Times* writes, "Dharavi is the grand panjandrum of the Mumbai slums." Dharavi, Asia's second-largest slum, is located in central Mumbai and houses over 1 million people. Slums are a well-known part of the city and have even become a growing tourist attraction in Mumbai despite the city's efforts toward modernization and development.

Most of the remaining urban population lives in chawls and on footpaths. Chawls are a quintessentially Mumbai phenomenon of multistory tenements. They are typically of a slightly higher quality than slums. Eighty percent of chawl residences have only one room. The term "pavement dwellers" refers to people who live in dwellings built on the footpaths and pavement of city streets. These are temporary structures made of cloth, cardboard, and sometimes wood and cement.

Rent control laws have helped to create a housing shortage. Most of the investors are looking to invest in ongoing real estate projects to get maximum returns. Figure 9.6 below shows the changes in property prices in Mumbai between 2003 and 2009.

Figure 9.6: Property Prices in Mumbai between 2003 and 2009

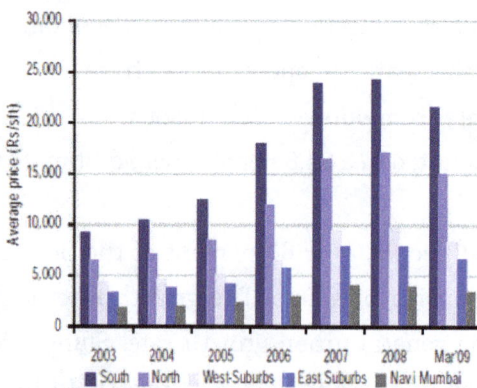

Source: India Real Estate (2009)

DELHI

Delhi has witnessed rapid suburban growth over the past decade. South Delhi, Gurgaon, and Noida have added thousands of apartment buildings, houses, shopping centers, and highways. New Delhi's famous Lutyens bungalows house the prime minister, members of his cabinet, top political and government leaders, military officials, senior judges, and top bureaucrats. New Delhi is also home to thousands of diplomatic staff of foreign countries and the United Nations. With India's growth, Delhi has developed into a business center, especially for outsourcing, IT consultancy, high tech, research, education, and healthcare services. Employees of these institutions are the source of growing demand for high-end housing provided by major builders such as Delhi Land & Finance. Roughly 18.7 percent of Delhi's population lives in slums, according to 2001 government statistics.

BANGALORE

In the 1990s the information technology boom hit Bangalore. Y2K projects in America's IT industry resulted in shortages of skilled computer scientists and systems programmers. Bangalore has transformed into the Silicon Valley of India with the creation of over 500,000 well-paying jobs for young college graduates. The demographics of the city changed; new high-rise residential buildings were built, campus-style office parks sprouted up, vast shopping centers began to thrive, streets became crowded with new cars, and gated expatriate housing estates emerged. Despite these changes, roughly 3 percent of Bangalore's population still lives in slums.

KOLKATA (CALCUTTA)

The most sought-after neighborhoods of Calcutta are generally centered on Park Street, Camac Street, Lower Circular Road, Sarat Bose Road, Salt Lake, Ballygunge, Anwar Shah Road, Chowringhee, and Golf Green. A recent building boom has converted sprawling British-era bungalows into high-rise condominiums and apartment buildings with modern amenities.

Kolkata is currently second to Mumbai in the number of high-rises and tall buildings. The highest of them is under construction and will be fifty stories when it is completed. New suburbs are constantly being developed in Rajarhat and along the Eastern Metropolitan Bypass. Once completed, these suburbs will include condominiums, complete with penthouses, many of which were designed primarily for nonresident Indians, expats, and wealthy residents. The tallest buildings in the city, the South City Towers, are also condominiums.

CHENNAI

In Chennai, houses are generally quite modernized. A basic single- or sometimes double-occupation flat in Chennai consists of a single bedroom with a hall, kitchen, and attached washroom. This ranges from one bedroom to five bedrooms or even eight bedrooms. According to a survey carried out by the census in 2011, of the large cities in India, Chennai has the second-lowest slum population, at 10 percent, after Bangalore.

HYDERABAD

In Hyderabad, housing in the twenty-first century is more modernized and developed than it was in the past. The housing sector in Hyderabad has a relatively sophisticated infrastructure and is suitable for gated communities and villas, as well as above-standard flats and condominiums. Hyderabad is home to several skyscrapers, including the Botanika and Lodha Belezza. Many residential infrastructure companies are well established in Hyderabad.

RESIDEX

The National Housing Bank launched the Residex, a housing price index, in 2007. It started with a few cities and is gradually expanding to cover tier one and tier two cities in India. Figure 9.7 below shows the residential real estate returns according to Residex data from 2007 to 2012.

Figure 9.7: Residential Real Estate Returns per Residex Data, 2007–2012

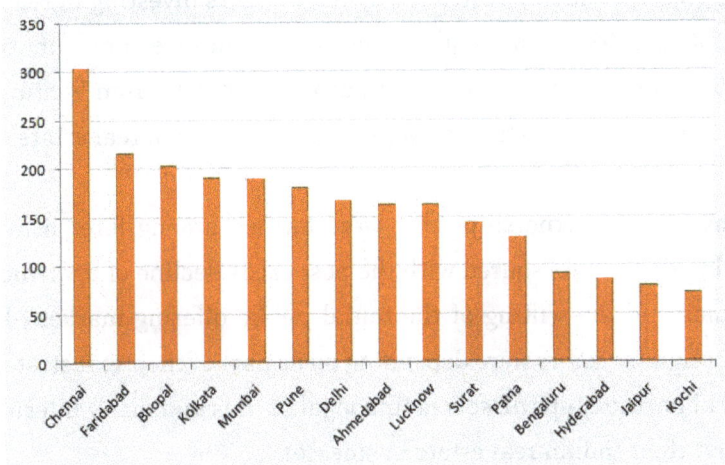

Source: Residex National Housing Bank

Figure 9.8 below shows the Residex values for the cities of Delhi, Bangalore, Mumbai, Bhopal, and Kolkata. These five cities were featured in the National Housing Bank's pilot study to examine the feasibility of preparing such an index at the national level.

Figure 9.8: Residex Values for Five Indian Cities

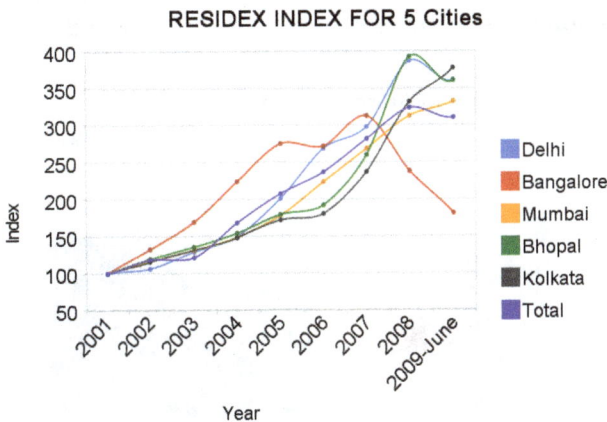

Source: Chauhan (2013)

Foreign investors flocked to India after the government passed new laws in 2005, greatly reducing restrictions on foreigners investing in real estate. From 2006 to 2008, private-equity funds and other investors pumped more than $15 billion into Indian property, according to data from Venture Intelligence. Sometimes investments were made directly into real estate companies.

Many of the partnerships that were formed among foreign investors and Indian developers soured with the post crisis decline of apartment and office sales and the wilting of the initial public offering market—both of which foreign investors were depending on as part of their exit strategies. A number of partnerships dissolved into legal battles and many international firms shut their Indian real estate businesses.

Today, developers and foreign investors believe the real estate sector in India is poised for a turnaround. They expect the government to undertake much-needed reforms that will help boost the economy, creating spending power for buyers and, ultimately, demand for both residential and commercial real estate (Anand, 2014).

Drawing data from the Residex chart for the five Indian cities mentioned above, the CAGR return for these cities could be calculated for 2001 to mid-2009. This is shown in Figure 9.9 below.

Figure 9.9: Average Return in Real Estate in India

Source: Chauhan (2013)

Favorable demographics, along with a large population of young people, rapid urbanization, and rising income levels are some of the key drivers of the Indian real estate market. Interest in the real estate market is not limited to domestic demand, as foreign investors and Indian expatriate community continue to invest in the sector. Figure 9.10 below shows the most popular growth drivers for Indian real estate in 2014.

Figure 9.10: Growth Drivers for Indian Real Estate

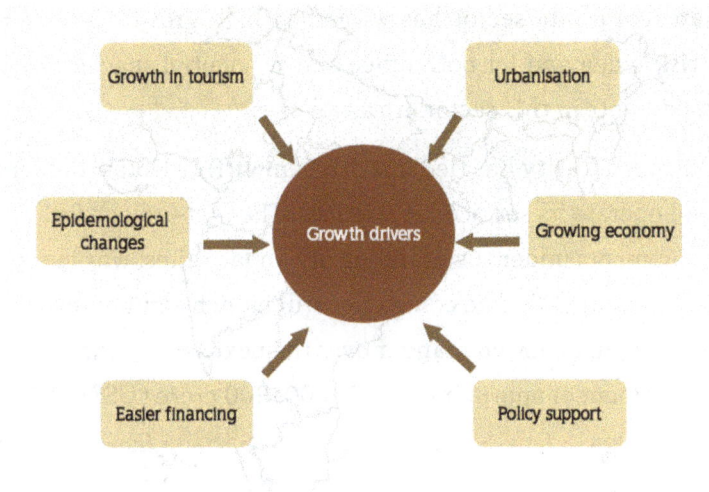

Source: IBEF (2014)

The Indian real estate sector has traditionally been an unorganized sector; however, with foreign investments and an increased number of corporate houses entering the sector, it is slowly evolving into a more organized one. In addition to the traditional asset classes, such as residential, commercial, and hotels, several new asset classes, such as student housing, senior citizen homes, luxury homes, holiday homes, and educational institutions are on the rise. Government policies have been instrumental in providing support to deal with sales volume, the increasing cost of raw material, reduction in margin pressure, and a strict regulatory environment.

With international real estate players making their foray into the Indian market, there have been multiple international best practices. Continued growth in this sector will require the introduction of a real estate investment trust and the phasing out of restrictive regulatory norms relating to foreign direct investment.

INVESTMENTS

The Indian real estate sector has witnessed high growth in recent times with the rising demand for both office and residential spaces. Some of the major investments in this sector are as follows:

◆ Assotech Realty has tied up with Lemon Tree Hotels to manage and operate its serviced residences. The first project, 210 apartments under the branding of Sandal Suites, was launched in Noida in 2015. The companies will launch eight to ten similar projects in a phased manner over the next seven years with an investment of approximately Rs 800–900 crore (US$129.37–145.57 million).

◆ Blackstone Group LP is all set to become the largest owner of commercial office real estate in India after a three-year acquisition drive in which it spent US$900 million to buy prime assets. Blackstone has acquired 29 million square feet of office space in cities such as Bengaluru, Pune, Mumbai, and Noida on the outskirts of New Delhi.

◆ L&T Infra Finance private equity plans to raise Rs 3,750 crore (US$606.54 million) in an overseas and domestic fund and launch a real estate fund.

◆ Infrastructure Development Finance Company Alternatives, Ltd., has sold two of its real estate investments to the private equity firm Blackstone Group LP. The assets—a special economic zone in

Pune and an information technology park in Noida—were sold for a combined enterprise value of Rs 1,100 crore (US$177.92 million).

♦ Goldman Sachs plans to invest Rs 1,200 crore (US$194.1 million) to build a new campus in Bengaluru that can accommodate 9,000 people. The new campus is being developed in collaboration with Kalyani Developers on the Sarjapur Outer Ring Road, Bengaluru.

♦ Snapdeal has entered into a strategic partnership with Tata Value Homes to sell the latter's apartments on its e-commerce platform. This is the first time an e-commerce company has tied itself to a real estate venture in India.

Total FDI in the construction development sector from April 2000 to April 2014 stood at around US$23.38 billion (Figure 9.11).

Figure 9.11: FDI in Construction Development Sector as a Percentage of India's Total FDI

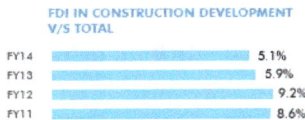

FDI IN CONSTRUCTION DEVELOPMENT
V/S TOTAL

FY14	5.1%
FY13	5.9%
FY12	9.2%
FY11	8.6%

Source: IBEF (2014)

GOVERNMENT INITIATIVES

According to M. Venkaiah Naidu, union minister of housing and urban poverty alleviation, "Under the Sardar Patel Urban Housing Mission, 30 million houses will be built by 2022, mostly for the economically weaker sections and low-income groups, through public-private-partnership, interest subsidy, and increased flow of resources to the housing sector."

The government of India and state governments have taken several initiatives to encourage the development in this sector. Some of them are as follows:

♦ The Securities and Exchange Board of India has announced final regulations that will govern real estate investment trusts and infrastructure investment trusts. This move will enable easier access to funds for cash-strapped developers and create a new investment avenue for institutions, high net-worth individuals, and eventually ordinary investors.

♦ The Telangana Real Estate Developers' Association (Treda) plans to host the Fifth Treda Property Show 2014 at Hitex Centre, Hyderabad. The show will be open to various groups, including prospective property purchasers, investors, architects, and others.

♦ The state government of Kerala has decided to make the process of securing construction permits smoother. It will be possible to go through the process online with the launch of software called Sanketham. This will ensure a more standardized procedure, more transparency, and less corruption and bribery.

♦ The government of India has proposed to release the Real Estate (Development and Regulation) Bill, which aims to protect consumer interests and introduce standardization in business practices and transactions in the sector. The bill will also enable domestic and foreign investment to flow into the sector.

THE ROAD AHEAD

As the Indian economy grows, the real estate sector continues to benefit. With the increase in foreign tourist arrivals every year, there is demand for real estate in the tourism and hospitality sector. Also, with the entry of major private players in the education sector, the large cities—Hyderabad, Bengaluru, Mumbai, Delhi, Pune, Chennai, and Kolkata—are likely to account for 70 percent of total demand for real estate in the education sector (shown in Figure 9.12 below).

Figure 9.12: Real Estate Demand in the Education Sector

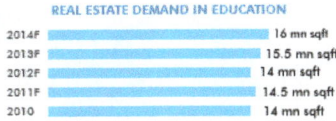

REAL ESTATE DEMAND IN EDUCATION

2014F	16 mn sqft
2013F	15.5 mn sqft
2012F	14 mn sqft
2011F	14.5 mn sqft
2010	14 mn sqft

Source: IBEF (2014)

CONCLUSION

THE INDUS VALLEY CIVILIZATION dates back more than 5,000 years. Archeologists have discovered bricks, bronze metals, and underground drainage systems, which existed in the prehistoric period. Present-day Afghanistan and Pakistan were once part of ancient India. Under Emperor Asoka of the Mauryan Empire (324–187 BCE), Taxila, in today's Afghanistan, was its capital, and the Taxila University was the oldest university in the world.

India's contributions to mathematics, astronomy, medicine, languages, and other areas of study are well known. The Indian subcontinent, through the centuries, experienced migrations, frequent invasions, and was colonized by the Moghuls, British, Dutch, and French; however, India and the Indian subcontinent have retained their unique cultural identity through the ages. Trade and cultural exchanges flourished through historical times.

The big question: Why has India, with her rich cultural heritage, not progressed in the application of science and technology, which in turn can translate into sustained overall development across the subcontinent? Countries that were late adopters of science and technology, for example, South Korea and Singapore, have done especially well with technology-induced development. The adoption gap still exists in India. Why? This is the conversation this book hopes to inspire in readers, perhaps reaching out to a general audience as well as scholars.

Sustained development is a commitment that requires all members of a society to participate in some measure. Work and professionalism are central to development in both agriculture and industrial sectors. Agriculture is a necessity for survival and for healthy living, but industrial production requires the application of science and technology, and exporting manufactured goods necessitates innovation and creativity for competitive advantage. In this sense, India's public policy, domestic markets, and private corporations are not providing the leadership—the institutions, including the educational system, are not keeping pace with international standards.

GDP is an overall measure of country's development and serves well to capture the creation of goods and services, on a yearly basis. However, GDP does not capture the lack of electricity or interrupted service, poor or inadequate roads for automobiles or trucks, lack of proper education and healthcare for the poor, and the lack of access to adequate drinking water for most of the day. For a country of more than one billion people, these challenges are enormous. On the whole, modern India, the largest liberal democracy in the world, has done well and is improving the delivery of the aforementioned services for her people.

This book is about opening the dialogue on India's management of organizations at all levels, including both government and nongovernment institutions. Development has multidimensional inputs and constituencies—and, of course, education, housing, electricity, manufacturing, healthcare, and others play a role. How could we frame these issues for discussion and debate? Yes, there are tough choices to be made, and yes, budgets have to be prioritized and allocated judiciously in the face of competing needs.

Development is also about intergenerational commitment and choices—that is, accumulated knowledge is passed onto succeeding generations. In education, the skills taught and learned should be relevant to local conditions and the needs of India and are to be practiced today and improved upon in the future. Are graduates applying for productive jobs and creating quality products and services in India? Do we measure their contributions or successes? How many masters and doctoral theses are applied to Indian contexts and conditions? How do the incentive systems work to promote high quality and productivity?

The title of the book, *India's Development Dilemma: Productivity or Bureaucracy?* poses this issue. What's the rationale for framing development as the choice between productivity and bureaucracy? It is because, for far too long, Indian leadership at all levels has treated development as a "feel-good phenomenon," and not as an inter-generational concept. Leadership should embrace the legacy that one generation leaves behind for succeeding generations. Ancient India, in many ways, has left its contributions in languages, arts, public planning, engineering, know-how in temple architecture, music, and other traditions, including religions. These are strengths and a lasting legacy for the Indian subcontinent.

In the application of science and technology for creating goods and services, there appear to be intergenerational deficits. The productivity in farming and agricultural products has not kept pace since the turn of nineteenth century, but recent efforts have improved this sector. In other industries, such as textiles, retail, transportation, real estate, banking, engineering, machinery, biotechnology, and information technology performance, productivity, and quality standards are uneven. Both government and private organizations are steeped in bureaucracy. The government has also created a work culture that is immune to productivity and a reward system that promotes lethargy and wastefulness. The K–12 educational systems and higher education do not promote creativity, innovation, and excellence. In many modern Indian households televisions, refrigerators, washers, dryers, laptops, and mobile phones are mostly imported. This means that in the supply chains of high-technology products, the exporting countries benefit, while Indian manufacturers suffer and do not participate in the knowledge creation for making such high-tech products. This deprives a generation of talented engineers of the know-how to make computers, mobile phones, cars, planes, and robots. It also means they will not have the knowledge to pass on to the next generation.

In the introduction, I mentioned that most institutions, such as courts, governmental agencies, and law enforcement, are riddled with perverse incentive structures, and therefore accountability is almost impossible. What is a perverse incentive? It is an incentive for inaction in the face of professional duty; for example, delaying the completion of work is rewarded, because someone gets paid beyond formal contractual obligations. By withholding performance on time, the threat of nonperformance is rewarded. This may not be the case in general, but excessive bureaucracy can tolerate nonperformance or delayed performance. For example, excessive teacher absences and the lack of relevant and practical curriculum in K-12. In the retail industry, the present structure needs to be improved, while at the same time keeping the Indian consumer and shopping culture intact and providing access to rural and urban populations.

PRODUCTIVITY OR BUREAUCRACY

India, in comparison to other dynamic modern economies, has a high level of bureaucracy in national, regional, and local governmental agencies. The governance of institutions, both public and private, is impacted by bureaucratic structure. It is clear that high productivity and minimal regulation with domestic demand for quality goods and services can lead to sustained development. Of course, this also requires political stability, rule of law, and executive leaderships from both private and public officials. This can be a tall order, but it is doable.

The manufacturing exports in developing countries have grown tremendously in recent years. Since the 1980s, developing countries are shaping their export pattern from commodities to manufacturing. The noteworthy effect is that they are accumulating a high rate of human and physical capital. Technology is also a factor in both human and physical capital accumulation in developing countries. India has a lesson to learn: these sustained economic developments due to productivity increases in manufacturing and agriculture sectors can provide a strategic path.

Development, in its broadest sense, occurs due to sustained application of accumulated knowledge passed on from one generation to the next. Yes, all societies, in some measure have undergone positive changes and development; however, in today's digitally globalized world, development has come under scrutiny. This book calls for a fresh look at what development is and what it might become if we carefully study bureaucracy and productivity and examine the measures that impact the outcomes of various Indian industries, businesses, and governmental agencies. With population increases, advances in healthcare, and the longevity of human lives, sovereign nations, including today's India, face challenges that earlier generations never encountered. Fortunately, with the globalization of knowledge, different countries and cultures have opportunities to learn from each other—and India can adapt and augment her past values with today's management strategy.

India, a country rich in resources, history, and culture, has the potential to be a major world power. It is clear from the data that one of the major factors holding the country back is the regulatory interference of its own government. Sectors where government policies are more liberal in regard to FDI have shown impressive growth. For example, India is a global competitor in the areas of biotechnology, Information Technology, and steel manufacturing. Sectors where there is greater government regulation, such as education and retail, are rife with inefficiencies. It's vital that India solves the issue of uneven development, because shortcomings in one area hamper growth in other areas; for example a lack of educational programs limits the number of qualified IT workers and antiquated systems for retail mean less profit for farmers in the agriculture sector.

Development of any nation is contextual to the country. It is a serious mistake to copy the prescriptions that work in other countries—including economic policies—and expect similar outcomes. India's domestic conditions are different from those of other countries. By and large, India has done well as the largest democracy in the world, but she can do better with improved work culture, enhanced productivity across all sectors, and professionalism among administrators, executives, and workers. Given the substantial population of young people, this will be a noble goal and a desirable one in the post digital world. When India solves its developmental dilemma and chooses productivity over bureaucracy, all of its citizens will thrive.

REFERENCES

Acharya, S., and R. L. Jogi (2004). "Farm Input Subsidies in Indian Agriculture." Institute of Development Studies Working Paper 140.

Costanza, R., M. Hart, S. Posner, and J. Talberth (2009). "Beyond GDP: The Need for New Measures of Progress." Pardee Paper no. 4.

Das, J., and J. Hammer (2004). "Money for Nothing: The Dire Straits of Medical Practice in India." Policy Research Working Paper 3269.

Fleurbaey, M. (2009). "Beyond GDP: The Quest for a Measure of Social Welfare." *Journal of Economic Literature,* 47(4), 1029–75.

Gole, S. (1990). "Size as a Measure of Importance in Indian Cartography." *Imago Mundi: The International Journal for the History of Cartography* 42(1): 99-105.

Government of India, Ministry of Finance (2004). "Central Government Subsidies in India: A Report."

Government of India, Planning Commission (2005). "Midterm Appraisal of 10th Five Year Plan (2002–2007)."

Kamau, C., and A. Rutland (2005). "The Global 'Order,' Socioeconomic Status and the Economics of African Identity." *African Identities* 3(2): 171–93.

Kremer, M., K. Muralidharan, N. Chaudhury, J. Hammer, and F. H. Rogers (2004). "Teacher Absence in India: A Snapshot." *Journal of the European Economic Association* 3(2–3): 658–67.

Kyrylych, K. (2013). "Problem of Uneven Economic Development of the World Economy: Essence and Causes." *Intellectual Economics* 7(3): 344–54.

Lewis, Martin W. (2010). "Uneven Economic Development in India." *GeoCurrents,* July 22

Mehta, P. B. (2003). *The Burden of Democracy.* Penguin: New Delhi.

Murgai, R., L. Pritchett, and M. Wes (2006). "India Development Policy Review—Inclusive Growth and Service Delivery: Building on India's Success." World Bank.

Paul, S. (2006). "Public Spending, Outcomes, and Accountability: Citizen Report Card as a Catalyst for Public Action." *Economic and Political Weekly* 41(4): 333–40.

Paul, S., S. Balakrishna, K. Gopakumar, S. Sekhar, and M. Vivekananda (2004). "State of India's Public Services: Benchmarks for the States." *Economic and Political Weekly* 39(9): 920—33.

Schwartzberg, Joseph E. (2008). "Maps and Mapmaking in India." In *Encyclopedia of the History of Science, Technology, and Medicine in Non-Western Cultures,* 2nd ed., edited by Helaine Selin, 1301–3. Springer.

Srinivasa Rao, A. (2011). "95 per Cent People below Poverty Line in Andhra Pradesh." *India Today,* December 17.

Valsan, B. (2014). "Continuous Water Supply a Massive Undertaking." *Times of India,* May 5.

World Bank (2003). "World Development Report 2004: Making Service Work for Poor People."

World Bank (2004). "India: Scaling Up Access to Finance for India's Rural Poor."

""World Bank (2006). "India: Development Policy Review—Public Health & Education; Lagging States; Sectors & People."

World Bank (2006). "Reforming Services in India: Drawing from Lessons of Success."

World Bank (2013). "India at a Glance."

World Bank (2014). "Citizen Report Cards."

World Bank (2014). "India Overview: Context, Strategy, Results".

World Bank (2014). "World Development Indicators—India."

AGRICULTURE

Cagliarini, A., & A. Rush (2011, June 1). "Economic Development and Agriculture in India." Retrieved November 23, 2014, from http://www.rba.gov.au/publications/bulletin/2011/jun/3.html

Chandrasekhar, C., and J. Ghosh (2011, August 9). "Women's Work in India: Has Anything Changed?" Retrieved November 23, 2014, from http://www.macroscan.org/fet/aug11/fet090811W.

Economic Survey, 2002—03 (2003, February 27). Retrieved November 24, 2014, from http://pib.nic.in/archive/ecosrvy/ecosrvy2003/ec.

"GDP of India" (2008, January 1). Trade Chakra. Retrieved November 23, 2014, from http://www.tradechakra.com/indian-economy/gdp.html.

"Indian Agro Products" (n.d.). India Exports and Business Trade Zone. Retrieved November 23, 2014, from http://www.india-exports.com/agro.html

"Land Use Map of India: National Institute of Hydrology" (2009, August 18). India Waterportal. Retrieved November 23, 2014, from http://www.indiawaterportal.org/articles/land-use-map-india-national-institute-hydrology.

NSSO (National Sample Survey Organization) (2006). "'Livestock Ownership across Operational Land Holding Classes in India, 2002–03.'", NSS Report no. 493.

World Bank (2004). "'India: Re-energizing the Agricultural Sector to Sustain Growth and Reduce Poverty.'" Report no. 27889-IN. Available at http://go.worldbank.org/BYIZWW8HO0.

World Bank (2014). Retrieved November 23, 2014, from http://databank.worldbank.org/data/views/reports/tableview.aspx.

TEXTILE

"A Brief Report On Textile Industry in India" (2014, May 1). Retrieved November 23, 2014, from http://www.cci.in/pdfs/surveys-reports/Textile-Industry-in-India.pdf.

Arumugam, S. (2013, June 25). "India's Textiles and Apparel Industry." Retrieved November 23, 2014, from http://www.citiindia.com/pdf/Overview of TC sector_June 2013.pdf.

Chellasamy, P., and K. Karuppaiah (n.d.). "An Analysis of Growth and Development of Textile Industry in India." Retrieved November 23, 2014, from http://www.fibre2fashion.com/industry-article/1/11/an-analysis-of-growth-and-development-of-textile-industry-in-india14.asp.

"Global Cotton Industry: Cotton Production and Consumption Worldwide" (2007, July 28). Retrieved November 23, 2014, from http://www.pbs.org/wnet/wideangle/episodes/the-dying-fields/global-cotton-industry/cotton-production-and-consumption-worldwide/1946/.

Sasi, A. (2014, July 3). "After Bangladesh Fire, India's Textile Exports to US up." Retrieved November 23, 2014, from http://archive.financialexpress.com/news/after-bangladesh-fire-india-s-textile-exports-to-us-up/1266372.

Textile Industry. (n.d.). "Country Wise Export of Hand Looms, 2002–03." Retrieved November 23, 2014, from http://www.texprocil.com/countrywise_exports.htm.

Textile Industry. (n.d.). Retrieved November 23, 2014, from http://www.dnb.co.in/Kolkata2008/Textile.asp.

"Textile Industry and Market Growth in India" (2014, October 1). Retrieved November 23, 2014, from http://www.ibef.org/industry/textiles.aspx

"Textile Industry in India" (n.d.). Retrieved November 23, 2014, from http://business.mapsofindia.com/india-industry/textile.html.

"Textile Industry Structure" (n.d.). Retrieved November 23, 2014, from http://www.india-crafts.com/business-reports/indian-textile-industry/textile-industry-structure.htm.

Textiles (n.d.). Retrieved November 23, 2014, from https://www.dnb.co.in/Axis_bank_SME_awards/Textiles.asp

Textiles and Apparel (2011, November 1). Retrieved November 23, 2014, from http://www.ibef.org/download/Textiles_and_Apparel50112.pdf.

RETAIL

"Frost & Sullivan Study Reveals India's Organized Retail Market Looks to Security Solutions as It Expects 44% Growth by 2012" (n.d.). Retrieved November 23, 2014, from http://www.sensormatic.com/instore/2009_Q1/fands.asp.

Hugh, E. (2008, February 9). "India Wholesale Inflation and Foreign Exchange Reserves." Retrieved November 23, 2014, from http://indiaeconomywatch.blogspot.com/2008/02/india-wholesale-inflation-february-9.html.

"Indian Retail Industry Overview" (n.d.). Retrieved November 23, 2014, from http://www.dnb.co.in/IndianRetailIndustry/overview.asp.

"India's Retail Market—Graphic of the Day" (n.d.). Retrieved November 23, 2014, from http://blog.thomsonreuters.com/index.php/indias-retail-market-graphic-of-the-day-2/.

"Retail Penetration in 2011" (2012, January 22). Retrieved November 23, 2014, from http://retailmantras.blogspot.com/2012/01/retail-penetration-in-2011.html.

BANKING

Anand, N. (2014, August 13). "Mobile Banking Zooms as India Gets Smarter." *Business Standard*. Retrieved March 2, 2015, from http://www.business-standard.com/article/finance/mobile-banking-zooms-as-india-gets-smarter-114081100826_1.html.

"Banking Sector in India" (2014, October 1). Retrieved November 23, 2014, from http://www.ibef.org/industry/banking-india.aspx.

"India Bank Loan Growth" (n.d.). Retrieved November 23, 2014, from http://www.tradingeconomics.com/india/loan-growth.

"Indian Banking Industry: An Excellent Long-Term Investment Option" (2012, May 9). Retrieved November 23, 2014, from http://www.economicsfanatic.com/2012/05/indian-banking-industry-excellent-long.html.

"India's Top Banks—Overview" (n.d.). Retrieved November 23, 2014, from http://www.dnb.co.in/topbanks_08/overview.asp.

"Monetizing Digital Media: Creating Value Consumers Will Buy—Who's Paying for Digital M&E?" (n.d.). Retrieved November 23, 2014, from http://www.ey.com/GL/en/Industries/Media---Entertainment/Monetizing-digital-media--creating-value-consumers-will-buy---Whos-paying-for-digital-M-E-.

SN, V. (2013, January 16). "Mobile Banking in India: Transactions vs. Amount Transacted in Nov 2012." Retrieved November 23, 2014, from http://www.medianama.com/2013/01/223-transactions-vs-amount-using-mobile-banking-india-nov-2012/.

ENGINEERING, MACHINERY AND TECHNOLOGY

"Engineering Industry in India" (2014, October 1). Retrieved November 23, 2014, from http://www.ibef.org/industry/engineering-india.aspx.

"Overview of India Engineering Industry" (n.d.). Retrieved November 23, 2014, from http://www.dnb.co.in/engineering/overview.asp.

"Heavy Engineering Equipment and Machine Tools Industry in India" (2013, June 24). Retrieved November 23, 2014, from http://swapsushias.blogspot.com/2013/06/heavy-engineering-equipment-and-machine.html#.VEkfWodptG4.

"India Exports of Electrical Machinery Etc." (n.d.). Retrieved November 23, 2014, from http://www.tradingeconomics.com/india/exports-of-electrical-machinery-etc.

"Automobile Industry in India" (2015, January 1). Retrieved February 19, 2015 from http://www.ibef.org/industry/india-automobiles.aspx.

"Biotechnology Industry in India" (2015, January 1). Retrieved February 19, 2015 from http://www.ibef.org/industry/biotechnology-india.aspx.

"Indian Pharmaceutical Industry" (2015, January 1). Retrieved February 19, 2015 from http://www.ibef.org/industry/pharmaceutical-india.aspx.

"Oil and Gas Industry in India" (2015, January 1). Retrieved February 19, 2015 from http://www.ibef.org/industry/oil-gas-india.aspx.

"Steel Industry in India" (2015, January 1). Retrieved February 19, 2015 from http://www.ibef.org/industry/steel.aspx.

Stephan, D. (2012, May 4). "Indian Specialty Chemical Industry Worth US $38 Billion in 2017." Retrieved November 23, 2014, from http://www.process-worldwide.com/management/markets_industries/articles/363065/.

"Chemical Industries in India" (n.d.). Retrieved November 23, 2014, from http://www.mapsofindia.com/maps/india/chemicalindustries.htm.

"India Exports of Miscellaneous Chemical Products" (n.d.). Retrieved November 23, 2014, from http://www.tradingeconomics.com/india/exports-of-miscellaneous-chemical-products.

"Trends in Commodity Exports" (n.d.). Retrieved November 23, 2014, from http://www.dnb.co.in/Exporters2012/Trends.asp.

"Chemical and Petrochemical" (n.d.). Retrieved November 23, 2014, from https://www.dnb.co.in/Axis_bank_SME_awards/Chemical_Petrochem.asp.

TRANSPORTATION

"4.7 Percent of Indian Households Own A Car" (2012, March 25). Retrieved November 24, 2014, from http://indiacharts.wordpress.com/2012/03/25/4-7-percent-of-indian-households-own-a-car/.

Srinath, P. (2013, July 2). "Hybrid Buses: An Exercise in Vanity Environmentalism." Retrieved November 24, 2014, from http://catalyst.nationalinterest.in/2013/07/02/hybrid-buses-vanity-environmentalism/.

"India Railway Map" (n.d.). Retrieved November 24, 2014, from http://www.mapsofindia.com/maps/india/india-railway-map.htm.

Dave, P. (2013, October 25). How Serious Are Indian States about '"Bus"'-Based '"Public Transport'?'" Retrieved November 24, 2014, from http://sustainablecitiescollective.com/pratik-dave/168386/JnNURM-India-bus-based-public-transportation

"WTO—International Trade Statistics for Commercial Services 2012—India Ranks Seventh" (2012, November 19). Retrieved November 24, 2014, from http://www.iitrade.ac.in/kmarticle. php?topic=WTO_-_International_Trade_Statistics_for_ Commercial_Services_2012_-_India_ranks_Seventh.

"Urban Passenger Travel Statistics in India" (2009, June 4). Retrieved November 24, 2014, from http://urbanemissions.blogspot. in/2009/06/urban-passenger-travel-statistics-in.html.

"India Domestic Airports" (n.d.). Retrieved November 24, 2014, from http://www.mapsofindia.com/air-network/domestic-airport-map. htm.

"Indian Airports Serve 169 Million Passengers in Last Year; Passenger Numbers Up 6% as AirAsia India Prepares to Launch" (2014, May 28). Retrieved November 24, 2014, from http://www.anna. aero/2014/05/28/indian-airports-serve-169-million-passengers-in-last-year/.

Singh, J. (2010, March 1). "Urban Transportation Market in India." Retrieved November 24, 2014, from http://www.slideshare.net/ jaaaspal/urban-transportation-market-in-india.

"Top Companies in India by Market Capitalization—BSE" (2014, November 21). Retrieved November 24, 2014, from http://www.moneycontrol. com/stocks/marketinfo/marketcap/bse/transport-logistics.html.

"Passenger Transport Demand—Outlook from WBCSD" (2007, August 29). Retrieved November 24, 2014, from http://www.eea.europa.eu/ data-and-maps/indicators/passenger-transport-demand-outlook-from-wbcsd/passenger-transport-demand-outlook-from-1.

Manshu. "India Registers First Quarter GDP Growth of 8.8%" (2010, September 1). Retrieved November 24, 2014, from http://www.onemint.com/2010/09/01/india-registers-first-quarter-gdp-growth-of-8-8/.

IT AND ITES

"Employability Gap in Indian IT Industry-Research Report" (2012, February 2). Retrieved November 23, 2014, from http://www.itpathshala.com/research-articles/employability-gap-in-indian-it-industry.php.

Heeks, R. (2010, January 5). "Indian IT Sector Statistics: 1980–2009 Time Series Data." Retrieved November 23, 2014, from http://ict4dblog.wordpress.com/2010/01/05/indian-it-sector-statistics-1980-2009-time-series-data/.

Madaan, M. (2012, March 9). "The Future of IT industry in India with Implication on the Recruitment Scenario." Retrieved November 23, 2014, from http://www.mmenterprises.co.in/hrblog/the-future-of-it-industry-in-india-with-implication-on-the-recruitment-scenario/.

"KPO Industry in India" (n.d.). Retrieved November 23, 2014, from http://www.socialproma.com/kpo-industry-in-india/.

"Software Technology Parks in India" (n.d.). Retrieved November 23, 2014, from http://www1.american.edu/initeb/mk5916a/cibercity.htm.

Tiwari, R. (n.d.). "Innovation Activities in India's IT Industry: Status Quo and Emerging Trends." Retrieved November 23, 2014, from http://www.global-innovation.net/projects/grd/india/ict/soft/.

"IT & ITeS Industry in India" (2014, October 1). Retrieved November 23, 2014, from http://www.ibef.org/industry/information-technology-india.aspx.

"A Brief Report on IT and ITES Industry in India" (2013, August 1).
   Retrieved November 23, 2014, from http://www.cci.in/pdfs/
   surveys-reports/IT-and-ITeS-Industry-in-India.pdf.

Deans, D. (2012, December 22). "Upside Market Potential for Internet
   Usage in India." Retrieved November 23, 2014, from
   http://blog.geoactivegroup.com/2012/12/upside-market-potential-
   for-internet.html.

"ITES and BPO Industry Insights" (n.d.). Retrieved November 23, 2014,
   from https://www.dnb.co.in/itesbpo/Industry Insights.asp.

Shetty, S. (2013, May 28). "Gartner Says Top Five Indian Providers Grew
   13.3 Percent In 2012, Exceeding Global IT Services Industry
   Growth Rate of 2 Percent." Retrieved November 23, 2014, from
   http://www.gartner.com/newsroom/id/2496815.

Illiyan, A. (2008). "Performance, Challenges and Opportunities of Indian
   Software Export." *Journal of Theoretical and Applied Information
   Technology* 4(11): 1108–6. Retrieved February 19 from http://www.
   jatit.org/volumes/research-papers/Vol4No11/11Vol4No11.pdf.

REAL ESTATE

Pawaskar, K. (2012, August 17). "Find the Best Real Estate Return in
   India—Residex." Retrieved November 23, 2014, from
   http://www.caporbit.com/real-estate-return-india-residex/.

"India Sees Third-Highest Rise in Housing Prices" (2012, June 6).
   Retrieved November 23, 2014, from http://www.business-standard.
   com/article/economy-policy/india-sees-third-highest-rise-in-
   housing-prices-112060600060_1.html.

Beniwal, H. (2012, December 2). "Can I Afford a House at Current
   Prices?" Retrieved November 23, 2014, from http://www.tflguide.
   com/2012/12/can-i-afford-a-house-at-current-prices.html.

"Delhi Leads World in Real Estate Price Rise" (n.d.). Retrieved November 23, 2014, from http://www.acreplus.in/news.php?id=15.

"Gurgaon—Registration Pricing" (2009, May 6). Retrieved November 23, 2014, from http://reliancesez.blogspot.in/2009_05_01_archive.html.

Chauhan, M. (n.d.). "A Close Look at Real Estate Returns in India." Retrieved November 23, 2014, from http://www.jagoinvestor.com/2009/12/returns-of-real-estate-in-india.html.

"Real Estate" (2013, March 1). Retrieved November 23, 2014, from http://www.ibef.org/download/Real-Estate-March-220313.pdf.

"India's House Prices Are Now Falling!" (2014, August 3). Retrieved March 3, 2015, from http://www.globalpropertyguide.com/Asia/India/Price-History.

"Indian Real Estate Industry" (2014, October 1). Retrieved November 23, 2014, from http://www.ibef.org/industry/real-estate-india.aspx.

Anand, S. (2014, August 5). "India Is Luring Real-Estate Investors Again." Retrieved March 3, 2015, from http://www.wsj.com/articles/india-is-luring-real-estate-investors-again-1407263766.

"Building New Dimensions for Real Estate Growth" (2013, September 1). Retrieved March 3, 2015, from http://www.ey.com/Publication/vwLUAssets/EY-Building-new-dimensions-for-real-estate-growth/$File/EY-Building-new-dimensions-for-real-estate-growth.pdf.

"NHB Residex" (n.d.). Retrieved March 3, 2015, from http://www.nhb.org.in/Residex/About_Residex.php.

LIST OF ABBREVIATIONS

AIVGA .... All India Vegetable Growers Association

ATM .... automated teller machine

BC .... business correspondent

BCA.. business correspondent agent

BCE.. Before the Common Era

BJP.. Bharatiya Janata Party

BMI ....Business Monitor International

BP... British Petroleum

BPO...business process outsourcing

CAGR...compound annual growth rate

CE.. Common Era

CGI.. Cancer Genetics, Inc.

CIFA.. Consortium of Indian Farmers Associations

CITI India...City Bank India

CSO.. Central Statistical Office

D&B .... Dun and Bradstreet

DBT.. Department of Biotechnology

DWT...deadweight ton

EIL ....Engineers India, Ltd.

EPC...engineering, procurement, and construction

FDI.. foreign direct investment

FY...fiscal year

GDP ....gross domestic product

GT .... gross tonnage

HDFC... Housing Development Finance Corporation

IAMAI....................................Internet and Mobile Association of India

IBEF .... India Brand Equity Foundation

iMaCS .... International Modal Analysis Conference

INR.. Indian rupees

IOCL .... Indian Oil Corporation, Ltd.

IT.. information technology

ITES .... information technology enabled service

JnNURM .... Jawaharlal Nehru National Urban Renewal Mission

JSW.. Jindal South West Holding, Ltd.

JV..joint venture

KCI ....Kanoria Chemicals & Industries, Ltd.

KOC .... Kuwait Oil Company

KPMG ....Klynveld Peat Marwick Goerdeler

KPO ....knowledge process outsourcing

LNG..liquefied natural gas

M&A ....Mergers and Acquisitions

MMbpd ....million barrels per day

MMF ....Man-made fibers

MMT ....million metric tons

MNC... Multinational company

MT.. million ton

Mtoe.. million tons of oil equivalent

MTPA.. million tons per annum

NASSCOM .... National Association of Software and Services Companies

NPCI .... National Payments Corporation of India

NSSO ....National Sample Survey Office

OVL .... ONGC Videsh Ltd.

PC..personal computer

PCPIR.............. petroleum chemicals and petrochemical investment region

PPP ....purchasing power parity

PSU .... public-sector undertaking

PWC.. PricewaterhouseCoopers

R&D	research and development
RBI	Reserve Bank of India
RIL	Reliance Industries, Ltd.
SAIL	Steel Authority of India, Ltd.
SBI	State Bank of India
SCB	scheduled commercial bank
SDF	Steel Development Fund
SIAM	Society of Indian Automobile Manufacturers
SMAC	social, mobility, analytics, and cloud
SSI	small-scale industry
TCS	Tata Consultancy Services
Treda	Telangana Real Estate Developers' Association
USB	ultra-small branch
USSD	unstructured supplementary service data
WA	Washington Accord
WIL	Welspun India, Ltd.
WSU	Wichita State University
WTO	World Trade Organization

LIST OF FIGURES

CHAPTER 1: THEORIES ABOUT UNEVEN DEVELOPMENT

CHAPTER 2: AGRICULTURE

CHAPTER 3: TEXTILES

CHAPTER 4: RETAIL

CHAPTER 5: BANKING

CHAPTER 6: ENGINEERING, MACHINERY, AND TECHNOLOGY

CHAPTER 7: TRANSPORTATION

CHAPTER 8: INFORMATION TECHNOLOGY AND INFORMATION TECHNOLOGY ENGINEERING SERVICES

CHAPTER 9: REAL ESTATE

INDEX

G

H

I

DISCLAIMER

Although the author and publisher have made every effort to ensure that the information in this book was correct at press time, the author and publisher do not assume and hereby disclaim any liability to any party for any loss, damage, or disruption caused by errors or omissions, whether such errors or omissions result from negligence, accident, or any other cause.

ABOUT THE AUTHOR

JAY NATHAN, PH.D. is a professor of management, Peter J. Tobin College of Business at St. John's University, New York. Previously, a tenured professor at the Kania School of Management at the University of Scranton, Pennsylvania. A Fulbright Scholar to Thailand, Poland, Kazakhstan, and Mongolia; honorable professor of Karaganda University of Economics, Kazakhstan; and author of *Kazakhstan's New Economy, Nomads and Eagle Hunters meet Technology and Management* distributed by the University of Chicago Press. Editor and past-president of the Global Awareness Society International. Professor Nathan has lectured under various fellowships, grants, and sponsorships in Japan, Brazil, New Zealand, England, France, India, Finland, Germany, Singapore, Sweden, Australia, Malaysia, Italy, Russia, Nepal, South Africa, Mongolia, Uzbekistan, Kyrgyzstan, Romania, and Lithuania. He is a life-time member of the Fulbright Association, was elected as a 1946 inaugural member of the Fulbright Society, and is on the Fulbright Association board of directors.

He has published peer-reviewed scholarly articles in the *Journal of Law, Medicine & Ethics, Hospital Management Quarterly, International Journal of Operations & Production Management, Journal of Management Sciences,*

Journal of Global Awareness, Journal of Production Planning & Control, and Wisconsin Academy of Sciences, Arts and Letters.

He is passionate about business education and contextualizing his international travel experiences in teaching, service, and research at local, regional, and national levels, especially in poor and developing countries around the world—and, he sees the world as one large campus.